SECURITY AND SOUTH ASIA
Ideas, Institutions and Initiatives

SECURITY AND SOUTH ASIA
Ideas, Institutions and Initiatives

.

Edited by
Swarna Rajagopalan

Routledge
Taylor & Francis Group

LONDON AND NEW YORK

First published 2006
by Routledge
512 Mercantile House, Kasturba Gandhi Marg, New Delhi 110 001

Simultaneously published in UK
by Routledge
2 Park Square, Milton Park, Abingdon, Oxon, OX14 4RN

Routledge is an imprint of the Taylor and Francis Group

Transferred to Digital Printing 2006

British Library Cataloguing in Publication Data
A catalogue record for this book is available from the British Library

ISBN 0-415-40106-2

Contents

Introduction

SWARNA RAJAGOPALAN

Stephen Philip Cohen has been many things to the universe of South Asian security analysis: scholar, institution builder (or 'rain-maker', as Kanti Bajpai once described him), mentor, possessor of contrary opinions, media favourite, innovator, and entrepreneur of projects and programmes. Steve Cohen's doctoral students at the University of Illinois at Urbana-Champaign author this anthology in his honour. To the ten of us who have contributed to this volume, he is, most importantly, our teacher. In the years since our graduation each one's relationship with him has metamorphosed, but in the spirit of the relationship that makes us a community, this is for our professor, thesis adviser, and committee chair.

ABOUT STEVE COHEN: A PERSONAL NOTE

The three short pieces that follow this introduction profile different aspects of Steve Cohen's career: his scholarship, the institutions he helped build, his role as a teacher, and his contribution to US South Asia policy. The temptation to add my little bit to that exercise is great enough that I will not resist the chance to mention a few things that have made it such a remarkable experience to work with him over the years.[1]

---

[1] I want to acknowledge Kanti Bajpai's contribution to this section.

Steve Cohen is one of three renaissance persons I studied with at Illinois, the others being his great friends and tennis companions, Marvin Weinbaum and Edward Kolodziej. Their wide range of interests and their absorption in different aspects of the human experience—from travel to family to the arts and sport—gives all three of them a perspective that allows students to grow as individuals rather than indoctrinated members of an epistemological club. Through the grim, unrelenting, life-texture-pulverizing years of scholarly boot camp—graduate school—Kolodziej's casual references to Moliere and Mozart in class, Weinbaum's commitment to performing music every week with his friends, and Cohen's enthusiasm for everything from trains and rickshaws to electronics to Aristotle, gave me hope that with a Ph.D. I could still be a person I would find interesting!

When everything is intrinsically interesting, everything and everyone with their individual quirks and baggage has intrinsic worth. Cohen is, contrary to the way he is sometimes perceived in the region, a respecter of persons. But respect in his book involves being honest to himself in what he writes and says, and while this honesty does not always find favour with his audience, he has the ability to respond graciously to criticism however proffered.

Cohen is criticized in India for being pro-Pakistani and in Pakistan for being pro-Indian. His commitment to both countries and affection for people he knows there is evident to those who get to know him. Cohen's bias, if any, lies in his standpoint as an American whose view favours US interests—surely not a negative for the realist-dominated national security elite of South Asia. There have been instances where his views reflected those held by some sections of Indians and Pakistanis: that nuclear weapons were not necessarily a disaster for South Asia; that US policies in Bangladesh in 1971 were faulty; that for the US, engaging Pakistan was important after the Cold War; and even in his criticism of the Emergency in India.

Cohen's years in South Asian security studies and in academics in general must be measured by the quality of friendships that the Cohens, as a couple, have built and sustained. Their relationships with the people whom Cohen has discussed, debated, and often disagreed with for four decades in this region, are personal, real, and warm. This is also true of Cohen's colleagues at Illinois—he might have nothing in common with some of them in terms of research (or politics), but it was always evident that their friendship and their well-being meant something to him.

Someone said to me right after I graduated, 'Don't tell me about your dissertation, that is your adviser's work. Tell me what you do.' I still find that shocking, because I worked with a person who allowed me to find my topic, feel my way through it, struggle with its challenges, and own the little triumphs of that struggle myself. Cohen got excited when I did, provided perspective when I lost it, kept faith, and promised me that there was light at the end of the tunnel. When personal challenges compounded the difficulties of the dissertation process, I even once got a 'Dear Abby' style note from him assuring me that since I was so miserable, I was close to the end! The secret of Cohen's success as a teacher of graduate students, I believe, lies in his secure sense of self that allows him to delight fully in his students' process and progress.

Cohen brings to his work (and his students') a rare combination of play and discipline. On the one hand, there is no idea too outrageous, no project impossible, no perspective untenable, and no approach beyond the pale; and no combination of any of these that is rejected out of hand. On the other hand, in the words of the Emergency rhetoric he abhors, 'there is no substitute for hard work' in the Cohen *gurukul*—we would rewrite, reconceptualize, remap till we wanted to retire! Cohen, by precept and practice, made it clear how things really do get better with multiple iterations and how editing is an important part of writing. There is, in his view, no final draft of any work. Superficially, this places a great burden upon the writer, but ultimately it liberates you from the burden of perfected completion and allows you to invest fully in the process and what it brings.

Cohen's dissertation advice was always practical and therefore invaluable. I would like to share a few instances with future dissertators who might read this volume:

- If you cannot get started, write a brief conclusion stating what you have found, pretending you are done. That will help you figure out what you mean to do.
- Doing interviews, know that you are doing well as long as people are talking!

- 'What is the shelf-life of this idea?' is a good measure for the endless reams of 'cutting-edge' literature that emerge as one writes. Cohen's yardstick is Aristotle's *Politics*, still going strong after a millennium or two.
- Write simply, without jargon or the popular phrases of the day. For me, this meant writing on identity politics without using the 'd-word' (discourse)!
- The fact that he used the bound copies of very long dissertations as doorstops and monitor stands in his office also reminded us of the virtues of brevity (a lesson I have not learned!).
- When you are tired, play some classical music and fix your footnotes and bibliography. This will give you a sense of accomplishment and energize you.
- Cure writer's block by 'generating text'. Most of it will be useless, but soon enough there will be something you can use.
- When you hate your dissertation, you are almost ready to defend it. So finish!

What made Cohen an award-winning teacher at the University of Illinois was that he took the same qualities into the undergraduate classroom. In the classroom Cohen's erudition was evident but accompanied by a sense of humour that made him very accessible. His respect for his students showed, and he would speak of every class as if it were made up of creative geniuses. Students sensed his ability to appreciate them as people and responded by giving the course their best. Regurgitation was not his style, and he brought the use of simulations and games into the undergraduate classroom. For me, though, one of the most exciting things about his pedagogy was that he would encourage students to substitute the research paper with a creative project. The bar was still high, but this allowed students to speak through their medium. Cohen taught a 'mass death' course in which he discussed the politics of human-made and natural disasters through history, and I remember that his office at one point contained several panels of a stomach-churning oil painting that had been submitted in lieu of a research paper.

Cohen's interest in South Asia is broad. He has the travel writer's appetite for local colour and for things unusual, and firmly believes in travel for research and study. He has the ethnographer's interest in stories and customs. He has the statistician's interest in aggregate numbers—what percentage would you say, or do you know how many? He has the historian's interest in change and the political scientist's facility with elite interviews and policy debate. Cohen reads widely and, I should add, every kind of text—academic, literary, cinematic, performance. He also has strong opinions on what he reads (he did not enjoy *Lagaan!*), but refreshingly, is genuinely interested in hearing the other person's view and their justification for it.

It is safe to say that no two students of Professor Steve Cohen are alike in sensibility, approach, temperament, or, most surprisingly, research interests! All of us arrived and left as individuals, who had now gained the skills and discipline to garner that individual creativity as we would. This volume is built around our shared identity as his students, but the chapters reflect some shared moments—in time or interest—with Cohen and for the rest, much as he allowed us to be, they are a reflection of the ten very different people whose growth he facilitated at one point in their lives. We share our connection with him and in some ways very little else. Therefore, the next task of this introduction will be to profile the contributors in terms both of the interests they share with Cohen and the range of their own interests.

The Cohen *Gurukul:* Horizons of History to Cutting Edge

During his tenure as professor at the University of Illinois, Professor Stephen P. Cohen taught thousands of students, guided scores, mentored dozens, advised several, and chaired the dissertation committees of eleven students (graduation dates in parentheses): C.V. Raghavulu (1976), Shivaji Ganguly (1977), [2] Sumit Ganguly (1984), Kanti Bajpai (1990), Kavita Khory (1991), Chetan Kumar (1995), Amit Gupta (1996), Swarna Rajagopalan (1998), Dinshaw Mistry (1998), Shonali Sardesai (2000), and Sunil Dasgupta (2002).

Cohen is best known for his academic writing on traditional security concerns in South Asia and his advocacy writing on US

---

[2]We were unable to locate Dr. Shivaji Ganguly as we put this volume together. His absence from this anthology is our loss.

foreign policy. Among his students, Shivaji Ganguly, Sumit Ganguly, Kanti Bajpai, Amit Gupta, and Dinshaw Mistry share this interest. Shivaji Ganguly's writings have centred on Cold War international affairs, India–Pakistan relations and US South Asia policy, and one might say that of all of us, his interests are most closely associated with Cohen's work. In recent years, Sumit Ganguly has emerged as an important voice on US South Asia policy, although this is not his sole interest. In common with Cohen, Kanti Bajpai uses a historical approach to writing theoretically on international relations. He is also the only one of Cohen's students to have worked on regional cooperation, even as Cohen has been an enthusiastic promoter and supporter of two important regional Track II initiatives—the Summer and Winter Workshops and the Regional Centre for Strategic Studies. Amit Gupta and Dinshaw Mistry share Cohen's interest in arms, arms production and procurement, and the arms race. The former has been writing on US South Asia policy as well.

Cohen sometimes talks about the 'hardware' and 'software' of security studies, meaning by the former, traditional areas of study such as war, foreign policy, and military affairs, and by the latter, the now-traditional area of ethnic or other internal conflict. As Sardesai mentions in her piece, it seemed to him his male students studied the former and his female students the latter. Khory, Rajagopalan, and Sardesai all wrote dissertations on ethnic conflict, lending credence to this notion. Khory examined the impact of ethnic conflict on foreign policy, Rajagopalan studied the national integration projects of three South Asian states from the point of view of communities with a secessionist history, and Sardesai's focus was on the modalities of conflict management in three internal identity-driven conflicts in the region. On closer examination, however, Cohen's male students have also shown an interest in this area. Sumit Ganguly has written on ethnic conflict as well, and now the politics of diasporic identities is a subject of research both for Amit Gupta and Kavita Khory. Gupta and Khory have different approaches to the politics of émigré South Asian communities; Gupta is interested in the political mobilization of the Indian–American community and its impact on US domestic politics and South Asia policy, while Khory's interests have ranged from the impact of ethnic conflict on foreign policy (her thesis) to the articulation of a community identity.

Notwithstanding Cohen's involvement with the most traditional areas of security policy and analysis, he has also been ahead of today's non-traditional security debates in his work with C.V. Raghavulu on natural disasters and the conceptualization of his popular Illinois course on the politics of mass death, which covered a wide range of human experiences from the Holocaust to famine to cyclones. That there is not a shred of orthodoxy to Cohen's thinking is also evident from his wholehearted support in the early 1990s for Chetan Kumar's thesis research on the role of the Internet in creating epistemic networks for social movements.

Military history is another field in which Cohen has done important work. Sunil Dasgupta's current research on insurgency and counter-insurgency operations follows that thread. However, history has been central to Cohen's work also as an approach to the contemporary. His first academic publication, a study of the relationship between rulers and priests in early Indian society, was preparation for his thesis work on civil–military relations in India. Rajagopalan's work on traditional Indian ideas on politics and security began as a paper for a seminar on regional security taught by Cohen.

Of the research areas that are significant in security studies today, feminist perspectives form the one topic that Cohen has not worked on. Perhaps surprising to some, Cohen has been an encouraging supporter of other people's work in this area. Long before it became fashionable, the Program in Arms Control, Disarmament, and International Security (ACDIS), under Cohen's leadership, offered space and support to a small Illinois reading group on women and war! Over the years, Illinois' Program in ACDIS, of which Cohen was one of the founders, has built its ties to the university's Women and Gender in Global Perspectives programme. Cohen was chair and discussant on the first panel on women, politics, and security in South Asia that my friend and I organized, and engaged with our papers as seriously as we could have hoped.

Thus, rather than produce clones of himself, Cohen has encouraged us to follow our interests, ensuring thereby (rather unintentionally) that on most issues relating to security in the region, at any level of analysis, you will find at least one Cohen student who takes an interest! This takes the Introduction to its final and most challenging task, to weave together analytically the rather disparately composed chapters in this volume.

PERSPECTIVES ON SOUTH ASIAN SECURITY

The articles in the substantive part of this book do not fall into easy categories, but link to each other in a chain of ideas and approaches.[3] Old-fashioned historical and institutional analyses, as well as qualitative textual or content analysis, are the tools used here to examine a wide array of subjects.

The first two articles, written by Rajagopalan and Bajpai, look most directly at ideas on security and strategic matters. How is security understood and how are important strategic relationships framed? they ask in contexts thousands of years apart from each other. The next three articles by Dasgupta, Gupta, and Mistry look at approaches to and choices made in the areas of military structure, arms production, and investment on science and technology. Khory and Kumar study how and why civil society groups are mobilized towards political ends. Khory examines ethnic mobilization in diaspora communities, while Kumar looks at non-official dialogue and initiatives towards a peaceful South Asia. Raghavulu's article on disaster management in India examines the role of state and non-state actors in preparing for and responding to natural disasters.

'Securing Rama's World' underscores the contextual and dynamic meaning of the term 'security'. It poses the three questions, now

---

[3]'South Asia' in this volume is, unfortunately, primarily India. Rajagopalan's essay alludes to ideas that predate the idea of India, South Asia, or, indeed, even a regional identity. Bajpai looks at Indian views of Pakistan. Khory's diaspora groups are located in North America, and they originate in and engage with the politics of India and Sri Lanka. Kumar searches for lessons from the India–Pakistan non-official peace process for Nepal and Sri Lanka. For the rest, the chapters are squarely concerned with India's problems and policies. While the essays span many subjects, from epic literature to armies to natural disasters, lack of a gender perspective is another lacuna. Neither shortcoming is reflective of the contributors' range of research interests outside this volume.

standard in security studies, of a text that was composed over several hundred years: whose security? security from what? and how is this referent to be secured from this threat? The Valmiki *Ramayana* depicts an epic age and remains in the Indian imagination as a repository of metaphors and values whose political salience has been resurgent in the last two decades. Exploring this text, Rajagopalan finds that for the universe of the Valmiki *Ramayana*, it is a certain value system that is the main referent. The characters in the story know what values they hold and what duties these make incumbent upon them. Living in more complex times, the emphasis on values still has resonance; the deepest fissures in South Asia today have to do with disagreements over political values—who belongs, democratic access and rights, the relationship between state and an ever-more diverse society.

Bajpai takes a different approach to the business of understanding how Indians think about security. He surveys fifty years or so of Indian writing and speeches on security and strategic affairs and identifies three schools of thought that he terms: Nehruvian, neoliberal, and hyperrealist. He identifies key premises of each, especially as they apply to war and the use of force. Applying these to the question of Pakistan and the challenge it poses to the Indian strategic policy elite, Bajpai concludes that the Nehruvian approach is most likely to last the duration and ups and downs of an India–Pakistan peace process. He draws on Boulding's three faces of power (threat, exchange, and integration) to support his argument that as difficult as dialogue is, it is the most enduring path to peace with Pakistan.

Bajpai's concern with the ideational underpinnings of contemporary strategic decision making is shared by Dasgupta, Gupta, and Mistry. What are the worldviews and values that inform the political calculus and motivate policy decisions?

Dasgupta carries forward Cohen's interest in regional militaries and examines the factors that limit the effectiveness of the Indian army both in internal and interstate conflicts. One of the factors he names is the inability of the political leadership to decide what the role of the army should be. He apportions blame equally to the political leadership for its failure to take seriously military decision making and to the military leadership for resisting structural reform in the name of preserving the military's autonomy from civilian interference in day-to-day affairs. Dasgupta argues for a clear-headed review of these issues, implicitly making the argument for openness to changing the way things have 'always' been. Similarly, Gupta argues that the continuation of socialist-era attitudes have limited the capacity of the Indian arms industry to compete in the global market. Examining the politics of arms production policy, he concludes that what the industry needs to survive is a realistic approach that acknowledges global trends.

Writing about India's science and technology choices, Mistry echoes Gupta's point that the world has changed and so must India's way of looking at its choices. More specifically, analysing the history of three projects in India's science and technology programme—the mission to the moon, the light combat aircraft (LCA), and the advanced light helicopter (ALH)—he identifies self-reliance and prestige as the two motivations behind India's choices. In recent years competitiveness and international collaboration are also making a difference to this calculus. He is of the opinion that these are better considerations from the point of view of improving India's technical outputs.

The old bases of decision making, whether socialistic ideals in the arms production industry or self-reliance and prestige in the case of science and technology policy, it is agreed, can only take India so far. Dasgupta, Gupta, and Mistry all press for openness to change and reform in the direction of clear and realistic objectives.

With Khory's article there is something of a shift in the realm of analysis. While the first five articles are concerned with the ideas and values that influence policy, Khory writes about how civil society organizations use the Internet to disseminate their ideas. She asks how the Internet has worked as an instrument of mobilization for diaspora communities seeking to garner support for political positions concerning their home countries. She finds that non-state actors with limited resources can make an impact disproportionate to their investment by using the Web. However, it cannot serve either as their only strategy nor even their chief strategy for mobilization. Further, it is not necessarily a democratic medium, with those able to access it still being limited and those being able to use it being even more limited. Either way, Khory is ambivalent about the Internet; however, she does not favour a security regime that centres on control, and thus, she throws open the technology, security, and politics debate.

With Kumar, civil society organizations remain at the core of the analysis of non-official (or Track II or people-to-people) efforts towards India–Pakistan peace; however, his interest lies in their activities and programmes rather than their methods of disseminating views. His survey of Track II activities suggests to him that South Asian states lack what he terms 'an architecture for peace'. By this he means opportunities and spaces in which people can learn about conflict resolution and peace building. He advocates capacity building programmes across state agencies and civil society in peace building, consensus formation, and negotiation.

The experience of disaster relief and management in India is the subject of Raghavulu's article. It assesses both the institutional response and the role of non-governmental organizations; 'Teach them how others have got it right' is also one of the lessons that emerge from this study. Raghavulu makes the point that the government wanting to help people in distress is a legacy of *dharmik* traditions (such as those in the Valmiki *Ramayana*). In reality, the same ills have plagued disaster relief efforts over the decades that he has been studying this area: corruption, lack of coordination, the push–pull of federal politics, and resistance to change and to changes in thinking about relief and reconstruction. The last is resonant of Dasgupta, Gupta, and Mistry's complaints. Raghavulu also underscores the lack of long-term commitment on the part of non-governmental actors, which puts the burden of relief and reconstruction squarely on the state. Like Kumar, Raghavulu advocates capacity building through public education on disaster responses.

These articles, written as a gift to a teacher, taken together constitute a study of the ideas and attitudes in specific historical contexts that impinge on policies and relationships that are more usually the substance of work in this field. They reflect a view of security as something that people choose to make for themselves through an exercise of agency that is rooted in the realm of ideas.

Stephen Philip Cohen: The Teacher

Shonali Sardesai

Dr. Stephen Cohen is the perfect guru, in my view. He made graduate school, often a bumpy experience, a little less gruelling for us with his constant support and encouragement. Once Dr. Cohen knew that a student was considering a Ph.D. focusing on South Asian politics at Champaign-Urbana, he contacted us and expressed interest in our work—a very reassuring step for those of us who were fresh out of undergraduate studies, still unsure of this major decision. It made us feel a little more comfortable that there was someone who would enable our professional growth once we began the dissertation journey.

In school Professor Cohen encouraged us to complete the required graduate coursework and pass qualifying exams so that we could get down to the real reason for being there—writing an original piece of work that in its small way would contribute to building knowledge on South Asia. As a teacher, Professor Cohen pushed us to think outside the box, explore our ideas, and grow professionally. His creativity was joyful and enthusiasm infectious. During the dissertation process, Professor Cohen would push us to think but leave us on our own once he thought we were on the right path. He would assuage anxieties during challenging times, share excitement as the dissertation took shape, and pull out much needed resources for fieldwork. He always had an open door policy and I do not think any of us was ever turned away when we needed advice or just a friendly face to make us believe that the dissertation would be done. In the process, he made the dissertation process an enjoyable and memorable one. He provided unflinching support to all his students, and one thing that never ceased to amuse him was that his female students seemed to work on topics on ethnicity, conflict, and South Asia, while his male students focused on topics such as weapons proliferation, nuclear policy, military, and South Asia.

Besides his keen interest in students working on South Asia, the South Asia Program on Arms Control, Disarmament, and International Security (ACDIS) was another example of his enthusiasm for the politics of the region. For us, his students, it gave us an opportunity to interact with some of the leading practitioners and academics from South Asia by learning from them as well as bouncing our ideas off them. Even now, Professor Cohen enjoys bringing his past students together and figuring out who graduated when and who overlapped with whom. In the process, he has fostered a sense of connection between us—his students and grand-students as he calls us.

Professor Cohen went beyond being our adviser in school by opening his home to us. Bobbie Cohen and he went out of their way to make us feel comfortable so far away from home and in the throes of crazy deadlines and pressures. It was so nice to unwind in their home, underlined by elephant motifs right from cushion covers to teacups! And, of course, how can one forget his child-like excitement for tennis and the latest techno gadgets?

South Asia has always been the flavour of the season for Professor Cohen, even when it was not in vogue to study the region, and he continues to be a close follower of events in the region, evidenced by his regular publications of books on South Asia. For us, members of his *gurukul*, it has been an absolute honour to interact with him as students, colleagues, and friends. As a last point, his students keep him youthful and he keeps us young, even though we may find it difficult to keep up with him.

Stephen Cohen: Academic, Adviser, and Institution Builder

AMIT GUPTA

S tephen Cohen's contributions to South Asian studies have come through his academic writings, his role as an institution builder, and in his training of a generation of South Asia scholars. His contributions to the growth of awareness about South Asia in the United States continue in Washington where he now heads the South Asia programme at the Brookings Institution.

STEPHEN COHEN: ACADEMIC

Stephen Philip Cohen's career as a South Asianist and political scientist has spanned five decades and led him, along with Paul Brass and Francine Frankel, to be one of the three pre-eminent American South Asia scholars of his generation. As a scholar, Cohen's work has covered both the domestic and international aspects of state security. His writings have examined civil–military relations, arms transfers and arms control issues, state capacity and the response to natural disasters, and American foreign policy towards South Asia. In the 1970s, when American scholars were shut out of India, he also briefly studied Japanese politics.

As is the case with any good scholar, quite a few of Steve Cohen's writings have stood the test of time and remain central to the study of South Asian politics and security. His book on the Indian Army is a classic and, five decades later, is still a must-read for anyone studying civil–military relations in India. His book on the Pakistan Army, while attempting to duplicate his work on India, was less persuasive—mainly because it had to compete with the work that preceded it. Pakistani scholars, however, with the exception of Hassan Askari Rizvi, have written little to counterbalance it, and it remains one of the essential texts on the study of civil–military relations in Pakistan.

The Indian Army: Its Contribution to the Development of a Nation was a seminal book on the military in India and provided an interesting contrast to the ongoing literature on civil–military relations that, in the late 1960s and early 1970s, focused on either the role of armies in national development or the failure of political systems and the subsequent takeovers by the military. Thus, Samuel Huntington, amongst others, wrote glowingly of the positive role to be played by militaries in institution building and political development. The costs of such military intervention to the democratic process were frequently ignored. Cohen's work, however, showed that a disciplined, apolitical military could be constructed in the developing world. In doing so, he explained why India would not follow the path of most other developing nations and allow the military to intervene in domestic politics.

Nearly a decade later, Cohen followed up with a book on the Pakistan Army. While not as convincing as the previous volume, the book was an important contribution to the understanding of the Pakistan Army. It explained why the military played the role it did in Pakistan, as well as the tensions between maintaining a professional military and intervening in the domestic political process. Interestingly, and this attests to its balanced approach, the book was criticized by both Indians and Pakistanis.

Cohen's work on civil–military relations was both credible and effective because he was, and continues to be, academically adventurous. In the 1960s, as a graduate student, he spent time in India doing field research. In the wonderfully open and small academic and political setting of the 1960s (Raj Thapar's autobiography *All These Years* brings out the flavour of what Delhi's intellectual life was like in the 1960s), Steve Cohen made a set of friends in the Indian establishment. In the late 1970s Cohen ventured into Zia ul-Haq's Pakistan, conducted a series of interviews with a general who was then an international pariah, and went on to write his second book on civil–military relations.

Given Cohen's early work in the field of civil–military relations, it is unfortunate that he has not revisited the subject in recent years. His comparative analysis of militaries would be especially useful at a time when armies both continue to determine state policies in some countries—as in Nigeria and Pakistan—while they have successfully permitted the transition to democracy in others—Brazil, Argentina, and Chile.

Professor Cohen's work on arms transfers and arms control issues is equally impressive and innovative. In this area Cohen was in the vanguard of discussing the consequences of the nuclearization of South Asia. In the late 1980s and early 1990s he brought out two volumes that examined the issue and discussed potential arms control and verification measures. At that point of time India had not conducted its second set of nuclear tests and the debate in both India and Pakistan centred on under what conditions either country would go nuclear. Cohen, however, was already heading research to find ways to stabilize the nuclear relationship and move both countries towards verifiable arms control—a problem that they now confront as they attempt to develop confidence building measures. Cohen was equally prescient when, in the early 1980s, he suggested that India and Pakistan attempt to resolve the Kashmir issue. The reaction in both countries at that time was that there was no Kashmir problem. He correctly argued that that was precisely the reason that both countries should seek a lasting solution since at that point of time the dormant conflict was not seen as affecting either country's vital national interests. Nearly two decades later one can only wish with hindsight that positive steps for conflict resolution had been taken then.

He subsequently went on to lead studies on the various nuclear and conventional military crises between India and Pakistan, and draw lessons from them about the nature of deterrence, crisis communication, and crisis prevention efforts in South Asia. This was all the more noteworthy since analysts and policy makers in both

India and Pakistan have, until recently, been reluctant to discuss such issues in a public forum. The Hamdoor Rahman Commission report on the crisis in East Pakistan and the subsequent 1971 war has yet to be publicly released in Pakistan. In India the Henderson Brooks report on the 1962 India–China war has yet to be released to the general public. By the late 1990s the Indian government became somewhat more transparent in the national security process. Following the 1999 Kargil conflict, the Indian government quickly put out an official report on the crisis and a number of books were written in India on the subject. On the other hand, there has been no serious public discussion in Pakistan about it. Similarly, the Indian government tasked its National Security Advisory Board to draw up a Draft Nuclear Doctrine and was to subsequently adopt the draft doctrine, with minor revisions, as official policy.

Steve Cohen retired from the University of Illinois in 1998, but has continued to remain an influential academic in South Asian studies. His last two books, *India: Emerging Power* and *The Idea of Pakistan*, have emerged as handy texts with which to educate both academics and policy makers about the policy process as well as the security issues that drive politics in South Asia. The book on Pakistan is particularly appealing since it discusses the issue of Pakistani national identity as well as the military's role in that country.

Cohen effectively discusses the transition of the Pakistani armed forces from a British-style fighting force to one with an American-type ethos. He then goes on to show how, since the 1970s, a Pakistani national military emerged and the challenges it continues to face. These include: preventing the Army from shifting from a professional fighting force to an Islamic fighting force; making the military an attractive career choice for the country's best and brightest; and, given its repeated intervention in politics, how to maintain the honesty and integrity of the military. Cohen summed up Pakistan's dilemma very well:

> Pakistan is a case in which an excellent army depends on a failing economy, a divided society, and unreliable politicians. The army lacks the capability to fix Pakistan's problems, but it is unwilling to give other state institutions and the political

system the opportunity to learn and grow; its tolerance for the mistakes of others is very low, yet its own performance, when in power, has usually dug the hole deeper. (2004: 130)

STEPHEN COHEN: INSTITUTION BUILDER

Steve Cohen's second major contribution to South Asian studies came in his ability to promote South Asian studies in the United States and in his attempt to create institutions that would systematize the study of the region. From the early 1970s there was a decline in interest in South Asian studies that saw a shrinking of South Asia programmes in American universities. In the new millennium, though, there has been a revitalization of South Asian studies in the United States. Moreover, most South Asia programmes concentrated on the teaching of history and culture. In that period Steve Cohen was one of the few American academics who was able to build a successful South Asia programme that focused on politics and security issues. While at the University of Illinois, Urbana-Champaign, he co-founded, in 1984, the Program in Arms Control, Disarmament, and International Security (ACDIS). Steve was able to negotiate grants from the Ford and MacArthur Foundations to create an academic research component for South Asian studies in ACDIS. He brought scholars from every major South Asian country to Urbana-Champaign and arguably made the University of Illinois the foremost centre in America for South Asian security studies.

As in any programme, the quality of scholars was uneven, but the South Asia programme was able to bring out a series of books and research papers that created a niche for South Asian security studies in the broader discipline. What made this all the more remarkable was the geographical limitations that Cohen was able to overcome. Most American think-tanks are based on either coast so the successful functioning of one in a small town in the Midwest was truly remarkable.

Steve Cohen's vision for ACDIS was constrained, however, not by his own actions, but by the University of Illinois' lack of interest in strengthening international programmes. The university's unwillingness to provide money to make ACDIS into a permanent centre means that the once the funding dries up, so too will the research on South Asia. After his retirement from the University of Illinois, Professor Cohen has built up a similar South Asia programme at Brookings and participated in the renaissance of India studies in the United States.

Steve Cohen's recognition of the importance of institutions was also seen in his pushing for the creation of a South Asia-based security studies centre that scholars from all the countries of the region could access. He was one of the people instrumental in setting up the Regional Centre for Strategic Studies in Colombo that has emerged as a major networking centre for South Asian scholars. The fact that it is located in Colombo has made it immune to the volatile swings in interstate relations in South Asia.

STEPHEN COHEN: ADVISER

Steve Cohen's contribution as a Ph.D. supervisor must also be acknowledged. His record is impressive because with the exception of one student, everyone who was advised by him completed their dissertation. Professor Cohen's effectiveness as an adviser lay in encouraging students to take on myriad subjects and to help bring these projects to fruition. Thus, as the editor of the present volume too has noted, there were dissertations that focused on traditional international relations issues of war and peace (Shivaji Ganguly, Kanti Bajpai, Sumit Ganguly, and Dinshaw Mistry), which addressed Steve Cohen's own concerns about peace and security. There were also studies of ethnicity and conflict (Kavita Khory and Shonali Sardesai), and one that took a constructivist approach to security matters in South Asia (Swarna Rajagopalan). There was also a unique and distinctive dissertation on the role of the Internet that was seen by its author as potentially shifting the paradigm in international relations (Chetan Kumar). While this did not happen, the blame cannot be laid at Stephen Cohen's doorstep. Steve not only mentored these scholars, but, with one exception, was able to provide the much needed funding to do field research. The quality of most of the dissertations was high and that led to their publication as books.

The students Steve Cohen advised have gone on to establish an academic presence in both the United States and India. It is a testament to his efforts that these students are now training the next generation of South Asia scholars with the values he instilled. Cohen trained his students to move beyond the petty and personalized attacks that mar so much of security studies in South Asia and not to make *ad hominem* arguments. Instead, he emphasized the development of arguments based on facts and reason. Steve Cohen also passed on his love for academic adventure to some of his students. Kanti Bajpai spent a year travelling around the nations of South Asia. Swarna Rajagopalan was to do the same. Itty Abraham spent a year in Brazil and India. By promoting such fieldwork, Cohen was able to help retain the role of qualitative research in a discipline that was becoming increasingly quantitative and, therefore, far less effective in explaining ongoing trends in international politics.

Stephen Philip Cohen has not only had a distinguished academic career, but he has served as a guide and mentor to an outstanding group of younger scholars. Further, his productivity, his sense of adventure, and his intellectual liveliness have made him one of the most influential South Asian scholars of his generation. This *festschrift* is a small token of gratitude from those of us who learnt from him and inculcated his values, academic skills, and personal integrity.

Steve Cohen's Contributions to American Policy Making

Sumit Ganguly

It can be safely stated that no other South Asia specialist of his generation has been as involved in the policy-making realm as Steve Cohen. He has performed this role as a private citizen, as an academic, and as a government official. As a private citizen his attempts to influence American policy can be traced as far back as the early 1970s. During the 1971 Indo–Pak crisis, which contributed to the genesis of Bangladesh, Steve played a critical role in focusing public attention on the gruesome acts of the Pakistani Army in the then East Pakistan. Using his own resources he travelled to Washington, DC, to meet with both Congressional staffers and policy makers in the Executive Branch to highlight the tragedy that was unfolding in South Asia and to critique ongoing American policies towards the region. This selfless act, which sadly went unnoticed in India, demonstrated his commitment to speak truth to power.

His academic writing has also had considerable policy impact. A short, pithy book that he co-authored with the late Richard Park of the University of Michigan, *India: Emergent Power?* (1978) contributed to a re-examination in Washington, DC, of India's role in the region and beyond. It required an unusual degree of perspicacity and foresight to recognize that India was on the verge of achieving great power status at a time when most of the American academia was paying scant attention to India. Indeed, they had, in large part simply written India off as a lost cause.

As a scholar and a keen observer of South Asian politics, he has also played a vital role in repeatedly providing Congressional testimony on a wide range of issues pertaining to South Asia. In his numerous appearances before Congress, he has never shied away from spelling out his strongly held views, even when they have not conformed to the prevailing wisdom of the day. For example, in the aftermath of the Soviet invasion of Afghanistan, he made a careful, limited, and calibrated case for American support for Pakistan. One can only speculate if General Zia ul-Haq, the then military dictator of Pakistan, was drawing on Steve's deft testimony when he described the renewed military and economic relationship with the United States as a 'handshake and not an embrace'.

In the aftermath of the Soviet withdrawal, when the United States lost interest in Pakistan, Steve remained one of the staunchest advocates of continuing engagement. It would be in interesting exercise in counter-factual history to see what might have transpired in US–Pakistan relations had his advice been followed in Washington, DC. In the event, it was not, and contributed to the rise of anti-Americanism within Pakistan as the Pakistani elite, with some justification, felt that they had been cast aside when vital American interests were no longer at stake in their country and its environs.

However, he was perhaps most influential in the policy-making world when he was a member of the US Department of State's Policy Planning Staff from 1985 to 1987. During these crucial years, when the United States was deeply involved in South Asia, Steve played a yeoman role in shaping the contours of American policy towards the region. While at the State Department, he tirelessly argued that it was possible for the United States, contrary to popular belief, to have good relations with *both* India and Pakistan. Such a position frequently put him at odds with many in the academic as well as policy-making communities who argued that the pursuit of such an option was little more than a fool's errand. Steve's insistence on this approach won out during the Reagan administration, which managed to court India while simultaneously maintaining a robust relationship with Pakistan.

After formally leaving academic life, Steve has been integrally involved in major policy debates on South Asia. At a time when the region looms increasingly large in American foreign and security policy concerns, his early advocacy for greater American interest in and involvement with the region has been finally heeded. Today an entire spectrum of American interests is increasingly implicated with South Asia. These run the gamut from the politically charged matters of outsourcing and weapons sales to more anodyne issues of democracy promotion and humanitarian assistance. It is heartening and reassuring to one and all of his students that Steve was at the forefront of promoting the cause of South Asia at a time when few, if any, academics, let alone policy makers, saw the signal importance of India and South Asia in the calculus of American global interests.

BIBLIOGRAPHY

Cohen, Steve and Richard Paul (1978). *India: Emergent Power?* New York: Crane Russak and Company.

Security Ideas in the
Valmiki Ramayana

SWARNA RAJAGOPALAN

Does security mean the same thing to people everywhere or does each culture have an indigenous understanding of what security means and what is to be secured?[1] This article is based on a larger study of political ideas in the *Valmiki Ramayana*. It explores the universe of threats and referents that are described in the text, with a view to answering this question in the context. A pilot effort, this presages a broader exploration of didactic and literary traditions in Indian history in order to ascertain what, if any, are the values and understandings of security that animate Indian, and more broadly, South Asian thinking.

The article begins with a brief survey of how security is now understood by disciplinary scholars, and then, identifying some key conceptual issues, reviews scholarly writing related to traditional Indian security ideas. Elucidating the importance of the *Ramayana* to

---

[1]Steve Cohen's first publication as a graduate student at the University of Wisconsin was an article placing contemporary civil–military relations in India in the context of the Brahmin-Kshatriya relationship of ancient Indian society (Cohen 1964). In 1994, for a regional security course he taught, I wrote the first and very simplistic version of this study. South Asian political and intellectual history remains a common thread in our research interests. Therefore, it is with pleasure and gratitude that I contribute a chapter on this topic to a volume in his honour.

Indian traditions, it provides a brief synopsis of the story. The article deals with the three-fold question of what is secured, who secures it, and why? The findings are summed up in the conclusion, providing a place for other studies of Indian security thought to start.

A UNIVERSAL UNDERSTANDING OF 'SECURITY'?

The global influence of Western social science and policy studies, which is both a consequence of colonialism and of post-World War II American academic domination, has rendered uniform the ways of seeing and theorizing 'security' in most academic and policy circles. Around the world, national security boards comprise military chiefs, defence bureaucrats, and diplomats, first and foremost, and institutes of security studies are essentially specialist centres for research into defence and foreign policy. Even those works that seek to accommodate a different political development trajectory than that of the Euro-American West, such as those by Mohammed Ayoob (1995), ultimately accept the focus on securing the state through foreign and military policy choices as natural and primary.

For the last decade or so Western scholars of security studies have engaged in definitional debates that have impinged largely on whether to expand the scope of the field. Several changes outside academe provided the impetus for this. First, and remotely, was an emerging global economic and security consensus (outside the US). Growing interdependence had made inequitable development inimical to both the more and less developed world. Further, security too was indivisible—one part of the world could not be held hostage to the rivalries of the other. Most recently, environmental issues have also been addressed from this interdependence standpoint. Articulated by landmark reports identified with Wilhelm Brandt (1980), Olof Palme (1982), and Gro Harlem Brundtland (1987), these views found institutional expression in the United Nations and other international fora. While American academics could and did ignore these developments, the second set of global events was compelling. The Soviet Union collapsed, ending the Cold War. It set in motion very rapid changes—the addition of new states to the international system and the dissolution of the Cold War division of Germany being only the beginning. Suddenly, it was as if the lid had been removed, and every world reality—hunger, injustice, conflict—that prioritizing the US–Soviet Union confrontation had concealed and contained was boiling right over. To add insult to injury, international relations scholars had failed to accurately predict the implosion of the Soviet system. The triumphal marches of the early 1990s were thus mixed with discordant notes of introspection and self-criticism.

All told, a fundamental review of the field was now called for. Barry Buzan's landmark *People, States and Fear* (1991) argued that beyond political and military security, there were three other salient dimensions—economic, societal, and environmental. However, he was quite clear that it was primarily the security of collectives, particularly the state, with which the field should remain concerned. Also within the realist tradition, Mohammed Ayoob (1995) challenged the focus on external threats, pointing out that to most new states, it was the process of state building itself that generated the most insecurities.

The opening up of other dimensions allowed discussion of issues hitherto well outside the scope of security studies or policy. Moving beyond Marxist critiques of core–periphery relations and the military–industrial complex, empirical research on the political economy of the trade in small arms, or what Peter Singer (2003) terms 'privatized military firms' (corporatized mercenaries), is now undertaken under the rubric of security studies. Similarly, identity politics, as it calls for the redrawing of boundaries within and across states, creates population movements, and results in violent conflict, is now part of the security studies mainstream (Brown 1993; Schmeidl 2002; Weiner 1993). Thomas Homer-Dixon's (2001) work on the relationship between resource scarcity and conflict has spawned a new area of research (also Klare 2002).

The realist/neorealist mainstream in international relations faced challenges from those who would stress the role institutional arrangements play to dilute power-seeking motivations or who would stress the importance of ideology. Marxists too challenged the discipline's conservatism by pointing to the iniquities inherent within the international system.

Critiques of security studies coming from outside mainstream international relations seek to further expand the scope of the field

(Krause and Williams 1997; Terriff et al. 1999). From peace studies comes a normative push to see peace as more than a state of 'no-war' and security as indivisible. Violence lies as much in structure as it does in the agency of an actor. Also in favour of an inclusive, non-hierarchical peace, feminism forces a further broadening of the agenda by arguing that a study of security should properly include the insecurities as well as the direct and structural violence that affect women primarily (Bertone 2000; Hudson and Den Boer 2002; Mazurana et al. 2002). Feminists also reject the inside–outside distinction, bringing issues like domestic violence and foeticide into the security agenda (Rajagopalan 2004).

Post-positivist approaches have also found their way to security studies. Challenging the idea that there can be 'one truth', that is, one way of seeing things, they point instead to the blurred lines between observer and observed, and reject the idea that the 'truth' can be objective observed and established. Knowledge in this universal without absolutes is socially constructed. Under this epistemological rubric fall several ideological schools, which would transform the field by insisting on deconstructive analysis, on evaluating work on the basis of its ability to help the troubled, and on examining the dialectic between the ideas and their material context. That 'securitizing' an issue is now a speech act that assures attention to a neglected issue is understood well, and adds impetus to this broadening drive.

The net result, much rued by many scholars of security studies including Steve Cohen, is an expansion of the scholarly agenda that is analytically ungainly even if it better reflects most people's reality. The dialectic of the field thus has a push–pull dynamic as some would enlarge its scope to include almost all of life itself and others would put back in place many of the old filters in order to create a more cogent policy agenda at least.

The puzzle is that those who expand the scope of this field have not thought to do so in terms of non-Western values and epistemologies. The expansionary drive, so to speak, drew on real world situations, but stopped short of taking into account civilizational diversity except insofar as diversity was seen to precipitate conflict. The relativism that has characterized the debate on other political issues is absent when it comes to security.

Moreover, positing difference and valorizing diversity are quite different from asking what it means to be secure or what it is that another society seeks most to secure—the task that this article undertakes.

INDIAN IDEAS AND CONTEMPORARY SCHOLARSHIP

Research has yielded only four works in which twentieth- and twenty-first-century scholars have shown interest in Indian ideas and arrangements related to security.

V.R. Ramachandra Dikshitar's *War in Ancient India* (1987, first published in 1944) focuses on war, militaries, and diplomacy. To Dikshitar, ancient India was a strife-torn world as a consequence of its society, which was divided along caste lines, equation of action with military campaigns, accent on heroism and adventure, imperialism, and a temperament combining aggression with defensiveness (ibid.: 8). Stephen Cohen's essay on civil–military relations studies caste structure and the Brahmin-Kshatriya equation to conclude that the king's role and powers were circumscribed by the 'all-pervasive religiosity of ancient Hindu society' (1964: 212), whereby the king (Kshatriya) remained the instrument of a purpose that was defined by the priestly caste (Brahmins). Stephen Rosen (1996), writing three decades later, places early India in a comparative context, seeking explanations for India's contemporary strategic culture. Rosen is persuaded that caste is an adequate answer in all historical periods. Unlike Dikshitar, whose life-work was an interpretation of early Indian ideas and texts, and Cohen, whose life-work has been the study of contemporary South Asian security and politics, Rosen's interest in India—early or contemporary—is only instrumental. This is most of all the case with Adda Bozeman. Bozeman's work epitomizes cross-cultural security studies to most Western scholars, but while she pioneered such study, her enthusiastic survey of cultural interactions over many periods and places is superficial and in places inaccurate. She does briefly discuss ancient India, but this is one of her weakest pieces. I only list her here because she is the name most associated with a study of this sort.

CAUTIONARY NOTES

One reason why there is so little work on this subject is that such research requires specialized language skills and historical context that most scholars in security do not possess. Further, those who do possess these skills are not interested in the same questions as security studies scholars are. Moreover, one faces important problems in the conceptual development of such a study, which I must very briefly highlight before we proceed.

The search for ideas about security in traditional Indian thought presupposes an understanding of what 'traditional Indian thought' is. This term is problematic because what constitutes 'India' or 'Indian' is defined anew everyday. Historically, 'India' was used to describe what has now come to be known as South Asia, of whose seven states it is only one. Political correctness is inimical to literary elegance; one can either use 'India' as one crosses the centuries to the mythic age of the *Ramayana* or clumsily use the very contemporary 'South Asia' to describe a time and a story whose consciousness does not even know Asia. Because the article seeks to define not India but security, I will simply use 'India' rather than South Asia. However, I will also clarify that the heritage of the *Ramayana* is, in my view, one to which every South Asian can lay claim and from which no one in this subcontinent may be rightfully alienated.

This brings me to the idea of 'tradition'. To identify Indian tradition with a single work, a single region, a single language, or a single faith is like identifying a yard of fabric with a single thread. The *Ramayana* thread in this civilizational fabric is one that recurs in different forms and shades. The epic is associated with Hinduism, but the story is known to both Hindus, and non-Hindus and its permeation of folk and classical arts knows no communal barriers. However, the civilization(s?) of South Asia comprise innumerable traditions; hence, the Rama story is a striking thread in one of the dominant traditions of the region, and the Valmiki text one of several written, oral, and performed renditions of the story.

If the claims that this article can make are limited by the enormous diversity of Indian traditions, the analytical time-travel adds further limits. Descriptions and ideas are presented here as if the millennia over which the *Valmiki Ramayana* acquired its present form were one moment in time. The *Valmiki Ramayana* acquired its present form over many centuries of remembered recitation. But the descriptions and ideas read in its text in 2004 are presented as if they occurred in one moment, were articulated in that moment, and remained true in that form for several centuries. Obviously, this is an analytical artifice. Nevertheless, all the researcher can do is to alert the reader.

Social science assumes a distinction between researcher and subject, and it also assumes that a researcher begins a study with a blank slate in that preconceived ideas do not impinge on the analysis. Transparency mitigates the absence of these criteria somewhat; therefore, I clarify, in the words of A.K. Ramanujam, 'In India and in Southeast Asia, no one ever reads the Ramayana or the Mahabharata for the first time. The stories are there, "always, already."' (1991: 46). This critical reading comes from a lifetime's intimacy with innumerable retellings—some mine, some others'—and not from an academic distance. As I began this study, I knew where I wanted to start looking, and it was only on second and third readings that I rediscovered forgotten passages and episodes that were also relevant. Moreover, my research into the secondary literature was like reading about myself. When *Ramayana* scholars wrote about the text, its consumers, and its narrators, I was all of them at once.

Finally, a study of this sort is prone to the fallacy of circular definition. How can you look for something unless you know what it is, and if you know what it is, will you find what you are looking for or what is out there? There is no exact equivalent of the term 'security'—which is hard enough to define in English itself—in Sanskrit, the language of the *Valmiki Ramayana*. Therefore, my search is dependent on my own previous training in security studies and on the way the understandings imparted thereby are mitigated by my own politics. What I ultimately bring to my exploration of the *Ramayana* is a broader understanding of security akin to the idea of 'human security'.

Why pursue a line of study that is so fraught with problems? Cross-cultural explorations of basic human values—justice, peace, security, freedom—lead to a cross-fertilization that can only be useful in an age of global regimes and global economics. In the South Asian context, all statutory warnings issued, it is particularly important as the region is home to more than a sixth of the world's population. Any globally-oriented security action that ignores the worldviews held by South Asians and their cultural underpinnings is doomed to rebound on its originators. Further, it is with every attempt to undertake cross-cultural investigations that we can hone the analytical tools we have for them.

WHY THE *RAMAYANA*?

This is a question no ordinary Indian would ask. There are many reasons why an exploration of Indian thinking is best begun with this popular and enduring story.

First, the Rama story is known around most parts of South Asia and many parts of South-East Asia, and over the millennia has become a part of their classical and folk, literary and performance heritage. The appeal of the *Ramayana* does transcend most divisions, as Paula Richman's (1992, 2000) anthologies on the various recensions extant show. The core plot is a simple, linear one and the dominance of the oral tradition has kept it fresh, as it changes with each telling and each hearing. Rama's triumph over his antagonist is a motif in the celebration of many Hindu festivals.

Second, the *Ramayana* offers a menu of ideals to the listener/ reader. First, the leading characters represent ideal types for the roles and relationships they portray. Rama is *maryada purushottama* (ideal man); his brothers and friends epitomize filial devotion and loyalty; his wife, Sita is represented as an ideal Indian woman;[2] and in addition, the epic features three of the five women considered in Indian mythology unparalleled in their integrity and spirit. In their behaviour, each of them holds up a standard against which Indians may measure themselves—as individuals and as members of a community (and it is this latter that is of interest to us). Second, the epic's rulers are praised for their standards of governance. Rama's

---

[2]On the *Valmiki Ramayana* and women, see Rajagopalan (2004).

rule, *Ramarajya*, is a utopian vision of perfect governance, yielding perfect health, prosperity, and virtue in the lives of its citizens. But he is not the only ruler exalted. His father is as well, and his father-in-law is that rare creature—a *rajarshi*—one who rules in perfect detachment and wisdom. There are passages throughout the Valmiki version that describe the fruits of such excellent governance as well as didactic passages where Valmiki, through the words of characters, advises rulers on rules and standards they should observe. These ideals still animate everyday conversations and political discussions in India at least.

Finally, the accessibility of the narrative and the appeal of its idealized protagonists makes it a useful tool for political mobilization. This is what has happened in the last two decades, as *Hindutvavadi* organizations mobilized support for their political agendas using the construction of a temple at the site said to be Rama's birthplace as their rallying point.[3] In the resulting polarization of Indian politics and society, *Ramayana* tropes and metaphors have been more or less appropriated by *Hindutvavadi* opinion makers. This lifts a study like this somewhat out of the academic and into the polemical realm, as we reclaim a text whose richness has lain in the freedom with which it has been narrated and interpreted. It is both a scholarly and political task to ask what the text actually says. In the specific context of security, it is important to be able to hold up actions undertaken in the name of these ideals to scrutiny by contrasting them with our reading of the text.

There are countless *Ramayana*s, and thanks to Paula Richman's two excellent anthologies, this is now recognized by the scholarly universe. Nevertheless, the *Valmiki Ramayana* is considered the '*adikavya*' or earliest literature (Basham 1967: 414; Warder 1975:175). Carried by Brahmins across the subcontinent, it inspired other regional recitations. This is why it forms the basis of this study.

---

[3]*Hindutva*, or Hindu-ness, is the ideological basis of the Rashtriya Swayamsevak Sangh (RSS), the Bharatiya Janata Party (BJP), and their allies, who are described as Hindu right-wing or Hindu nationalist organizations. I prefer to use the term 'Hindutvadi', a term they use, because the English terms do not fit exactly. For more, see Rajagopalan (2003).

THE STORY IN BRIEF

On the banks of the Sarayu, the town of Ayodhya stood like a beacon. Many generations of excellent Ikshvaku rulers had built a kingdom full of happy, prosperous, healthy, and virtuous people. The present ruler, Dasharatha, was no exception. His four sons, born after the performance of a sacrifice seeking the blessing of an heir, were outstanding young men, exceptional in their devotion to each other. They married princesses from Mithila, and life was idyllic until the eve of the eldest prince Rama's installation as heir-apparent. Rama's stepmother used two boons granted to her in the early years of her marriage to have her son Bharata replace Rama and the latter exiled for fourteen years. Ever obedient, Rama departed for the forest; however, he did not leave alone as his younger brother Lakshmana and his wife Sita insisted on accompanying him.

The beginning of the exile was a sylvan idyll. The royal trio visited sages, enjoying their company and hospitality, and delighting in being able to protect their hosts from disruptive *rakshasas* (ogres). This ended when an ogress, Soorpanakha, saw Rama and fell in love with him. She took their ironic responses for flirtation and offered to kill Sita, the impediment to her happiness. Provoked, Rama had Lakshmana mutilated her by cutting off her nose and ears.

This act set the rest of the epic's events in motion as Soorpanakha was the sister of Ravana, the *rakshasa* king of Lanka. Ravana had deputed his brothers to harass the denizens of this region, and she ran first to them for justice. In a series of confrontations, the brothers killed everyone who came to defend her, so she finally went to Lanka and sought Ravana's help. She also described Sita's beauty, inflaming passions of fury and lust in her brother. Weighing his options, he chose to heed those who enthusiastically advocated revenge over those, like his brother Vibheeshana, who asked him to desist.

Ravana abducted Rama's wife through an elaborate deception. He bore her away to Lanka and tried to win her favours by alternately seducing and threatening her. She was steadfast in her refusal to entertain his suit.

Discovering her disappearance, Rama and Lakshmana followed first a trail of tossed ornaments and then clues given by friendly creatures for some distance. Directed to the *vanara* (monkey or forest-dweller) kingdom, they formed friendships with the *vanara* king Sugriva and his counsellor Hanuman. To honour this friendship, Rama killed Sugriva's brother and rival Vali, while remaining in hiding—one of the most contentious acts in the epic. In return for this, Sugriva sent out a search party, and Hanuman crossed the sea to Lanka and finally found Sita.

War ensued, and Rama, Lakshmana, and the *vanara*s won. The second contentious act of Rama was to tell Sita that he had rescued her to prove his manhood, but having lived with another man for a year, she was free to go where she would. But an ordeal by fire established her fidelity, and the trio returned to Ayodhya, their exile also completed.

Rama's virtue was so great that during his reign everything in his kingdom and in his subjects' lives was perfect. One day he learned that some of his subjects were still sceptical of Sita's fidelity. He exiled her although she was pregnant, and the epic culminates in his reunion with their children, his insistence on her proving herself once more, and her decision to return to her mother, the earth (that is, to die).

'SECURITY' IN THE *RAMAYANA*

The substantive core of this article, this section is based on a close reading of the *Valmiki Ramayana* in translation. Who secures what from whom/what and why, to put it very simply, are the questions posed of the text. The story itself, descriptions within the text, and didactic passages where one of the characters makes a point to another are used as the basic database. Incidents are not discussed as they appear in the narrative but in the order devised for analysis.

As this section begins, acts of support, refuge, protection, and vengeance will be listed as variations of the act of 'securing'. This is an instance of the circular definition trap I described earlier—in order to answer any of these questions (whose aim is to define security), I must first offer a working definition of security. I do so in these minimal terms and interpret them broadly to somewhat redress the fallacy. Further, if you place support, refuge, protection, and vengeance on a continuum, there are other values and behaviours that belong on the same continuum. Nurture, defence, justice, creation, and peace itself are tucked away in some of the intervals. Therefore, while primarily narrating instances of support, refuge, protection, and vengeance, we might do so knowing these other values are likely implicit and might also constitute security, either instrumentally or intrinsically.

Traditionally a discussion of security in a particular setting is a description of security measures, where what is to be secured and from what are considered axiomatic. Here, because we take none of these prior understandings as sacrosanct, the questions posed are more fundamental, and armies, spies, and military tactics are considered relevant only as instruments to secure whatever is to be secured. In this short paper they are not discussed at all.

Acts of Support

The encounter between Rama and the *vanara* king Sugriva was immediately sealed with a friendship pact between the two. Sugriva was hiding from his brother Vali. Presuming Vali dead, Sugriva ascended his throne and took his wife; however, Vali was alive. Unable to give his brother the benefit of the doubt in these circumstances, Vali now wanted revenge. Rama promised to kill him and free Sugriva, while the latter promised to find Sita and help rescue her. Overseen by Hanuman, this friendship pact lasted through the war to the very end of the Rama story when all of the *vanaras*, except Hanuman, who knows no death, followed Rama to his end.

Alliances of mutual support are thus important as each ally helps the other eliminate threats or cope with losses. While the story describes the bonding of Rama and Sugriva as individuals, their friendship is tantamount to an inter-group alliance by another reading. What this underscores is the centrality of cooperative action to security. Notwithstanding the brothers' military prowess and Rama's divinity, the friendship of Sugriva and the *vanara*s is essential to each turn in their mission—the search for Sita, the building of a bridge across the sea, Hanuman flying out to get life-saving herbs for an unconscious Lakshmana in the middle of the war, and not least, the provision of an infantry.

Acts of Refuge

In the build-up to the war, Ravana's brother Vibheeshana tried to convince him to return Sita and avert the defeat and destruction that fighting Rama would bring. Unsuccessful and insulted, he and a few companions sought refuge in Rama's camp. Rama consulted his allies on the question of offering refuge even as he told them:

> In the name of humanity one should not strike even an enemy arrived at one's door and piteously soliciting protection with joined palms, O scourge of your enemies! An enemy come for protection against his enemies, be he distressed or [even] proud, should be protected [even] at the cost of one's life by one who has subdued one's mind. If from fear or folly or even from desire [of some gain] a man does not justly protect a refugee according to his capacity, the sin incurred by him is despised in the world. [Nay] if, remaining unprotected, a refugee perishes before the eyes of the man who is able to protect him, the former makes away all his merit....
>
> I vouchsafe *security* against all living beings to him who comes to me only once and seeks protection [from me], saying 'I am yours': such is my vow. Bring him [hither], O jewel among monkeys, be he Vibhisana or Ravana himself, O Sugriva! *Security* has [already] been granted in his favour by me.' (SVR II Yuddha XVIII: 27–30, 33–34, 281–82) (emphases mine)

In other words, offering refuge is an integral part of security. The person who seeks it is in search of security and the person approached is morally bound to provide it. A variation on this theme appears in the *Uttarakandam*[4] where the importance of responding promptly to

---

[4]There are two volumes of the Gita Press translation of the *Valmiki Ramayana*, which is the version used in this paper. The first contains four books of the text (*Balakandam, Ayodhyakandam, Aranyakandam,* and *Kishkindhakandam*) and the second three (*Sundarakandam, Yuddhakandam,* and *Uttarakandam*). Of these, the Balakandam and the Uttarakandam are considered later interpolations. I cite extracts in the following format: SVR (for *Srimad Valmiki Ramayanam*), I or II to indicate the volume, the abbreviated name of the book (*Bala, Ayodhya, Aranya, Kishkindha, Sundara, Yuddha, Uttara*), canto number: verse number, page number in that volume. The full citation follows in the bibliography.

petitioners in search of help or justice is emphasized more than once. Security is then to be found in the prompt and full response made to a situation of need—where the need is insecurity, and the response its alleviation in the best circumstances.

Acts of Protection, of Others and Oneself

Protection is a very prominent part of Rama's view of his life-purpose, and this view reflects the larger purpose of his incarnation (of which he remains mostly unaware) as well as his caste duty as a Kshatriya.

Protection of Others

While the heirless king of Ayodhya, Dasharatha, was getting ready to perform a sacrifice in the hopes of begetting a son, deities and heavenly beings complained that they were afraid of him, protected as he was by a boon that none of them could kill him.

Even as Dasharatha was praying for a son, gods and other heavenly beings were seeking Vishnu's help against the ogre Ravana's unchecked strength. Ravana was protected against death at the hands of any other than a human. Vishnu promised to kill Ravana on the battlefield in their interests (SVR 1 Bala XV: 29, 48) and his incarnation as the human prince, Rama, was the vehicle for this.

When Dasharatha's sons were still young, the sage Vishwamitra arrived at court. Asked what he would like, Vishwamitra demanded that Rama and Lakshmana accompany him in order to protect him and other ascetics whose penances were being disrupted by ogres. Faltering at the prospect of his young sons face to face with ogres, Dasharatha was reprimanded for failing to keep a promise. Moreover, protection was (is) the duty of kings (and princes). In this instance, it was both protection of the ascetics, as well as protection of *dharma*[5]

---

[5]The word '*dharma*' is related to the word for holding or sustaining. It is traditionally used in any of three senses: (*a*) the ideational order that underpins society and the institutions it spawns, (*b*) an individual's own roles and duties that are partly intrinsic and partly based upon her or his place in that order, and (*c*) a more abstract sense of right and righteousness. In contemporary times the word is also used for 'religion' in the Semitic sense of the term, even though Indic belief systems and faiths do not conform to the symbolic and institutional features of Semitic faiths. This becomes a source of conceptual confusion in the political discourse. This paper uses the term '*dharma*' in its traditional rather than newer sense.

itself, which was maintained in part by the performance of sacrifices and austerities. The protection of *dharma* was the protection of the state; a state without *dharma* was (is?) doomed to decline. The two boys went with the sage, helped him, furthered their spiritual and military education, and brought themselves back brides.

In the course of their journey the boys learnt the story of Vishwamitra. Born a Kshatriya and king, Vishwamitra chose the path of penance and austerities following a conflict with the sage Vashishtha, who incidentally was the guru of Rama's family, the Ikshvakus.

The conflict arose over Vishwamitra's coveting Vashishtha's wish-giving cow, Shabala. Claiming he had a right to it as sovereign over the region, Vishwamitra had her carried away. In each of the violent confrontations provoked by Vishwamitra's sons and soldiers, Vashishtha's smallest exercise of spiritual energy prevailed and the king was left, defeated, enraged, and admiring. Attempts to equal Vashishtha's prowess culminated in Vishwamitra's transcending his own objective. For our purpose, what is important is to note that the protection of the cow, which we are told was as a daughter to Vashishtha, was both a protection of property and kin. From Vishwamitra's point of view, the conflict was about suzerainty and then revenge. Finally, this conflict becomes rivalry, at least in the mind of Vishwamitra, who is determined to equal, if not surpass, Vasishtha's power and status.

Forest ascetics requested protection from the exiled princes (for instance, SVR I Aranya VI). On that occasion, in one of her longest speeches, Sita made a plea for non-violence. She cautioned him against cruelty without enmity or provocation. She sought to protect his *dharma* while he protected the ascetics. She warned that carrying a weapon corrupts a person by tempting them into cruelty (SVR I Aranya IX: 23, 572–73). Rama's response is that he is bound by his promise and his duty as a Kshatriya to carry weapons and offer protection against those who threaten them and their penances (SVR II Aranya X: 3, 15–20, 574–76).

The mutilation of Surpanakha is one of the most grotesque episodes in the epic and it sets the stage for Rama's encounter with Ravana (SVR I Aranya XVIII). Rama and Lakshmana flirt with her cruelly, but when she offers to hurt Sita, the protection impulse goes to work and she loses her nose and ears. In the Tamil *Ramayana* by Kambar, she loses her breasts. The sequence of events that unfolds culminates in the abduction of Sita by Ravana.

The deception that made this possible was the appearance of an enchanted golden deer near Rama's hermitage. Sita pleads with Rama to capture the deer for her. The deer leads him a distance before Rama, realizing that it is an ogre in disguise, kills him. The deer is restored to its ogre form and lets out a dying cry in Rama's voice, 'Lakshmana!' Hearing this, a distressed Sita insists on her brother-in-law running to Rama's aid.

Most oral renditions of this story will say at this point that, reluctant to break his word to protect her, Lakshmana drew a line— Lakshmana *Rekha* or the line of Lakshmana—around the hut, placing a protection charm on it. He strictly forbade her to step across this line. At this point the storyteller could adopt one of two storylines. Ravana comes calling on Sita in the guise of a mendicant. The first has Sita step across the line to pour rice into Ravana's begging bowl. The second has her invite him in to accept alms. Either way, it is the violation of this charmed line of protection that makes her vulnerable. The idea of a 'Lakshmana *Rekha*' is deeply entrenched in the Indian vocabulary. It is used regularly to denote either a set of taboos or a self-restraint. However, the Lakshmana *Rekha* story is not found in the *Valmiki Ramayana*, the *Kamba Ramayanam*, or Tulsidas' *Ramcharitamanas*; it appears to come from a more recent text, the *Adhyatma Ramayana*.

In the *Valmiki Ramayana*, Lakshmana leaves asking the deities of the forest to take care of Sita. When the brothers return to find her gone, Rama reprimands Lakshmana for allowing Sita's anxiety to make him break his promise. A 'reproachful act' has been committed by 'leaving alone Sita, who deserved protection' (SVR I LVII: 14–19, 693–94). It is an 'error that is grievous in every respect' (SVR I LVIII: 15, 695–96). He dismisses Lakshmana's explanation, saying that it was wrong to leave Sita alone and unprotected just because she spoke anxiously and angrily (SVR I LIX: 21–27, 697–98).

Once hostilities have broken out and casualties sustained on both sides, Ravana makes a renewed threat assessment and it is not an optimistic one. Finally taking cognizance of the power and fighting prowess of Rama's allies and armies, he asks battle survivors to keep the doors and outer gates of the citadel closed and defend it vigilantly. He asks them to keep watch on all entry and exit points at all times and to remain at their posts with their troops at all times. Ravana reaffirms the importance of knowing where the enemy is at all times— that is, the importance of assiduous intelligence gathering (SVR II Yuddha LXXII: 8–16, 487–88).

Protection of Self

The most immediate sense in which we usually understand security is self-defence. Three acts of self-protection in the *Ramayana* may be listed here. All three involve killing an ogre who has attacked Rama or Lakshmana. In two out of three cases, the ogre is a fallen creature from heaven and the act of self-defence becomes an act of redemption.

The princes and Sita encounter Viradha in the early part of their exile. Rama and Lakshmana attack him when he lecherously picks up Sita. This provokes him to drop her and pick them up. When they manage to kill him for attacking them, he reveals his identity. The story of Kabandha is very similar. He looks to eat Rama and Lakshmana, but they escape by cutting off his arms. This releases him from his curse. Ayomukhi is an ogress who is attracted to and propositions Lakshmana. He cuts off her nose, ears, and breasts in response—similar to the response Surpanakha received.

Sugriva's wish to have Vali killed also falls into this category. Vali has been hunting him for years and Sugriva wishes to be free.

Protection of the Social Order

Beyond a Kshatriya's duty to protect others and the human impulse to protect oneself, lay the duty to protect broader principles and values of society that devolved on kings. In the *Ramayana*'s last and interpolated book, the *Uttarakandam*, this duty is performed on two occasions. Debate on the first has always existed, but the second is also now contentious.

The first occasion arises when Rama is told that people in his kingdom are speculating about the hold Sita has on him, allowing him to overlook her year spent in another man's palace and take her back. Notwithstanding her trial by fire at the end of the war, they question her fidelity and lament the fact that his action in reuniting with her sets a (binding) precedent on them to accept their unfaithful wives. We are told that Rama does not essentially doubt Sita's fidelity, but he cannot stand to have aspersions cast on either his detachment or his ability to be impartial in meting out punishment. Detachment and impartiality of the king are the underpinnings of the social order. Her exile is the price of his good name (SVR II Uttara XLIV–XLV).

When one sets the issue of Sita's fidelity against other women's stories in the *Valmiki Ramayana*, another issue emerges: controlling the behaviour of women is essential to the maintenance of a *dharmik* society. Ahalya is a willing party to the seduction that ends in extramarital intercourse. She is turned to dust as a punishment. Kaikeyi uses her husband's especial affection for her to win the exile of Rama and the ascension to the throne of her own son. She is vilified harshly by everyone except Rama who sees her as a mere agent of fate. Women who articulate their desires and assert their right to have them fulfilled are inimical to social order as Valmiki valued it. So the idea that Sita could have had a choice of men at some point and the chance to exercise that choice was untenable. Further, that Rama should be able to accept this suggested that he was not the ideal protector of the order it threatened.

Rama killed Shambhuka for performing austerities forbidden to him as a Shudra. As the story unfolds, a petitioner approaches Rama in court to say that his governance is not so perfect for his child has died. A visiting sage, Narada, tells him this has happened because someone is violating caste rules by engaging in spiritual activities. Rama scours the kingdom and chances upon Shambhuka. When Shambhuka honestly identifies himself as a Shudra, Rama informs him that he will lose his life for this violation of caste prohibitions. As a sign that the social order has been restored, the child is revived (SVR II Uttara LXXV).

Acts of Punishment and Vengeance

Where the study of government is called '*dandaniti*', or the law of punishment, acts of vengeance and punishment cannot be separated from definitions of security.

The first 'crime and punishment' story in the epic is that of Ahalya, wife of a sage, and Indra, the king of heaven. An enamoured Indra took the form of Ahalya's husband and approached her. Although she recognized him, she was flattered and curious, and allowed him to seduce her. Her husband caught them as Indra was leaving. He cursed them both. Ahalya was turned to dust and Indra was covered first with a thousand phalluses and then, on divine intercession, a thousand eyes. In Ahalya's case the curse would end by the touch of Rama's feet. Thus, there was instant punishment, but it had to be somewhat proportionate and it had to have an end.

Parasurama is considered the divine incarnation preceding Rama's and their encounter marks the passing of the mantle from one to the other. There are two stories of punishment associated with Parasurama's life, but only one of them features in the *Ramayana*, which is the one this discussion focuses on. One day while meditating, Parasurama heard his mother call twenty-one times for help. Upon visiting the *ashrama* of Parasurama's parents, he found that the king of that realm, Kartavirya Arjuna, had carried away the gift-giving cow Kamadhenu. Parasurama restored the cow and its calf to his parents, but not before defeating the royal army and killing the king. The sons of Arjuna visited the *ashrama* in Parasurama's absence and killed his father to avenge the killing of theirs. Parasurama then single-handedly killed twenty-one generations of Kshatriyas and having rid the earth of its ruling caste, handed its kingship to a Brahmin sage. The cycle of vengeance then abated and Parasurama retired to purely spiritual pursuits.

News of Rama stringing Shiva's bow provoked him to issue a fresh challenge to avenge what he thought might be an insult to the singularity of the weapon. Could Rama repeat the feat with its twin, the bow of Vishnu, now in Parasurama's possession? That Rama could established the authenticity of the Rama incarnation, and put an end to the Parasurama incarnation.

When Surpanakha was mutilated, she ran to her brothers Khara and Dooshana to complain. In order to avenge the wrong done to her, they first sent their armies to attack Rama and Lakshmana. When their soldiers were defeated, they themselves went into battle and lost their lives (SVR I Aranya XIX–XX, XXII–XXX). The cycle of revenge and injury and revenge set in motion by the mutilation of Surpanakha resulted in the abduction of Sita and the destruction of Lanka. Losing Khara and Dooshana, she ran to her most powerful brother, Ravana. She taunted him for being unable to protect her, and she described to him the beauty of Sita. As a result, Ravana was not only outraged at the fate of his sister, but also intrigued that there was a beautiful woman he had not won over himself.

Rama explained to Vali that he had been killed not as he supposed as a quid pro quo for the rescue of Sita, but as punishment for his unrighteous expulsion of his brother Sugriva and his consorting with the latter's wife. It was the king's right and duty to punish all wrongdoing and Rama was acting as the agent of his brother Bharata.

The war in Lanka was the ultimate punishment or act of vengeance. Ravana had abducted Sita, and for this, Lanka would pay. The sins of the king visit on his subjects—some things never change. At the end of the war, Rama was granted a boon and asked for the lives of all those who fought for him. There was no amnesty for those who fought on the wrong side of the war.

The question of proportionality in all these cases is a difficult one. What is disproportionate by the standards of our age—the turning to dust of Ahalya for two ages—is within the universe of the protagonists apparently proportionate. What we need to take out of these examples are not the individual equations but the principle that there is something such as inadequate and something such as excessive punishment. There is room for repentance and for merciful commutation of sentences.

Acts of Redemption

Viewing each birth as one pause in the self's journey towards self-actualization, one looks to secure good things for this life and the ones after. The *Ramayana* includes many instances in which an accursed existence is ended by meeting Rama or death at his hands assures release from the cycle of rebirth. This, of course, is closely tied to Rama's characterization as an incarnation of Vishnu. There are allusions to this, and Rama feels himself transformed on two occasions. But essentially, in the *Valmiki Ramayana*, he remains ignorant of his true identity and on two occasions he is reminded of it. Both times he has doubted his wife Sita, who is in turn the consort or *shakti* (energy) of the reincarnated Vishnu.

Release from a curse is similar to return from exile because essentially the curse interrupts one life with another, and the release is a restoration. Similarly, as facilitating a traveller on a journey secures the traveller's ends, so does the encounter with Rama facilitate the journey of the self in the *Valmiki Ramayana*. Rama attributes this to his acting on behalf of a good king, but we as consumers of the story know it comes from his divine nature.

Three of the four instances where Rama is the agent of redemption have already been discussed in this article. Ahalya (SVR I Bala XLVIII–XLIX) and Kabandha (SVR I Aranya LXIX–LXX) are both released from a curse through Rama's arrival in their lives. Both pass also from corporeal to ethereal existence with his grace. Vali is punished by Rama, but he recognizes that by killing him, Rama has given him a chance at immortality.

It is Sabari we encounter for the first time as we close this section. Sabari has waited through the ages, deferring her own death for the chance to meet Rama (SVR I Aranya: 74). She has prepared for hundreds of years to host him and having done so, is freed from the cycle of mortality.

WHAT UNDERSTANDING OF SECURITY MAY WE DERIVE FROM THIS?

Filtering the preceding discussion through the four questions raised in this one, we are offered a glimpse of what the *Valmiki Ramayana* might offer the definitional debates in security studies.

What is Secured?

Any study of security first begins by identifying the referent of the term 'security'. Who or what is secured in the *Valmiki Ramayana* and, ergo, what we might conclude about who or what should be secured are the points of departure for the last section of this article. The preceding analysis of the story suggests three main referents: *dharma*, the individual, and least frequently, proprietary rights. The most important of these is *dharma*. In both its sense as the underpinnings of the social order and the quality of righteousness, *dharma* is to be secured.

There is, in Indian thought, a close relationship between *dharma* as a set of values and principles that are the foundation of a society and the righteous behaviour of individuals. The two are related at the level of ideas in that one aspect of the social order is the definition of *svadharma*—an individual's own *dharma*—which is determined by age and station (or life-stage and caste, more specifically). The two are also symbiotically related insofar as a society based in principle on *dharma* is not really '*dharmik*' if it consists of unrighteous people or, worse, is ruled by an unrighteous king. The righteousness of the people follows the example set by the king—*yatha raja tatha praja* (as the king so the people), the saying goes. Therefore, the king's own character and behaviour must embody righteousness. This means always doing what is right, disregarding his own preferences, being available to those in need, and applying the law as equally as it is set out.

On the other hand, *dharma* itself was something larger and higher than, as well as separate from, the collective of righteous people and righteous king. All of them were subject to and instruments of this higher value system (or if you would, morality or ideology). Such a moral framework is why the *Ramayana* tradition is replete with debates over incidents that are morally ambivalent. Anyone may constantly be judged against the standards of this unarticulated but overarching morality.

The purpose of the Rama *avatara* (incarnation) was the protection of *dharma*, both in its broader societal sense and in the individual one. A scholarly and devout king, Ravana was ambitious, and enjoyed and asserted his power, even in the heavens. His growing power threatened the continuance of a particular order, kept in place by certain gods and certain social and ritual practices—a certain *dharma*. Further, his own conduct fell short of what was considered righteous. On both counts an intervention was called for, and since Ravana was protected by a boon from death at the hands of every creature save a human, this was accomplished through Vishnu's human incarnation as Rama:

> They call it 'Dharma', for it sustains [the world]. The created
> beings are sustained by 'Dharma.' Since it supports the three

worlds together with all the movable and immovable things. He [the king] sustains [even] his enemies, puts them on the right path and delights his subjects by 'Dharma.' Therefore he [his rule] is known as 'Dharma.' This act of 'Dhrana' or sustaining is 'Dharma'—this is the conclusion. O king Sri Rama, this is the highest Dharma which yields compassion, honouring noble men, straight-forwardness in behaviour, O Rama! This is the 'Dharma' in this life and the life hereafter that accrues from protecting the subjects. (SVR II Uttara Interpolated Canto II: 7–10, 852).

As the basis of the social order, *dharma* is to be protected at all costs. As youth and later during their exile, Rama and Lakshmana undertake to guard ascetics during the conduct of rituals and austerities. *Dharma* is invoked here in two ways. First, it is their *dharma* to protect all in their care, as these ascetics living in forests within their domain are. Second, in the proper and undisturbed conduct of such austerities lies the ultimate defence of the social order—who gets to perform them, whether they are performed properly, and whether they are performed at the right times are determinants of whether the gods will bless the people of the kingdom. Both in the *Balakandam* and the *Aranyakandam*, *dharma*, the basis of the social order, is an important referent of security.

In the last and interpolated book of the epic, this order is protected through the punishing of one alleged transgression and one actual transgression. By showing himself impartial in the first instance (which involves his wife Sita) and prompt in the second (the killing of Shambhuka—by stopping only to state the cause of death to the offender), the king goes beyond removing the cause of the decline in *dharma*. He also manages to reaffirm his credentials as king and restore confidence in his kingship. The latter is an important element in the preservation of the social order because people follow the lead of the king.

The second dimension of *dharma* is righteous behaviour on the part of the individual. As the individual is the unit upon which society and *dharma* both depend, bad moral choices on his or her part are also detrimental to the continuance of a given order. What is interesting is that all the three instances of individual misbehaviour that are punished relate to fidelity and adultery issues. Ahalya is punished for following her curiosity. Vali is punished for cohabiting with his sister-in-law. The sack of Lanka follows the abduction and captivity of Sita. Sita's later expulsion relates to her fidelity during captivity. Shambhuka's is the sole exception; it is unrighteous behaviour that unsettles the *dharmik* basis of society by violating caste rules.

The second referent of security is the individual whose survival and safety are to be secured. Acts of support, refuge, and protection were carried out to keep individuals safe. Vibheeshana and Sugriva sought safety through refuge and alliance with Rama. In encounters with *rakshasa*s, the brothers protect themselves and Sita from getting hurt. As the prospect of defeat looms nearer, Ravana urges the soldiers and citizens of Lanka to protect the citadel and thereby protect themselves.

There is one instance where ownership is protected—that of Sabala by Vashishtha. However, Rama's campaign to recover his wife also has shades of proprietorship about it, and when he tells her he cannot accept her after she has spent a year in Ravana's custody, he effectively tells her he has just protected his honour.

From What is the Referent Secured?

In the *Valmiki Ramayana rakshasa*s are the agents of death, destruction, desecration, and dissipation—all sources of insecurity to the denizens of Rama's universe. In the most literal sense, then, the main threat to Rama's world stems from *rakshasa*s whose magical powers and strength are used always for evil.

At several points through the text, these magical powers—to fly, to change form, to change size—are described. What are wonderful qualities in heavenly beings like *gandharva*s are dreadful in *rakshasa*s who are also described as ugly, grotesque, and frightening. Theirs is a brute strength, animated by a bestial nature. As he enters Lanka, Hanuman is struck both by the grandeur of its palaces and the wild abandon of the revelries within them. Unfettered by shame, scruples or the need to obey social strictures, the *rakshasa*s are self-indulgent in ways for which humans and *vanara*s are punished. They thus represent the quintessential 'other'—the natural enemy. *Rakshasas* threaten the princes and others with death, either so that they may be consumed or out of anger. The threat of sexual assault and also violent jealousy must also be prevented from fruition. *Rakshasas* desecrate as sport the austerities and penances of ascetics. This last does not merely destroy the efforts of the ascetics but over time, it undermines the ritual and spiritual underpinnings of society, i.e., *dharma*.

The survival of characters and their safety from violence, including sexual, is an important concern throughout. After all, this is an epic that precipitates its culmination through the abduction of the chief female protagonist. Theft and arbitrary rule are also punished, but the epic does not waste a great deal of time discussing private ownership as a value or the right to rebel. Insults and revenge also reduce security by fostering a climate of conflict.

However, one really important category in this discussion of threats is the question of immoral conduct. In keeping with the value that is placed on controlling one's senses—a value that is even greater for kings—the *Ramayana*'s people are most unforgiving when dealing with those who indulge their passions. Ahalya and Vali pay for their own mistakes; the people of Lanka pay for Ravana's lust for Sita and for revenge against Rama.

Related to this is the threat posed by unrighteous conduct ranging from dissolute self-indulgence to violating caste rules. Vibheeshana defects to Rama's side, unwilling to be part of Ravana's intransigence on restoring Sita to her husband. Rama exiles Sita rather than be regarded as partial to her and unable to do what is right—even though he has done what is right.

In short, Rama's world is most threatened by *rakshasas* who, among other things, undermine the *dharma* that is essential to its survival. It is the threat of *adharma* that looms largest, in other words, and this threat is made real by the *rakshasas*.

By Whom is the Referent Secured?

Agency in the matter of creating security is the preserve of very few, all male. The most important agent of security is Lord Vishnu in his incarnations. He took the form of Parasurama to rid the world of an abundance of arbitrary rulers and then took the form of Rama to eliminate Ravana.

In this story of Rama, it is Rama and his brother Lakshmana who are responsible for most of the security actions. In each category—support, refuge, protection, and punishment—the brothers work together.

Finally, the very patriarchal (even misogynistic) bent of this epic invests in kings, husbands, and brothers the right to make rules, interpret, and enforce them. The right to avenge dishonour also vests in them. Whether it is Ahalya's husband who punishes her and her lover, Parasurama's father who orders his wife killed, the brothers of Soorpanakha or Rama acting as Bharata's agent to kill Vali, none of them owe the subject of their actions any warning or justification.

To What End?

The answer to this question is drawn out of the responses to the preceding three. The purpose of any security-related action—support, refuge, protection, punishment, and redemption—is ultimately the preservation of *dharma* in all the senses discussed in the response to the first question on referents.

Many actions are undertaken in the epic for survival and safety as well. Further, the assertion of ownership and manhood and wreaking vengeance are also motivations for acting in ways that increase or decrease security.

However, all roads, all anecdotes and discussions lead back to the question of *dharma* and of maintaining the ethical foundations of society.

Postscript

The centrality of *dharma* explains also the reason why acts of redemption are included here. This is a moral and didactic text, and most Indians read it not as story or analytical object, but as a record of grace on earth. Therefore, it is important to note that in this epic the transcendental dimension of security is also served. Ahalya, Kabandha, Sabari, and Vali, among others, achieve immortality and release through Rama's grace. This releases them from the endless burden of mortal life after mortal life, and they merge with eternity.

In the Hindu-Buddhist framework, to not be born again is freedom from no small burden.

FROM VALMIKI'S TEXT TO OUR TIMES

What is security, then, if we were to base our understanding on the values and priorities of the *Valmiki Ramayana*? Then, as now, security pertained to many things, but none more vitally than the protection and preservation of *dharma*. *Dharma* referred to both the foundational value system of a society as well as prescribed and actual individual behaviour. Beyond *dharma*, security was survival and safety, protection of honour and property, and sometimes an end to arbitrary rule. Self-indulgent behaviour, arbitrariness, unrighteous choices, and *rakshasa*s posed the greatest threats to society. The right to act was confined to divine incarnations and other male authority figures.

The first step in applying what we can learn from Valmiki for our own times is to define what our *dharma* is. What is our foundational ideology or value system—at least in India? This brings us back to the debate currently polarizing Indian political discussion—what are India's fundamental values? Traditionally, Indians have not spent centuries making lists of these values, but as in Valmiki's time, each of us could now come up with a list of our own, adding a rivulet to the larger debate.

Beyond forcing this question on us, Valmiki's epic is remarkable for its disinterest in military issues. Unlike the other great Indian epic, the *Mahabharata*, the *Ramayana* glosses over details of military preparations or the great rituals performed to expand a king's sovereignty. It is the continuance of a value system at one level and the righteous conduct of individuals that make a society secure. The king, as an agent of *dharma*, is charged with enforcing both and protecting individuals against *adharma*, within them or in their surroundings. To step a little beyond the scope of this article, examples of well-governed polities in the *Valmiki Ramayana* are essentially descriptions of communities whose people are prosperous, happy, healthy, and virtuous. Their well-being is a product of *dharma* being successfully preserved. Thus, a secure society is not a militarily powerful one—to the exclusion of good, value-based governance.

Finally, the emphasis placed on individual morality and behaviour as an appropriate referent for security action is in sharp contrast to our times, where the louder the rhetoric on accountability, the less accountable the elite actually are. There was zero tolerance in Rama's time for moral transgressions, and the number of politicians who would meet his standards in their own personal conduct is probably rather pitiful today.

Not all the news is positive though. This is a deeply misogynistic text, and its values are clearly precursors of many continuing problems faced by women in South Asia. From male preference to the denial of female agency, not much has changed since Valmiki composed these verses. Moreover, Valmiki's epic is a firm believer in the caste rules we now say we reject. This really underscores the importance of understanding what our own *dharma* is today as a society. It brings us back to the first question raised in this concluding section.

The hallmark of a great book is that you can reread it ad infinitum, read it with absorption and still engage with it each time in a totally different way. This story, beloved to millions of South Asians, is a great book and a repository of many of the most enduring values and metaphors in Indian political discourse. Its ideas about security, as well as governance and polity, deserve more than one exploration, and this article is an attempt to open up the opportunity for such explorations.

BIBLIOGRAPHY

Ayoob, Mohammed (1995). *The Third World Security Predicament*. Boulder: Lynne Rienner.

Basham, A.S. (1967). *The Wonder that was India*. Calcutta: Rupa.

Bertone, Andrea Marie (2000). Sexual Trafficking in Women: International Political Economy and the Politics of Sex. *Gender Issues*, 18(1), pp. 4–22.

Bozeman, Adda B. (1960). *Politics and Culture in International History*. Princeton: Princeton University Press.

———— (1992). *Selected Essays: Strategic Intelligence & Statecraft*. Washington, DC: Brassey's.

Brandt, Wilhelm (1983). *Independent Commission on International Development Issues (Brandt Commission). Common Crisis North-South: Cooperation for World Recovery*. Cambridge, Mass: MIT Press.

Brown, Michael (1993). *Ethnic Conflict and International Security*. Princeton: Princeton University Press.

Brundtland, Gro Harlem (1987). *The World Commission on Environment and Development (Brundtland Commission). Our Common Future.* Oxford: Oxford University Press.

Buzan, Barry (1991). *People, States and Fear.* Boulder: Rienner.

Cohen, Stephen P. (1964). Rulers and Priests: A Study in Cultural Control. *Comparative Studies in Society and History,* 6(2), pp. 199–216.

Dikshitar, V.R. Ramachandra (1987). *War in Ancient India.* Delhi: Motilal Banarsidass.

Homer-Dixon, Thomas (2001). *Environment, Scarcity, and Violence.* Princeton: Princeton University Press.

Hudson, Valerie M. and Andrea Den Boer (2002). A Surplus of Men, A Deficit of Peace. *International Security,* 26(4), pp. 5–38.

Kautilya (1987). *The Arthashastra,* translated by L.N.Rangarajan. New Delhi: Penguin.

Klare, Michael T. (2002). *Resource Wars: The New Landscape of Global Conflict.* New York: Owl Books.

Krause, Keith and Michael C. Williams (1997). *Critical Security Studies: Concepts and Cases* (Borderlines Volume 8). Minneapolis: University of Minnesota Press.

Mazurana, Dyan E., Susan A. McKay, Khristopher C. Carlson, and Janel C. Kasper (2002). Girls in Fighting Forces and Groups: Their Recruitment, Participation, Demobilization, and Reintegration. *Peace and Conflict.* 8(2), pp. 97–124.

Palme, Olof (1982). *Independent Commission on Disarmament and Security Issues (Palme Commission). Common Security: A Blueprint for Survival.* New York: Simon & Schuster.

———— (2004). Epic Roots: Governance, Democracy and Women in the Valmiki Ramayana. Paper presented at the Seventh Sustainable Development Conference, Islamabad, Pakistan, 9 December.

Rajagopalan, Swarna (2003). Secularism in India: Accepted Principle, Contentious Interpretation. In William Safran ed., *The Secular and the Sacred: Nation, Religion and Politics.* London: Frank Cass.

Ramanujan, A.K. (1991). Three Hundred Ramayanas: Five Examples and Three Thoughts on Translation. In Paula Richman, ed., *Many Ramayanas: The Diversity of a Narrative Tradition in South Asia.* New Delhi: Oxford University Press.

Ramayana (1981). Translated by Kamala Subramaniam. Bombay: Bharatiya Vidya Bhavan (first edition).

Richman, Paula, ed. (1991). *Many Ramayanas. The Diversity of a Narrative Tradition in South Asia.* New Delhi: Oxford University Press.

———— ed. (2000). *Questioning Ramayanas: A South Asian Tradition.* New Delhi: Oxford University Press.

Rosen, Stephen P. (1996). *Societies and Military Power: India and its Armies.* Ithaca and London: Cornell University Press.

Schmeidl, Susanne (2002). (Human) Security Dilemmas: Long-term Implications of the Afghan Refugee Crisis. *Third World Quarterly,* 23(1), 7–30.

Singer, Peter (2003). *Corporate Warriors: The Rise of the Privatized Military Industry.* Ithaca: Cornell University Press.

Srimad Valmīki-Rāmāyana, Part-I (SVR I) (2001). Gorakhpur: Gita Press (sixth edition).

Srimad Valmīki-Rāmāyana, Part-II (SVR II) (2001). Gorakhpur: Gita Press (sixth edition).

Srimad Valmīki-Rāmāyana, Volumes I, II and III (1974). Gorakhpur: Gita Press.

Teriff, Terry, Stuart Croft, Lucy James and Patrick M. Morgan (1999). *Security Studies Today.* Cambridge: Polity Press.

Warder, A.K. (1975). Classical Literature. In A.L. Bosham, ed., *A Cultural History of India*, pp. 170–96. Oxford: Oxford University Press.

Weiner, Myron (1993). *International Migration and Security.* Boulder: Westview.

Indian Strategic Culture and the Problem of Pakistan

Kanti Bajpai

The future of South Asia will depend heavily on India. As the largest country in the region, its choices and actions will condition the policies of its neighbours and of the non-regional powers that have a stake in the subcontinent. India's policies are likely to affect actors well beyond South Asia as well. The life-chances of over 1 billion Indians and perhaps another 2 billion people around its periphery, from Afghanistan and Pakistan in the west, to Nepal and China in the north, to Bangladesh and Burma in the east, and a number of other countries in the Asia-Pacific and Indian Ocean littoral, will be affected in varying degrees. How will India behave in the years to come? Observers claim that Indian diplomatic rhetoric and moves have changed considerably since the end of the Cold War; but in what respects exactly? One way of answering that question is by understanding Indian strategic culture. What are the basic perceptions and precepts of India's strategic community? What do they tell us about how India might behave over the next decade or so? This article attempts to delineate Indian strategic culture in the post-Cold War period and to show that there are three distinct approaches to India's most important South Asian neighbour—Pakistan.

Indian strategic culture, which was dominated by the worldview of its first prime minister, Jawaharlal Nehru, is in ferment. With the end of the Cold War, at least three different streams of thinking are vying for dominance. These three schools may be called Nehruvianism, neoliberalism, and hyperrealism. To call them 'schools' is perhaps to overstate the case somewhat. Those who hold to the views associated with the three perspectives do not call themselves by the names I have used, although the usage of the term 'Nehruvian' is common enough in Indian discourse. I claim, however, that these three viewpoints exist and that if one abstracts from Indian security texts, they can be assembled in the way that I have done here.

Such a claim will be controversial even in India. It is a commonplace of the discourse on Indian security that India does not have a strategic culture and that Indians have historically not thought consistently and rigorously about strategy. At the very least, Indians have not recorded their strategic thinking in written texts, the only exception being the ancient classic, *Arthashastra* (Kautilya 1987). That India does not have a tradition of strategic thinking is not altogether incorrect. On the other hand, since the country's independence in 1947, it has had to deal with a number of security challenges, and the volume of writings on these issues is enormous. Newspaper and magazine commentary is probably the largest single source on Indian thinking. In addition, the strategic community has produced a corpus of scholarly writings on security. A number of journals publish regularly on security matters. Finally, there are the texts of Indian prime ministers and other leaders who have over the years written and spoken publicly on security policy.

I argue that Indian strategic culture can be understood in terms of an identifiable set of basic assumptions about the nature of international relations, some of which are shared between the three schools and some of which are not. With Alastair Iain Johnston (1995), we can refer to these assumptions as constituting the central strategic paradigms of the three perspectives. In addition, the three perspectives can, once again in terms of Johnston's schema, be described by their grand strategic prescriptions on the means that should be used to make India secure.

This article focuses on the problem of Pakistan in India's security and describes the differences between the three schools of thought on what to do about this rather turbulent and troublesome neighbour.

Pakistan is the perennial concern of India's security. The two countries have fought four wars, have accused each other of interfering in their internal affairs, and have nuclear weapons. Commentators on India's security either argue that Indian strategy remains unchanged and that it has always dealt with Pakistan in more or less the same way; or that India's approach to Pakistan is ad hoc and reactive. We will show that India's perspectives on Pakistan are neither monotonic nor ad hoc and reactive. Differences over Pakistan, I argue, arise from deep-rooted beliefs and assumptions about the regulation of international relations as also social relations more broadly.

My article relates to Steve Cohen's work in a number of ways. Since the 1960s his central concerns have been with India and then Pakistan. His first book was on the Indian Army and Indian security (Cohen 1971 [1990]). In the 1970s and 1980s he turned his attention increasingly to Pakistan and its strategic views and debates (Cohen 1984 [1998]). Throughout most of his career, when few, if any, scholars outside South Asia wrote about Indian and Pakistani security and fewer still took the issue of their strategic cultures seriously, Cohen kept these concerns alive. In 1980 he published an essay on what he called 'the strategic imagery of elites', which dealt with Indian and Pakistani views of security and is part of the first generation of strategic culture studies (Cohen 1980).[1] Over forty years, his writings on civil–military relations in India and Pakistan and on South Asian security have contributed to our understanding of the political and strategic cultures of the two major subcontinental powers (Cohen 2001).[2] My article here is intended to continue in the Cohen tradition of taking South Asian security thinking and practice seriously.

The article is organized in the following sections. The first briefly answers the question, 'What is strategic culture?', and shows how it can be used for India. The second section outlines the basic assumptions and arguments of Nehruvianism, neoliberalism, and hyperrealism, the three schools of strategic thinking that I argue are the dominant ones in India after the Cold War. Section three then goes on to

---

[1] On the various generations of strategic culture studies, see Johnston (1995:4–22).
[2] Cohen's latest works on India and Pakistan continue to deal with issues related to political and strategic culture (see Cohen 2001, 2005).

describe how the three schools view Pakistan, and what India should do to manage the strategic challenge that it poses. The article then suggests that the three schools of thought have their roots in larger bodies of thought on international relations and the organization of human relations. I conclude with some thoughts on which school offers the most hope for dealing with Pakistan.

WHAT IS STRATEGIC CULTURE?

What is strategic culture? Johnston defines strategic culture in the following terms:

> Strategic culture is an integrated set of symbols (i.e. argumentation structures, languages, analogies, metaphors, etc.) that acts to establish pervasive and long-lasting grand strategic preferences by formulating concepts of the role and efficacy of force in interstate political affairs, and by clothing these conceptions with such an aura of factuality that the strategic preferences seem uniquely realistic and efficacious. (1995: 36)

A strategic culture can be described in two parts:

> The first [part] consists of basic assumptions about the orderliness of the human environment—that is, about the role of war in human affairs (i.e., whether it is aberrant or inevitable), about the nature of the adversary and the threat it poses (i.e. zero-sum or positive sum), and about the efficacy of the use of force (i.e., about the ability to control outcomes and eliminate threats and about the conditions under which the use of force is useful).

> The second part of strategic culture consists of assumptions at a more operational level about what strategic options are the most efficacious for dealing with the threat environment as defined by answers to the three sets of questions. These lower level assumptions should flow logically from the

central paradigm....Thus the essential components or empirical referents of a strategic culture will appear in the form of a limited, ranked set of grand strategic preferences. (ibid.: 37)

In short, strategic culture consists of a central strategic paradigm (the basic assumptions about orderliness) and a grand strategy (secondary assumptions about operational policy that follow from the prior assumptions). These may be gleaned from various texts written over time by statesmen, soldiers, scholars, diplomats, and commentators.

Johnston's conception of strategic culture will inform this enquiry into Indian strategic culture. First, we will use his distinction between central strategic paradigm and grand strategy to parse Indian strategic culture. Second, we will follow his lead in describing strategic culture by interpreting various written texts rather than by inferring cultural traits or constants from behaviour. However, we will also depart from his schema and methods in various ways. First, while Johnston could turn to a series of well-known ancient Chinese military classics for his work on China, this is not possible in the Indian case where there are no established canonical texts except for the *Arthashastra*. Instead, we will turn to the post-Cold War writings of some of the most important voices in the Indian strategic community. This is probably more appropriate in any case, given how difficult it is to establish the influence of ancient texts on contemporary thinking and choices.

Second, Johnston's conception of strategic culture and grand strategy places great emphasis on the role and deployment of force. The use of force is clearly the key issue in any conception of strategy; it may well be less important in grand strategy, which refers to the coordination of a nation's military, political, diplomatic, and even cultural resources for the purposes of security. Grand strategies vary not just by differences in how force is used, but also by the extent to which other instruments are deployed. Johnston allows for this, for instance, in his discussion of an accommodationist grand strategic posture, but the issue of the efficacy and disposition of force is pervasive in his study of Chinese strategic culture (Johnston 1995:

112). The other instruments of grand strategy in Johnston's study figure mostly as elements that contribute to the husbanding of force—for instance, the mobilization of domestic economic resources to prosecute war more efficiently. However, a grand strategy may use economic or cultural capacities to change the entire terms of discourse between two states and societies, and may in that sense rival military capacities as an instrument of grand strategy. Thus, economic resources must be allocated wisely for the purposes of war making, but they may also be deployed coercively or otherwise to change the interests of adversaries and thereby transform the entire nature of the relationship. This is the fundamental premise of functionalist and liberal arguments about interstate relations.

We will also need to relax some of Johnston's methodological injunctions, at least for the purposes of this paper. Johnston grants that there may be different streams of strategic thinking, but he suggests that in order to establish the existence of a strategic culture it is necessary to show that there exists a set of strategic preferences that are consistently ranked above others in some canonical texts, that the different streams in effect can be ordered from the most to the least important. He also insists that the link to actual behaviour must be established, by showing that the preferences of a strategic culture 'anchor' the thinking of decision makers and that their thinking then determines the course of government policy.[3]

While Johnston is correct to insist on such rigor, this is not possible at the present stage of research on Indian strategic culture. For one thing, as noted earlier, in India there are no canonical texts across which one would test for consistency of preference ranking. The researcher on Indian strategic culture must, therefore, take a more collage-like approach to textuality, fashioning a composite text out of scattered writings in the press, academic journals and volumes, think-tank publications, biographies and autobiographies, and so on. Thus, we will be content here to delineate the three dominant approaches culled out of this collage of materials and ask what the relationship of these various Indian writings is to other bodies of

---

[3]For relevant discussions, see Johnston (1995: 32–39, 52–60, 109–10).

thought on international relations and social affairs. The extent to which the Indian writings highlighted here represent the thinking of policy makers and to what extent they have influenced them in the actual conduct of relations with Pakistan, I leave aside for the present.

THREE STRATEGIC PARADIGMS: NEHRUVIANISM, NEOLIBERALISM, AND HYPERREALISM

According to Johnston, a core strategic paradigm provides answers to the following questions:

- What is the role of war in international relations?
- What is the nature of the adversary and the threats it poses?
- What is the utility of force?

Indian strategic thought does not address these questions systematically and explicitly enough for a Johnstonian analysis. There are no ancient 'military' classics as far as we know apart from Kautilya's *Arthashastra*. As for the *Arthashastra*, it does not have the status of the Western or Chinese military classics. It would be hard to show, for instance, that its tenets were widely known historically. Nor are there any modern classics of strategy and grand strategy, though Jawaharlal Nehru's writings on international affairs and Indian foreign policy does constitute a corpus of influential materials. More recently, the writings of K. Subrahmanyam and, in nuclear matters, of General K. Sundarji, have been influential. Subrahmanyam's views in particular, because of his extensive newspaper writings, are widely known.

In the Indian case, therefore, the central strategic paradigm cannot be delineated with the kind of textual richness and interpretive rigor that Johnston was able to bring to bear in the Chinese case. What this article will do, therefore, in this section is to sketch in the broad approach to international relations that is embodied in the three Indian schools of thought. To do this it will be necessary to reconstruct that thought and then to extrapolate from it to the three questions located at the heart of a central strategic paradigm.

BASIC ASSUMPTIONS AND ARGUMENTS OF
THE THREE SCHOOLS

Before we proceed to reconstruct Nehruvian, neoliberal, and hyperrealist approaches to international relations in terms of their differences, it is important to note their areas of agreement. For while they disagree in key respects, they also proceed from a core set of common assumptions and arguments.

First of all, all three paradigms accept that at the heart of international relations is the notion of the sovereign state that recognizes no higher authority. In such a system, each state is responsible fundamentally for its own security and well-being. Above all, states strive to protect their territory and autonomy. Second, all three paradigms recognize that interests, power, and violence are staples of international relations. States cannot avoid the responsibility of pursuing the national interest, however that is defined. Nor can they be indifferent to the cultivation of power—their own and that of other states. States must in some measure accrue power in a competitive system. Finally, conflict and war are a constant shadow over interstate relations. While the three paradigms differ on the causes of conflict and war, and on the ability of states to control and transcend these forces, all three accept that disputes and large-scale organized violence are a regular feature of international relations. Third, all three paradigms accept that power comprises both military and economic capabilities at a minimum. States need both. While they differ on the optimum mix and use of these capabilities, proponents of the three views are in agreement that military and economic strength are vital for security. Beyond this common base, the three paradigms differ.

Fundamental to Nehruvianism is the argument that states and peoples can come to understand each other better and thereby make and sustain peace. Nehruvians accept that in the international system, without a supranational authority, the threat of war to settle disputes and rivalries is in some measure inescapable. States must look after themselves in such a world in which violence is a regrettable last resort (Krishna 1984: 270–71). However, Nehruvians believe that this state of 'anarchy' can be mitigated, if not eventually supervened. International laws and institutions, military restraint, negotiations and compromise, cooperation, free intercourse between societies, and regard for the well-being of people everywhere and not just one's own citizens, all these can overcome the rigors of the international system.[4] Furthermore, to make preparations for war and a balance of power, the central objectives of security and foreign policy is, for Nehruvians, both ruinous and futile: ruinous because arms spending can only impoverish societies materially and create the very conditions that sustain violence and war; futile because, ultimately, balances of power are fragile and do not prevent large-scale violence, as the two world wars so catastrophically demonstrated (Nehru 1981: 536–48).

Neoliberals also accept the general characterization of international relations as a state of war. That coercion plays an important role in such a world is not denied. The lure of mutual gain in any interaction is also, however, a powerful conditioning factor amongst states, particularly as they become more interdependent. Neoliberals often express their distinct view of international relations by comparing the role of military and economic power. According to them, states pursue not just military power but also economic well-being. They do so in part because economic strength is ultimately the basis for military power. Economic strength can, in addition, substitute for military power: military domination is one way of achieving one's ends; economic domination is another. Economic power can even be more effective than military power. Thus, in situations of 'complex interdependence' force is unusable or ineffective.[5]

Most importantly, though, neoliberals believe that economic well-being is vital for national security in a broader sense. An economically deprived people cannot be a satisfied people, and a dissatisfied people cannot be secure (Baru, no date: 4–5). The key question, then, is: where does economic strength and well-being come from? In the neoliberal view, it can only come from free market policies. Free market policies at home imply, in addition, free trade abroad. Free

---

[4]Many of these themes are evident in Nehru's speeches. See, for instance, his thoughts on the importance of the Commonwealth and United Nations (Nehru 1961: 132–81).
[5]See Raja Mohan (2001b) on how China, in contrast to India, has used trade and economic relations more generally to 'leverage' relations with the US. Also see Baru (1998a: 66–67).

trade is a relationship of mutual gain, even if asymmetric gain, and is therefore a factor in the relations between states. Indeed, where Nehruvians see communication and contact as the key to the transformation of international relations, neoliberals believe that trade and economic interactions can achieve this.[6]

Hyperrealists harbour the most pessimistic view of international relations.[7] Where Nehruvians and neoliberals believe that international relations can be transformed—either by means of communication and contact or by free market economic reforms and the logic of comparative advantage—hyperrealists see an endless cycle of repetition in interstate interactions. The governing metaphor of hyperrealists is threat and counter-threat (Karnad 1994: 2). In the absence of a supranational authority that can tell them how to behave and is capable of enforcing those commands, states are doomed to balance of power, deterrence, and war. Conflict and rivalry between states cannot be transformed into peace and friendship (except temporarily as an alliance against a common foe); they can only be managed by the threat and use of violence (Chellaney 1999: xviii).

From this, hyperrealists conclude that the surest way of achieving peace and stability is through the accumulation of military power and the willingness to use force (ibid.: 528). Hyperrealists reject the Nehruvian and neoliberal concern over runaway military spending and preparedness, arguing that there is no very good evidence that defence derogates from development (ibid.: 531). Indeed, defence spending may, in the Keynesian sense at least, boost economic growth and development. Hyperrealists, like neoliberals, are also sceptical about the role of institutions, laws, treaties, and agreements. For hyperrealists, what counts in international relations is power in the service of national interest; all the rest is illusion. The neoliberal faith in the power of economics is equally one that hyperrealists do not share. Hyperrealists invert the relationship between military and economic power. Historically, they argue, military power is more

---

[6]On the importance of economics and the market in strategy, see Gupta (2001), *Indian Express* (2001), Raja Mohan (2001b), and Ramesh (1999).
[7]I use the term 'hyperrealist' to signify that the proponents of these views value force and unilateral methods much more than a prudential realism would allow.

important than, and probably prior to, economic power. A state that can build its military power will safeguard its international interests and will build an economy and society that is strong (Chellaney 1999: 529–34; Karnad 1994: 2).

War, the Nature of the Adversary, and the Utility of Force

What can we say from this reconstruction of Nehruvian, neoliberal, and hyperreal approaches to international relations in relation to the role of war, the nature of the adversary, and the utility of force?

For Nehruvians, war is a choice that states can and will make. While Nehruvians accept that the international system is anarchic and that states pursue their interests with vigour, violence is not inevitable.[8] Wars, as Nehru affirmed, are made in the minds of men, and therefore it is in the minds of men that war must be eradicated. War is not a natural, inherent activity. It can be avoided and limited even when it occurs. The state of war—the fear, expectation, and preparation for war—can be overcome by wise, cooperative policies amongst states (Nehru 1963: 1–3).

The adversary, in the Nehruvian view, is not a permanent one. War arises from misperceptions and ideological systems that colour the attitudes of states and societies and spread fear and hatred. The adversary either does not comprehend India or is misled about Indian goals and methods. Its leadership may be at fault. Ordinary citizens may support their governments out of ignorance or illusion created by government propaganda. The adversary, therefore, can be made into a friend by communication and contact with India and Indians, at both official and non-official levels (Dubey 1999: 23–25).

It is this—communication and contact between governments and peoples—rather than force that will end conflict and make India more secure. International organizations and interstate negotiations are ways of institutionalizing communication and contact. The threat or use of force, particularly in a coercive, offensive way, is counter-productive and will generally be reciprocated by the adversary, leaving the basic

---

[8]See Krishna (1984: 270–71) on Nehru's use of the term 'anarchy' in the context of international relations. On the pursuit of national interest and the necessity of defence, see Nehru (1963: 45–46).

quarrel unchanged. Both parties can only be weakened and harmed by a relationship built on force. All issues are negotiable in the end. India must dispose of enough force to defend itself, but it should not have so much that it makes others fearful. Certainly, force must be absolutely the last resort, even if it is used coercively (Nehru 1963: 35, 45–6).

Neoliberals, too, admit that war is a possibility between sovereign states. However, it is not the only inherent condition in the international system. Given that societies have different comparative advantages and that there is a global division of labour, states cannot escape the logic of interdependence (Baru, no date: 13–14). Interdependence makes for more pragmatic policies internationally. In their external relations, states worry not just about war but also about trade, investment, and technology (ibid.: 14–17, Baru 1998a: 67; Baru 1998b: 90–91; also, Subrahmanyam 1999: 12 on globalization, interdependence, and war avoidance).

In the neoliberal imaginary, therefore, adversarial relations are produced by two factors. First, like Nehruvians, neoliberals hold misunderstanding miscalculation as being responsible for enmity. If governments and peoples were more clear-headed and did their cost–benefit calculations correctly, they would probably see that rivalry and violence is irrational and that the benefits of economic relations untrammelled by quarrels over territory are far greater than anything that may be gained from conflict. Second, military enmity is fundamentally an old-fashioned condition that cannot be sustained as economic globalization goes forward. India itself is guilty of seeing its relations with various countries in the old geopolitical way because it has not understood the logic and power of globalization (Baru 1998a: 66–70, Baru 1998b: 88–103; also Subrahmanyam 1999: 12).

Force is an instrument of declining utility, therefore. For neoliberals, force is an outmoded and blunt instrument unsuited to the new world order. States must have enough force to defend themselves, but it is economic power and the capacity to innovate in a global economy that eventually makes societies secure. Force in the service of expansionism is irrelevant. Territorial conquest and control, in a world where capital, information, and even skills flow across national boundaries, is anachronistic. States must be attentive to defence needs, but on the whole India's economic growth and modernization, and its integration into a globalized world economy is its greatest source of strength (Raja Mohan 2001b). India would do better to use its increasing economic power as a way of influencing others than to use force in such a role.[9]

Hyperrealists offer quite different perspectives on war, adversaries, and force. War is a constant possibility in an anarchical system and, while it can be destructive and painful, is also the basis for a state's autonomy and security. War is not, therefore, an aberration but a natural tendency of international relations. Preparing for war is not warmongering; it is responsible and wise statecraft. War comes when rival states calculate that the other side is either getting too powerful or is weakening.[10]

In the hyperrealist view, the international system is a lonely place. States have no permanent friends. Anyone can be an adversary. The adversary, as much as India, must prepare for war in the service of its interests and survival. Other things being equal, neighbouring states are more likely to be adversaries: conflicts over territory, status, and power are ever-present possibilities in intimate relationships. No amount of communication and contact or economic interaction will transform the relationship because it is zero sum. Only a balance of power can regulate relations with nearby or distant rivals (Chellaney 1999: 558).

Force, in the hyperreal view, is an indispensable instrument in international relations. It is the only means by which states can truly achieve their ends against rivals. States must accept that violence may be necessary in the national interest. Force may be deployed purely defensively, but the best defence is often offence. It may even save lives on both sides. Control of territory is not old-fashioned, but rather militarily imperative, especially in conflicts with neighbours. In the end, force may have to be used to destroy the adversary's military formations and to control or wrest contested territory. No political or military leadership can responsibly avoid planning for the

---

[9]'Economic policy can itself be an instrument of foreign policy if it enables a country to win friends and influence people' (Baru 1998a:67).
[10]On the importance of national power or strength, see Chellaney (1999: xviii).

coercive use of force. Only 'idealists' of various stripes—Nehruvians or neoliberals—could fool themselves into thinking that a more aggressive posture is always bad.[11]

THE PAKISTAN PROBLEM IN INDIAN STRATEGIC CULTURE

Grand strategic thought, as Johnston emphasizes, is focused on the issue of means rather than ends. How do the three schools of thought deal with the operational challenges of security with respect to Pakistan? The strategic paradigms have indicated the general predispositions of different streams of Indian thinking. What prescriptions do they offer more specifically on India's dealings with Pakistan?

Nehruvianism and the Problem of Pakistan

Nehruvians believe that India and its various neighbours, including Pakistan, can and will live in peace. With the smaller states there is little or no prospect of violence. With Pakistan, on the other hand, there is a long history of violence. Nehruvians see Pakistan as an aggressive state, as do the neoliberals and hyperrealists. In the Nehruvian view, Pakistan is an artificial state, created on the basis of the erroneous 'two-nation theory' (Dhar 2001; Khan 1993: 23). A state based on Islamic precepts and on its difference with India cannot hold together. Compounding the problem is the absence of democracy. Feudal overlords and the military together control the country. They perpetuate their domination by casting India in the role of a mortal threat (Kotru 2001; Nakra 2001). Having demonized India, Pakistan must constantly enlist powerful protectors against its bigger neighbour. During the Cold War, this meant allying with the US and China. Pakistan's alliances with Washington and Beijing gave Islamabad an inflated sense of its military and diplomatic strength. Backed by American and Chinese power, Pakistan became obdurate and aggressive.[12]

---

[11]See Chellaney (1999: 536) on why India needs to adopt a more 'punitive', less 'reactive' posture vis-à-vis Pakistan.

[12] See the statement of Indian Ambassador Arundhati Ghose, quoted in Ram and Muralidharan (1998: 31).

In the Nehruvian view, India's policy towards Pakistan must take account of these complexities. While relations with Pakistan are daunting, they are not hopeless. Given the intricacies of the relationship, India's moves must be geared to patient, long-run diplomacy rather than dramatic breakthroughs. The Nehruvian diagnosis rests on the view that enmity and hostility towards India comes from misunderstanding and delusion. The original Partition ideology—the two-nation theory—is a mass delusion that was propagated by Jinnah and the Muslim League (Dhar 2001). The enemy image of India sustained and elaborated by the feudals and the military is also false. The primary aim of Indian policy is, of course, to defend the country from military aggression and subversion. In the longer term, though, it is to undermine the two-nation theory and to break down the image of India as a hostile state. Communication and contact between India and Pakistan is the only way of doing this (Bidwai 1999: 110–11; Dixit 2001b; Parthasarathy 2001).

Various lines of policy follow. First of all, an adequate defence against aggression is vital. India cannot afford to be surprised and overcome militarily. The accent in the Nehruvian programme, though, is on the word 'adequate'. Nehruvians, we should remember, are sceptical of the use of force and of a balance-of-power politics. India, they believe, should be able to defend itself against its enemies, but should not dispose of so much force that it frightens others.[13] In addition, Nehruvians believe in the efficacy of international institutions and rules in preventing and limiting violence among states, for violence can only compound violence.

Thus, a second important line of policy is to use international law and institutions as well as bilateral treaties and agreements to bring Pakistan round to a more pacific and cooperative stance. Not surprisingly, it was Jawaharlal Nehru and India that took the Kashmir issue to the UN in 1948. It is also India that has repeatedly sought to codify relations with Pakistan in treaties and agreements—most importantly, the Simla Accord, and most recently, the Lahore Declaration. While Nehruvians no longer have much faith in the UN

---

[13]Nehruvians in effect support what is called 'defensive' or 'non-offensive' defence. On these notions, see Gates (1991) and Moeller (1992).

in the matter of Kashmir and more generally in dealing with Pakistan, they insist that bilateral agreements have an important place in resolving conflict. The Simla and other agreements, including the various cooperative and confidence building accords, in their view, must be the touchstone of India's Pakistan policy (Dixit 2001a).

A third line of Nehruvian policy is to wean Pakistan away from its external backers and supporters, and to discourage those powers from interfering in the region. Weaning Pakistan away from its external dependencies will require it to shed its hostile image of India and restructure its domestic politics. Discouraging external powers from meddling in regional affairs can be achieved by pursuing a policy of non-alignment. By adopting a principled stand on great power behaviour and by refusing to permanently ally with one power or other, India can persuade those powers to leave it and the region alone.

Finally, the core of the Nehruvian approach is to change Pakistani attitudes towards India. The only way of accomplishing this, in the end, is through communication and contact with both the Pakistani government and people. No matter what the provocation by Pakistan, Nehruvians argue, New Delhi must hold firmly to a policy of engagement and negotiation. Summitry is one way of keeping an official conversation going with Pakistan. Trade and the benefits from it can be instrumental in showing Pakistanis that diplomatic normalization with India is profitable. People-to-people interactions (sports, culture, intellectual exchanges) can serve to demystify India in the Pakistani imagination. In sum, only a multifaceted relationship with Pakistan can bring about lasting accommodation and a robust peace.

Neoliberalism and the Problem of Pakistan

When neoliberals think about India–Pakistan relations they approach the issue differently from Nehruvians. Where Nehruvians emphasize a multifaceted process of communication and contact, neoliberals look essentially to strike bargains to the advantage of both sides.

In the neoliberal view, Pakistan is a threat to India's security but can be brought round to a more accommodative view of the relationship if New Delhi uses an approach built on the promise of mutual gain, particularly economic gain (Dattar 2001). Neoliberals argue that ultimately Pakistan's leaders and people are not above the logic of costs and benefits. Whatever their sense of national identity and their fear of India, Pakistanis will eventually measure their policies towards their neighbour in terms of the advantages and disadvantages of alternative courses of action. Ultimately, economic well-being is paramount for any society, and Pakistan will come round to the view that it must cut a deal with India in order to give its people a better life (Raja Mohan 2001a).

Neoliberals do not reject the entire Nehruvian programme. The Nehruvian insistence on an adequate but not threatening defence posture and a multifaceted relationship with Pakistan is congenial to neoliberals who place great emphasis on economic well-being via free market policies. An overly ambitious defence posture, in their view, will channel government and private expenditures into non-productive areas and cramp economic growth (Abraham 2001; Subrahmanyam 2001). In this respect, they do not differ greatly with the Nehruvians. Neoliberals also support the Nehruvian view of working towards a broad relationship with Pakistan and Pakistanis. The core of the neoliberal approach is based on the primacy of economics and, therefore, anything that goes beyond the traditional focus on military and diplomatic interactions is helpful.

However, neoliberals differ with Nehruvians in two key respects. First of all, neoliberals are not great believers in the effectiveness of international institutions and laws as well as bilateral treaties and agreements.[14] The Nehruvian 'obsession' with institutions, laws, treaties, agreements (for example, in the UN, especially in the early years), and the various bilateral accords with Pakistan are, in their view, a negotiatory dead end. The Nehruvian way constitutes a formalistic, old-fashioned approach to diplomacy and statecraft and has been the bane of India's foreign policy. UN resolutions are ineffective, even against the humblest of states. And bilateral accords

---

[14]In this respect, Indian neoliberals are not the same as Western academic neoliberal institutionalists who set great store by the possibility of rules, norms, and institutions. Perhaps the best-known Western academic neoliberal theorist is Robert Keohane. See Keohane (1989). On the debate between neorealists and neoliberals in international relations theory, see Baldwin (1993).

with Pakistan, while welcome, are in the end mere paper commitments, which Islamabad can ignore, even tear up at will. New Delhi should be prepared to scrap any or all of these accords if and when it is necessary to do so; the Nehruvian insistence on sticking by them in rote fashion for all time is unimaginative and unhelpful. Neoliberals do not necessarily reject these accords, but they want India to adopt a more flexible, 'non-dogmatic' approach.[15]

The second difference with Nehruvians is on the regional role of the great powers—the US, Russia, China, Japan, and the Europeans. Neoliberals argue that keeping the great powers out of the region is futile and, worse still, positively harmful to the Indian cause. Great powers by definition are hard to keep out of strategic arenas and, in the case of the US, virtually impossible. Indeed, great power involvement in South Asia could be turned to India's advantage (Gupta 2000). After the Cold War the great powers perceive India and Pakistan quite differently. An India that is booming economically in the wake of economic reforms, that is a non-expansionist power, and that is a stable multi-ethnic democracy is an asset to them and to the international order as a whole. By contrast, Pakistan, with its economic problems, its revisionist agenda in South Asia plus its support of revolutionary Islamic groups, and its chaotic, Islamic polity is a potential failed state and an international mischief-maker if not danger (Subrahmanyam 2001). India should cultivate the great powers in this new geopolitical situation and encourage them to lean on Pakistan as a way of bringing Islamabad round to a deal. From the neoliberal perspective, what India needs is omni-alignment, not non-alignment: an engagement and rapprochement with all the great powers, even China, in the service of a regional order that suits New Delhi's interests and that is not inimical to great power preferences (Raja Mohan 1998).

For neoliberals, then, Pakistan policy must be geared to bringing Islamabad to the negotiating table. Whereas Nehruvians want to fundamentally change Pakistani thinking, neoliberals are more 'pragmatic' and 'worldly', insisting that an economic logic will eventually engineer accommodation. Economic development in

---

[15]C. Raja Mohan made this point at a panel discussion on India's relations with Nepal at the India Habitat Centre, New Delhi, 22 November 2001.

Pakistan will do more to transform elite and popular attitudes than anything India can do by way of political, social, and cultural engagement. For Pakistan to come to the table will, in addition, require India to become an economic powerhouse. The example of India's economic growth, the gap in capabilities that will open up as a result, and the potential opportunities for Pakistanis in an accelerating Indian economy will give New Delhi the power to make Pakistan an offer it cannot refuse. When the economic foundation for a new relationship is built, as it increasingly has been over the past decade of reforms, flexibility in India's diplomatic stance will be crucial in encouraging Pakistan to reciprocate with its own brand of new thinking. Finally, the pressures exerted by the great powers on India's behalf will put Pakistan in a mood to negotiate seriously.

Hyperrealism and the Problem of Pakistan

The hyperrealist prescription for dealing with Pakistan is not to worry overly about the intensity of communication and contact with that country or to rely on the imperatives of economic change or even to turn to others for help. Instead, hyperrealists argue, India must focus on the 'fundamentals' and on policies that have stood the test of time in the international system.

In the end, according to hyperrealists, the only language that Pakistan understands and heeds, like any other country, is the language of power and violence. The core of India's policy, therefore, must be to build its military strength (Chellaney 1999: 527–95; Karnad 1994: 1–15). (This is a necessity beyond Pakistan, for India has other strategic challenges, namely, China and, in the long run, the United States.) Given that India is eight times Pakistan's size, it should be in a position to overawe Pakistan militarily. From a position of dominance, New Delhi should dictate terms to Islamabad. With military strength will come an array of options that can be used to raise the costs of Pakistan's intervention in Kashmir. These options should be exercised sooner rather than later. Taking the fight to Pakistan rather than reacting to Pakistani provocations is the essence of a workable, effective policy (Chellaney 1999: 541).

What does it mean to take the fight to Pakistan? Hyperrealists argue that India should repay Pakistan in the same coin militarily, but politically and economically in addition. Militarily, India should make Pakistan pay a much higher cost for the conflict in Kashmir. At the very least, Indian forces should be more aggressive in counter-insurgency operations, as they were in Punjab. Beyond this, Indian forces could begin to test the Line of Control or even the international boundary. Artillery fire, air strikes, and 'hot pursuit' attacks into Pakistan-held Kashmir would serve notice that India was no longer willing to fight a purely defensive internal war. Finally, at the limit, India should be prepared to attack across the international boundary to threaten Pakistan's heartland. The fact that India and Pakistan are nuclear powers does not bother some hyperrealists who would seriously contemplate the possibility of 'limited war under nuclear conditions', arguing that India's nuclear superiority will give it 'escalation dominance', that is, the ability to control the pace and direction of military action. Politically, hyperrealists argue, there is no reason why India cannot do what the Pakistanis are doing in Kashmir. New Delhi could begin to fund and arm various dissident groups in Pakistan, including separatists or ethnic rebels in Baluchistan and Sindh, as well as unhappy religious groups in Punjab. India could increasingly play host to prominent dissident leaders as well, especially Sindhis, but also those from the Pakistani side of Kashmir (Chellaney 1999: 541). In addition, India could resort to economic warfare to raise the costs of conflict. New Delhi could meddle with Pakistan's currency and stock market. It could increase its own defence spending, compelling Pakistan to raise its expenditures and driving its economy into a fiscal meltdown. As the US drove the Soviet Union out of business, so India could spend Pakistan into oblivion.[16]

Hyperrealists, therefore, in effect imply that the collapse, destruction, or surrender of Pakistan is the only truly viable solution to India's Pakistan problem. In their view, Pakistan is an implacable foe, and with every setback or defeat, it will only rebuild itself for the next round of conflict. After 1971 that should have been clear to

---

[16]These were arguments made at various seminars and brainstorming sessions held in Delhi amongst security specialists that I attended in the weeks and months after the Indian and Pakistan tests of May 1998 and up to the Kargil war. These sessions brought together a number of security specialists.

India. Pakistanis see compromise and negotiation, restraint and cooperation as signs of weakness and incoherence in India. Unless Pakistan is reduced to a state of permanent chaos or debility, it will, phoenix-like, rise from the ashes to challenge India again and again.

To sum up: Nehruvians, neoliberals, and hypernationalists have quite different prescriptions for how to deal with Pakistan. Nehruvians trust patient, long-term diplomacy that builds on existing treaties and obligations, defensive defence, society-to-society contact and communication, and non-alignment. Neoliberals prefer a pragmatic, flexible approach to Pakistan, a reliance on economic contacts and India's growing economic strength to bring Pakistanis round, a restrained military posture, and alignment with the great powers (especially the US) rather than non-alignment. Hyperrealists want India to rely on power and force rather than treaties and economic links to take the fight to Pakistan, to subvert it from within, and eventually to bring about its surrender or collapse.

CONCLUSION: UNDERSTANDING INDIAN STRATEGIC CULTURE

Is Indian strategic culture unique to India? Do these various perspectives come from 'native' modes of thinking? I would argue they do not. They are quite comprehensible and familiar to strategists anywhere in the world. The work of Kenneth Boulding, the maverick economist and peace activist, is useful in showing that three Indian perspectives have a more universalist provenance or affinity. The essay might have rendered the intellectual underpinnings of Indian strategic viewpoints in some other way.[17] Boulding's schema is attractive because it goes quickly to the core of the contending arguments and prescriptions.

The lenses through which Indians view Pakistan can be understood in terms of three metaphors used by Boulding. He uses these to describe the nature of social relationships in general. He argues that the interactions between humans are regulated by one of three things:

---

[17]For instance, the three strategic positions can be related to differences in political ideology. See Bajpai (2001).

threats, exchange, or integration. Human beings, he notes, could organize themselves by the use of coercion and, in particular, by promises of mutual violence. They could, alternatively, organize themselves on the basis of exchange: the desire for reciprocal gains and the interdependence it produces might regulate human interactions. Finally, humans could structure their behaviour towards each other by means of various integrative instruments. Empathy, dialogue, and reconciliation are well-known integrative methods available to humans. Boulding acknowledges that these are Weberian 'ideal types': no human interaction is based purely on threats, exchange, or integration. In the actual world any human relationship, from the biological family to the family of nations, comprises a mix of these elements (Boulding 1987: 48–59; Boulding 1989).

In international relations, interactions dominated by threats and coercion are familiar enough. Indeed, the staple of international relations is what Jean-Jacques Rousseau long ago called the 'state of war'—the fear, expectation, and actual experience of organized violence. In the discipline of international relations, this is the view of political realists.[18] We increasingly describe the relations between states in another language, though, and this is the language of exchange. The vocabulary of interdependence, trade, and other forms of collaboration in an interconnected world is part of the idiom of exchange relations. Liberals in international relations argue that interdependence arising out of a division of labour can impel states to cooperate amongst themselves. In general, liberals look for the possibility of mutual gains in any relationship, no matter how conflictual. As long as both sides can gain, there is a basis for cooperation if not friendship.[19] Beyond mere cooperation, there is a view in international relations that states and societies can achieve various levels of integration with other states and societies. Communication and convergence is at the heart of the view that this

---

[18]On Rousseau's international writings, see Hoffman (1965: chapter 3). The canon of political realism is long, but in modern international relations writings the pride of place goes to Carr (1964), Morgenthau (1997), and Waltz (1979).

[19]For a classic liberal argument, see Angell (1913). In more recent scholarship, see Nye and Keohane (1977).

is possible. As states and societies talk to each other, as peoples visit each other and learn about each other, they draw closer and can settle differences without fighting. In international relations arguments of this kind can be grouped under the rubric of cosmopolitanism.[20]

Indian strategic thinking mirrors the three perspectives on international relations. Indian arguments about relations with Pakistan reflect these larger prisms. Boulding's threat metaphor and the arguments of political realists rather aptly describe the views of those I call hyperrealists. His exchange metaphor and the arguments of liberals are similar to those of neoliberals in India. And his integration metaphor and the arguments of cosmopolitan thinkers converge with the contentions of the Nehruvians.[21]

Historically, Nehruvianism dominated Indian strategic thinking. Nehruvians were criticized in some measure—sometimes more and sometimes less—by earlier liberals and hyperrealists, but to no great effect. After the Cold War, neoliberals and the new breed of hyperrealists have grown in influence, and the Nehruvian view has come in for greater criticism. An understanding of these alternative, 'insurgent' views is therefore vital.

Which of the three strategic pathways is the surest road ahead in dealing with Pakistan? An answer to this must await a careful weighing of the various claims and arguments. Meanwhile, the Boulding schema can be used to offer some initial thoughts on the most effective and enduring route to regional order. The use of threats is the most primitive method of constructing social relationships. A threat system suffers from at least two limitations. For one thing, coercion is a highly inefficient way of organizing social life. For another, its constant deployment debases its usefulness: put differently, increasingly large doses of coercion are necessary to produce the same effects. In an age when the instruments of violence include weapons of mass destruction, the graduated use of coercive strategies could end in catastrophe.

---

[20]Immanuel Kant's writings on war and peace represent a Cosmopolitan viewpoint. They are usefully excerpted in Forsyth et al. (1970). In contemporary international relations, see Beitz (1979). In India, Mahatma Gandhi probably best exemplifies cosmopolitanism. See Anadkat (2000: chapter 2).

[21]Bull (1977), renders these three approaches in terms of the 'Hobbesian', 'Grotian', and 'Kantian' perspectives on international society.

Exchange is a more attractive method of regulating social life. Its chief limitations are that the gains from it may be unequal as between the contracting parties and the basis for its continuation may eventually be exhausted. Some may do better from exchange than others, and what we can get from each other may be finite in a material sense. When inequality reaches unacceptable levels or exchange possibilities are exhausted, social life may revert to a more primitive, coercive state. Boulding, therefore, suggests that integration is the most lasting—and, admittedly, the most demanding—basis for social life. Empathy and dialogue can construct a world in which we draw closer and come to a richer and more permanent accommodation of each other. Hard as the Nehruvian road to peace with Pakistan may be, it is, on this analysis, the most durable.

BIBLIOGRAPHY

Abraham, Amrita (2001). Mission Possible. *Indian Express,* 28 June.
Anadkat, Nalin (2000). *International Political Thought of Gandhi, Nehru and Lohia.* Delhi: Bharatiya Kala Prakashan.
Angell, Norman (1913). *The Great Illusion.* New York: Putnam's (fourth edition).
Bajpai, Kanti (2000). Nuclear Weapons, Grand Strategy, and Political Values in India. Seventeenth P.C. Lal Memorial Lecture of the Air Force Association of India, New Delhi.
Baldwin, David (ed.) (1993). *Neorealism and Neoliberalism: The Contemporary Debate.* New York: Columbia University Press.
Baru, S. (no date). National Security in an Open Economy. Report of the Indian Council for Research on International Economic Relations (ICRIER), http://www.icrier.com
———— (1998a). Economic Diplomacy. *Seminar,* 461, 66–69.
———— (1998b). The Economic Dimensions of India's Foreign Policy. *World Affairs,* 2 (2), 88–103.
Beitz, Charles R. (1979). *Political Theory and International Relations.* Princeton: Princeton University Press.
Bidwai, Praful (1999). Lessons from Pakistan. *Frontline,* 19 November.
Boulding, Kenneth (1987). Peace and the Evolutionary Process. In Raimo Vayrynen with Dieter Senghaas and Christian Schmidt, (eds.), *The Quest for Peace: Transcending Collective Violence and War Among Societies, Cultures and States,* pp. 48–59. Beverly Hills, CA: Sage Publications.
———— (1989). *Three Faces of Power.* Beverly Hills, CA: Sage Publications.
Bull, Hedley (1977). *The Anarchical Society: A Study of Order in World Politics.* New York: Columbia University Press.
Carr, E.H. (1964). *The Twenty Years' Crisis, 1919–1939.* New York: Harper Row (Second Edition).

Chellaney, Brahma, ed. (1999). *Securing India's Future in the New Millennium*. New Delhi: Orient Longman and the Centre for Policy Research.
Cohen, Stephen P. (1971 [1990]). *The Indian Army: Its Contribution to the Development of a Nation*. New Delhi: Oxford University Press.
———— (1980). The Strategic Imagery of Elites. In James M. Roherty, ed., *Defence Policy Formation: Toward Comparative Analysis*, pp. 153–73. Durham, Carolina Academic Press.
———— (1984 [1998]). *The Pakistan Army*. New Delhi: Oxford University Press.
———— (2001). *India: Emerging Power*. Washington, DC: The Brookings Institution.
———— (2005). *The Idea of Pakistan*. New Delhi: Oxford University Press.
Dattar, Ashok (2001). Will We Agree to Disagree One More Time? *Indian Express*, 13 July.
Dhar, P.N. (2001). Let Us Not Bury the Future in Our Past, *The Telegraph*, 13 July.
Dixit, J.N. (2001a). Bring Back Shimla Spirit. *Indian Express*, 22 June.
———— (2001b). No Euphoria Please. *The Hindustan Times*, 11 July.
Dubey, Muchkund (1999). India's Foreign Policy: Aims and Strategies. In Nancy Jetly, ed., *India's Foreign Policy: Challenges and Prospects*, pp. 10–25. New Delhi: Vikas.
Indian Express (2001). Business, Not Politics. Editorial, 11 January, http://www.expressindia.com/ie/daily/20000915/shekhar2.htm.
Forsyth, M.G., H.M.A. Keens-Soper, and P. Savigear, eds. (1970). *The Theory of International Relations: Selected Texts from Gentili to Treitschke*, pp. 181–258. London: George Allen and Unwin.
Gates, David (1991). *Non-Offensive Defence: An Alternative Strategy for NATO?* New York: St. Martin's Press.
Gupta, Shekhar (2000). Don't Fear the K-Word. *Indian Express*, 18 March.
———— (2001). The Real Battle Will be for the Market, *Indian Express*, 13 January, http://www.indian-express.com/ie/daily/20010003/shekhar.htm.
Hoffman, Stanley (1965). *The State of War: Essays on the Theory and Practice of International Politics*. London: The Pall Mall Press.
Johnston, Alastair Iain (1995). *Cultural Realism: Strategic Culture and Grand Strategy in Chinese History*. Princeton: Princeton University Press.
Karnad, Bharat, ed. (1994). *Future Imperilled: India's Security in the 1990s and Beyond*. New Delhi: Viking.
Kautilya (1987). *The Arthashastra*, edited by L.N. Rangarajan. New Delhi: Penguin Books.
Keohane. Robert O. (1989). *Institutional Institutions and State Power*. Boulder, Co.: Westview.
Khan, Rasheeduddin (1993). Fundamentalism/Communalism in South Asia. *World Focus*, 14, (11&12): 21–26.
Kotru, M.L. (2001). Indo–Pak Dialogue, *News Time*, 23 June.
Krishna, Gopal (1984). India and International Order: Retreat from Idealism. In Hedley Bull and Adam Watson, eds., *The Expansion of International Society*, pp. 269–87. Oxford: Clarendon Press.
Moeller, Bjorn (1992). *Common Security and Non-Offensive Defence: A Neorealist Perspective*. Boulder, Co: Lynne Rienner.

Morgenthau, Hans (1997). *Politics Among Nations: The Struggle for Power and Peace.* New Delhi: Kalyani Publishers (sixth edition). First published 1991.

Nakra, J.C. (2001). Indo–Pak Relations and the J-K Problem. *National Herald,* 22 June.

Nehru, Jawaharlal (1963). *India's Foreign Policy, Selected Speeches, September 1946– April 1961.* New Delhi: The Publications Division, Ministry of Information and Broadcasting, Government of India. First published 1961.

————— (1981). *The Discovery of India.* New Delhi: The Jawaharlal Nehru Memorial Fund and Oxford University Press. First published 1946.

Nye, Joseph and Robert Keohane (1977). *Power and Interdependence: World Politics in Transition.* Boston: Little, Brown.

Parthasarathy, Malini (2001). Agra, Just a Beginning, *Hindu,* 12 July.

Raja Mohan, C. (1998). Nuclear Balance in Asia, *Hindu,* 11 June.

————— (2001a). Pakistan as a Bridge State? *Hindu,* 21 June.

————— (2001b). Trade as Strategy: Chinese Lessons. *Hindu,* 16 August.

Ram, N. and Sukumar Muralidharan (1998). India Must Say 'No' to CTBT and FMCT. *Frontline,* 3 July.

Ramesh, Jairam (1999). Yankee Go Home, But Take Me With You: Yet Another Perspective on Indo-American Relations. *Economic and Political Weekly,* 34 (50): 3532–34.

Subrahmanyam, K. (1999). Asia's Security Concerns in the 21st Century. In Jasjit Singh, ed., *Asian Security Concerns in the 21st Century,* pp. 7–23. New Delhi: Knowledge World.

————— (2001). Invitation to Peace: Pakistan, Not Kashmir is the Issue, *Times of India,* 18 June.

Waltz, Kenneth N. (1979). *Theory of International Politics.* Reading, MA: Addison-Wesley.

The Indian Army and the Problem of Military Change*

SUNIL DASGUPTA

At a time when the developing world was being brought increasingly under military rule, Stephen Philip Cohen (1971) made a novel argument about the Indian Army, which, he said, had transformed successfully from an instrument of colonial policy to a legitimate national military institution of independent India because its officer corps had been progressively Indianized since World War I. Together, the two World Wars turned a colonial constabulary force into a large and powerful expeditionary army that perforce had to recruit Indians into leadership positions, thereby laying the foundations for its later coherence and subservience to the political class. Following independence in 1947, the nationalist leadership accepted the Indian Army as legitimate because there already existed a competent and apolitical officer corps that shifted its allegiance from the king to the nation.

In making this argument, Cohen's analysis clarified a number of theoretical and empirical puzzles. The Indian Army had not only sought and gained national legitimacy, but also refrained from

*The author is grateful to Ned Bagley, Rajesh Basrur, Anit Mukherjee, and Swarna Rajagopalan for their comments. The usual disclaimer about their responsibility applies.

intervening in politics, which was unlike other developing world militaries of the time. How was it possible that an institution that should have been discredited with independence became a nationalist force overnight? Why was it that Indian Army officers did not develop political ambitions even as they saw their erstwhile colleagues now in Pakistan take over the government? Whereas Samuel Huntington (1968: 219–21) saw the professional military as a vanguard of conservative change, Samuel Finer (1976: 20–26) and Alfred Stepan (1973: 47–65) argued that the same professionalism led to coups, militarism, and possibly fascism. Cohen's representation of the Indian Army provided a third model that attributed positive aspects to a military's role in nation building without the downsides of armed forces assuming political power.

Using Cohen, later analyses of the Indian Army investigated the specific causes and consequences of the country's civil–military harmony in explicit and implicit comparison with the unhappy situation elsewhere, particularly the rest of South Asia (see Cohen 1988, 1990; Ganguly 1991; Kukreja 1991; Kundu 1998). But these efforts have been one-dimensional. They have looked at civil–military relations, but not the flip side—at military effectiveness. The two-sided character of civil–military relations is a central expectation of existing theory. Feaver (1996: 149–150) captures the essence of the civil–military dilemma when he writes that the challenge lies in creating a force strong enough to defend, but not so strong as to threaten society itself. It is also the implication of Cohen's empirical work. The British decision to Indianize the Army was made in pursuit of military effectiveness. Faced with a global challenge, the British had to transform an army hitherto limited to internal policing and border skirmishing into an expeditionary force capable of fighting in Europe and the Middle East. The Army opened recruitment to new sections of society and commissioned more Indians as officers to lead the growing numbers of men. The civilian authority responsible for the empire in India protested the resulting dilution of British control over the Army, but the military imperative prevailed. After independence, similar tensions have gone unresolved. The Army has suffered from a long identity crisis that dissipated its energies between constabulary and external defence functions. Thus, while India has shown exemplary political supremacy over its armed forces, it has suffered in military effectiveness. Recent scholarship, however, has focused exclusively on India's civil–military balance while ignoring military effectiveness. The question whether the civil–military balance has come at the cost of military effectiveness remains unanswered.[1]

This chapter attempts to fill this gap in the literature, bringing the analysis of the Indian Army back in line with Cohen's initial scholarship. In doing so, it arrives at certain judgments about the Army's effectiveness. My preliminary conclusion is that the Indian Army may have come a long way in the past fifty years, but it has not been very successful at making institutional changes on a scale comparable to the changes that allowed its Indianization under the British. The identity crisis between constabulary and expeditionary roles has been more trenchant in the post-independence period and exacerbated by a peculiar civil–military arrangement that has kept political leaders from intervening in the internal affairs of the Army and the military leadership out of higher defence planning (on problems with civil–military relations in India, see Dasgupta 2001). The arrangement has choked serious reforms not only in strategic planning, but also in institutional matters such as recruitment, training, and promotion. The net result is a force that has been unable to win decisive victories—with one exception—or serve as an effective instrument of compellence. My conclusions are necessarily tentative given that the concept of effectiveness itself is theoretically contested and the evidence here is simplified and abbreviated to meet space constraints. The chapter, therefore, is more an argument for further research on Indian military effectiveness than a substantive critique.

But why should we care about the Indian Army today? Recent economic growth, political change—the rise of the conservative

---

[1]The connection between effectiveness and control occurs implicitly in a variety of arguments, the most important of which come from Indian Army officers complaining about the country's higher defence planning. But there is little explicit examination of the compensating relationship between control and effectiveness, and even lesser willingness to accept the idea that intrusive political control over armed forces might be necessary for military reform. See Feaver (1996).

nationalism—and technological advancement—the advent of nuclear weapons, among others—have revived hopes and fears within and outside the country of the rise of a new Indian Army and the emergence of India as a great power. It is a measure of this expectation that scholars have increasingly turned to a more systematic study of the Indian Army. Notably, Stephen Rosen's *Societies and Military Power: India and its Armies* (1996) points out that military effectiveness is a function of institutional cohesion enabled by separating armed forces from the rest of the larger society and its divisions. He argues that the compulsion of democratic governments in India to create representative institutions was likely to hurt the country's military capability. Similarly, George Tanham's (1992, 1995) analysis of India's security policy and the Indian Air Force argued that Indian power remains bound by cultural and social incapacity. Indian experts, typically, have analysed the deficiencies in their country's defence as rooted in the lack of national willingness and the inability to mobilize collective action that could be resolved through greater institutional centralization (Singh 1999: 9–58, 292). Historically, Indian political leaders have shied away from security entanglements in order to maintain national focus on economic development. Cohen (1971: 104–05) writes, for example, that Jawaharlal Nehru 'rejected the military and militarism as viable instruments or targets for the nationalist movement'. Nehru has been the fountainhead of an intellectual tradition that has abjured military and military means even as the country had been thrust with war. Whether India will emerge as a great power, with the Army as a centrepiece, will depend on the political, bureaucratic, and military establishments bringing about institutional change. While some of the issues involved, such as the relative importance of the Army vis-à-vis the Indian Air Force and the Indian Navy, are widely mentioned, missing from the debate is a study of the Army's capacity to innovate.

Towards that end, I examine the Indian Army's record and portents of military change by first laying out the concept of military effectiveness and change, and then applying them to its performance in external and internal wars. This is followed by a more explicit evaluation of the Army's attempts to make military change.

MILITARY EFFECTIVENESS AND CHANGE

Military change is commonly believed to occur out of necessity, usually during war. Though the Taliban was thoroughly defeated, for example, the regime's forces performed better in the later stages of the war, using camouflage and adopting well-known fire and manœuver practices (Biddle 2003: 36–41). Traditionally, military change, innovation, and effectiveness are associated with this kind of learning during war. The best armies, if they did not preempt an attack, absorbed the initial offensive and changed their fighting styles to reverse early losses. Equally, offensive operations have sought ways of defeating the enemy in one swift blow in order to deny opposing armies the opportunity to learn. In World War II the German blitzkrieg precluded the possibility of military learning for France. The British managed to escape at Dunkirk, regrouped, and innovated—with air power, alliance politics, and colonial defence strategy—to alter the course of the war. In recent history, the scope of learning during war has reduced dramatically as wars have become shorter for political and technological reasons. This has made war preparation more critical than ever before. War preparation is used to substitute for war itself when leaders want to pursue compellence—to shock and awe the challenger with the show of asymmetrical power.

War preparation is usually of two types: linear rearmament (more and larger weapons, armies, budgets) and leapfrogging innovation (a different way of doing things that alters war itself). Innovation can range from technological developments such as mobile warfare and air power to organizational changes like recruitment and training. While Stalin rightly said that 'quantity has a quality all its own', linear rearmament, typically, has proven poor defence. Military professionalism, the military revolution, and now the revolution in military affairs are all rooted in the belief that quality matters. Linear rearmament is not only of poor quality—witness the three Battles of Panipat—but also visible, imitable, and possibly countered. The naval competition between Britain and Germany before World War I showed the fruitlessness of linear expansion. As World War I amply demonstrated, neither side was able to gain any significant advantage. Military innovation, on the other hand, is less visible, more difficult to evaluate, and definitely harder to imitate and counter. The impact of Germany's innovation in mobile tank warfare before World War II, for example, did not become evident to the French or the British until the blitzkriegs of 1939 and 1940, when it was too late. As weapons have become deadlier and international norms against conquest have strengthened, the scope of learning during war has contracted, making peacetime innovation critical for any country seeking to use military power effectively. The history of peacetime military change, however, is mixed because most armed forces end up preparing for the last rather than the next war.

Who is responsible for military change? French historian Marc Bloch (1949) blamed the collapse of his country in 1940 on the failure of the French society to provide the military with adequate resources. The implication is that the onus for military change rests with society at large. Democratic polities in particular hold that society—acting through the political leadership—provides the military with the objectives of and resources for the common defence. The military is seen not only as being difficult to change, but also designed not to change so as to withstand the shock of war. Governments around the world, for example, house defence research and development outside the services because they believe military culture not to be disposed to innovation. This view, however, is contested. Elizabeth Kier (1997) has argued that the French military saddled itself with a defensive doctrine, partly as a result of what it saw were social constraints but also in tune with its internal dynamics more generally. Stephen Rosen (1991) found that important military innovations came from the armed forces themselves. He found that innovation required strong internal advocates to shift priorities, deprive existing programmes, and invest in new thinking. The high failure rate of innovation efforts, moreover, made the pursuit risky and expensive. Successful innovators commanded credibility within the service and possessed the knowledge necessary for bringing about change. Usually such a reformer rose from the ranks (ibid.: 251). Alan Millett, Williamson Murray, and Kenneth Watson (1988: 2) split the responsibility for military change between political and military leaders. They define effectiveness as the ability of armed forces to convert available resources into military power. The implication is that while the military does not—should not—have to provide its own resources, it is certainly responsible for how it uses what is available.

While there is little doubt that the military is at least somewhat responsible for the state of its effectiveness, the question really is how far military leaders can go to in pursuit of military change. Should the military, like the German Army, seek to alter the very relationship between the military and the society in an effort to become more effective? Or should the military, like the inter-war French forces, leave the question of reform primarily to outsiders such as politicians? There are dangers in both directions. One leads to military coup and the other to defeat in war. Though the absolute standard is that civilians have the right to be wrong, there can be no predetermined level of military involvement in decision making. The pre-World War I debate over whether the British Indian Army was a constabulary or an expeditionary force was resolved in favour of the military commander-in-chief rather than the political chief executive, but with no major upset in civilian supremacy over the military. In the US, military leaders play an important role in determining national security objectives and requirements (Rosen 1991: 251). The military playing this role without raising fears of intervention is a sign of a consolidated democracy (Karl 1990; Pion-Berlin 1997: 215). The civil–military question in consolidated democracies is not one of intervention, but of the proper involvement of armed forces in making national security policy. The military is a legitimate—and often competing—actor alongside the civilian bureaucracy and the political leadership. In India the balance tipped far in the direction of control and away from effectiveness due to a peculiar set of circumstances.

THE CASE OF THE INDIAN ARMY

As with most militaries, the Indian Army's leaders and political masters have intensely debated the question of its proper role. The origins of the Army lie in the native forces raised by the British East India Company to conquer the subcontinent. The British imported Europe's military revolution of standing armies, drilled infantry, and massed attacks with devastating effect to win the subcontinent by

1840 (the best history of the formation of the modern Indian Army is Mason 1974; see also Lynn 2003: 145–78 for the roles of the Indian and British influences). The shock to British supremacy came not from a competing sovereign, but from the native troops who had fought and won these victories. In 1857 the Sepoy Mutiny almost dislodged the British from India in a bloody revolt that took almost two years to subdue. Thereafter, the British reorganized native forces into a purposively reliable imperial constabulary capable of policing recalcitrant Indians and fighting limited border conflicts. Since political loyalty and control was of primary concern, the Army was carefully organized on the basis of caste and class to preclude mutinous collective action (Cohen 1971: 38–39). Recruitment was restricted to groups such as Sikhs, Rajputs, and Gurkhas—later called the martial races—that sided with the British in the mutiny (Roy 2001: 939). The officer corps was nearly all British—the role of the Indian officer class that had intermediated between the British and native troops contracted beyond recognition—and Indians were excluded from technical arms such as the artillery (Cohen 1971: 54–55).

As British rule consolidated in India by the end of the nineteenth century, however, military competition heated up in Europe. Lord Kitchener, who came to India as commander-in-chief in 1902, was intent on transforming the army in India into a force that could fight with the Allies in a European war. He wanted a dramatic increase in size and capability, which implied expanding the recruitment pool by going beyond the martial races, training Indians into the technical arms, and, most controversially, commissioning Indians as officers (ibid.: 22–28). Lord Curzon, the viceroy and political head of government in India, feared that Kitchener's expansion would destabilize the Army and the empire in India. He also worried about costs since Calcutta, not Whitehall, paid for the British Indian Army (ibid.). The debate in the highest circles of government in Britain and India was intense and, eventually, insecurity in Europe gave Kitchener victory and allowed him to transform the Army's recruitment, weapons, training, leadership, and logistics. The Indian Army recruited over a million troops during the course of World War I and served in theatres from France to the Middle East as one of the Allied largest forces in the conflict (Jeffrey 1981: 374).

Despite Kitchner's military transformation and India's subsequent independence, the Army's constabulary role did not end. Even under Kitchener's hand, the Indian Army comprised a field army of 152,000 and an internal security force of 82,000 (Singh 1969: 217). The British used the Army sparingly for policing in the waning years of the empire, but it was never absent. The most infamous incident occurred in Amritsar's Jalianwallah Bagh in 1919 when a British officer ordered his Gurkha soldiers to fire into a park full of protestors, killing 379 and wounding hundreds (Swami 1997). Following independence, the first task of the Indian Army was to police the chaos of the Partition as the Punjab Boundary Force (Menezes 1999: 432). In 1948, the new nationalist government ordered the Army to wrest the princely state of Hyderabad whose ruler prevaricated over acceding to India (Menezes 1999: 455). Thus, the Indian Army has suffered from an identity crisis from doing dual service in constabulary and external defence functions. Over time, the identity crisis only exacerbated. Between 1947 and 1998, twelve of the Army's eighteen major campaigns were internal (Singh 1999: 142–43).

The impact of the identity crisis has been made worse by India's civil–military arrangement. At the turn of independence, India's political leadership made a strategic choice of adopting a low-key defence posture and political non-alignment in order to escape the security dilemma (Tellis 2001: 13). The nationalist movement had won independence by abjuring military means. No major political leader had military experience, though a number of them thought about military matters (for examples, see Cohen 1971: 88–113). The new nationalist government was fundamentally concerned with the Army's acceptance of political supremacy. The history of other developing countries was hardly inspiring in this respect and subsequent coups in Pakistan worsened these fears. From these conditions emerged an implicit agreement between the military and political leaderships that allowed the Army freedom of action within the institution in return for it submitting to the new nationalist leadership on political-strategic matters. Cohen (1971: 29) writes of this as a legacy of the British philosophy of 'separate spheres' of political and military authority, which is in fact the Clausewitzian model on which Huntington (1957: 189–92) based his notion of 'objective civilian control'.

In the mid-1950s, however, defence minister V.K. Krishna Menon disturbed the balance, interfering in internal appointments and budget allocations. With Nehru's support, Menon promoted a group of generals supportive of government initiatives, including the forward policy that led to a lost war against China in 1962. The political leadership was devastated. Nehru was never the same afterwards and died two years later. A chastised political leadership thereafter turned away from the Army's internal matters, but allowed the civilian bureaucracy to establish stringent oversight norms over the Army because they still feared military ascendancy.

The arrangement met the theoretical standard of civil–military relations, but failed to serve the cause of military effectiveness. It gave the Army operational autonomy, which was fine for linear change, but failed to create the conditions for transformation when it was required. The Army stuck to—and still continues—its caste- and race-based recruiting policy despite the Indian Constitution banning this kind of discrimination. Over- and under-representation both have incurred real costs. The Sikh mutiny following the Army's attack on the Golden Temple in Amritsar in 1984 came to be seen as one of the scariest episodes of military uprisings in the history of independent India because the community is heavily overrepresented in the Army (Kundu 1991: 69–84, 1996: 46–69). On the other hand, Muslim underrepresentation has raised legitimacy issues, particularly when the Army has been deployed in Muslim-majority areas (Khalidi 2003). The Army continues to suffer from an acute shortage of junior officers, as many as 13,000, or about 30 per cent of the officer corps (Singh 1999: 112), but it has failed to take remedial measures such as promoting from the lower ranks or devolving command responsibility. Instead, it has focused its institutional effort to make the service a more competitive career option by lobbying the government for pay rises. While the services can compete with the private sector for enlisted men, it is self-defeating to compete with a booming private sector for officer candidates on material terms. The significant pay increases in the last twenty years have only served those already inside, which is important for morale, but has hardly mitigated the officer shortage. Yet pay hikes are viewed as the solution to the problem. Similar problems exist with inconsistency in command performance that should be traced back to failures in training and promotion practices.

But the public discourse surrounding the military does not connect results of military action with the Army's structure. Reflecting the initial civil–military agreement, questions of how the Army organizes itself must ultimately be left to the Army itself. Except in a few rare cases such as K. Subrahmanyam, outsiders—politicians, bureaucrats, and certainly academics—are not considered competent to comment on military structure. The commentary on defence matters is usually conducted largely at an abstract political level rather than on the specifics of military organization. The questions in the public domain are often about proper institutionalization of higher defence planning, but not about combat organization.

Indian military leaders themselves blame the absence of reforms—and their performance—on inept politicians, a controlling civilian bureaucracy, and their own exclusion from higher defence planning. The implication is clear: the fault lies outside, not within the military. There can be little doubt the Army has been severely constrained by the political leadership and the civilian bureaucracy, but the absolution the Army confers itself is questionable. Military leaders have been remarkably unwilling to make the hard choices necessary for internal reforms. In this, the Army has behaved as a classic conservative institution that sees no need for unsettling reforms such as commissioning officers from its lower ranks. In the conversion view of military effectiveness offered by Millet et al. (1998: 2), it would seem that Indian Army leaders abdicated their larger responsibility for building an effective force in order to secure the limited gains of operational freedom.

The inability of the Indian Army to convert national resources into military power is particularly evident in the linear mode of expansion during the three major episodes of military reorganization—in the 1960s, the 1980s, and the late 1990s. Though these efforts were justified with arguments about changing threats and responses, closer examination shows they may have been led by the weapons that were procured rather than some strategic purpose. The purchase of new tanks and armoured vehicles in the 1980s, for example, enabled the creation of strike forces, the capstone achievement of that decade's reorganization. The irony is that India has since not needed to fight a tank battle. The country's security environment has deteriorated instead due to unconventional threats. To understand the relationship between military structure and war outcome, I examine the Army's record and follow it up with a discussion of how it was affected by organization.

ASSESSING INDIA'S MILITARY EFFECTIVENESS

External Wars

The Indian Army has won one unquestionable military victory, against Pakistan in 1971, and then too the gains were limited to the eastern theatre. It won a smaller victory in 1999, also against Pakistan, but after taking considerable losses. With the exception of the war in 1962, India has not fought a power of comparable or greater national capability. This is a consequence of astute political management of regional and global politics, but the inability of the Army to press home its advantages against a smaller power such as Pakistan even when the opportunity presented itself shows, at the very least, inefficiencies in how the country and the Army converted national resources into military power. The poor conversion most visibly manifests in command performance, particularly at echelons requiring greater prospective planning and wartime coordination across units, arms, and services. The Army's public record shows its leadership unable to exploit gains on the ground when given the opportunity. Clearly, the Indian Army has had exceptional officers, but the incentive structure within the institution has not promoted them. Indeed, promotion practice within the Indian Army is a long-standing and unaddressed issue of complaint. The net effect of these internal problems is that the Indian Army has not demonstrated any serious innovation in how it fights with the exception of the 'lightning concept' in the eastern theatre in 1971. Reorganization efforts have added more tanks and guns, but these have seldom brought fresh advantages against real or potential opponents. Arguably, the Army drew incorrect lessons from past conflicts. These shortcomings can be traced back to those in the organizational structure of the Army, but public discourse on the connection between structure and performance is conspicuous by its absence. The military leadership's determination to keep so-called 'political interference', for example, has come at a cost: without political leaders developing a stake, military reforms cannot occur. To understand how these weaknesses played out, a short narrative of the wars is necessary.

Free India's wars began early, in October 1947, with a single brigade hurriedly inserted into the Kashmir Valley to stop Pakistani raiders from reaching the capital city of Srinagar.[2] The brigade won a series of battles in November and December that fixed the outcome of the war. A winter lull followed when neither side could reinforce, but regular Pakistani troops, which came in to support the irregulars, held off the push back next spring. The result was a stalemate. India failed to regain the western and northern territories it had already lost. Most battles in the war were set-piece confrontations, with one side besieging the other inside fortifications. There was little militarily sensible movement. Pakistani irregulars stopped to loot Baramulla en route to Srinagar, allowing the entering Indian brigade to take up positions around the city that eventually saved the war for India. Following the success of the Tithwal offensive in the fall of 1947, the Indian Army failed to press the advantage. Given the fact that the country was in a tumult after independence and the Army was unprepared for assault by the raiders, its record in the First Kashmir War was even. The war won the Army more Param Vir Chakra medals—the highest gallantry award—than any other since.[3] Notwithstanding the rearguard action fought by the Army, kernels of later problems such as the inability to concentrate forces and manœuver around the enemy and the doctrinal disposition to set-piece battles can be seen in the campaign.

Following this, the Indian Army fought internal security campaigns until 1962, when it was humiliated by China. The war

---

[2] The history below is mainly derived from the Indian Army's official Website of major operations, http://indianarmy.nic.in/armajop1.htm. See also IDR Team (1990), Maxwell (1970), Praval (1990), Palit (1991), and Sardeshpande (1992). This is not an exhaustive coverage of the literature. A Pakistani perspective can be found in Amin (2001).

[3] See Indian Army website, http://indianarmy.nic.in/armajop.htm

with China came after almost a decade of political mismanagement of the military when defence budgets were cut, the country's first procurement scandal was exposed, and politically compliant generals were appointed to key posts. Neville Maxwell (2004), who wrote the definitive book on the war with help from senior Army officers, indicts the political leadership and its handpicked generals mishandling India's defence. The war itself was a walkover for the Chinese, who rolled down the mountains and overran Indian posts often with less than a dozen soldiers. The 'penny-packet' positions suggest the use of constabulary practice in external war. At one point, the Chinese threatened to cut off the entire north-eastern part of India. The commander of the new IV Corps created to spearhead the counter-attack in the north-east was a political appointee who sought to fight the war from across the country sitting in New Delhi (ibid.: Part III). The political interference in this war instilled fear into the hearts of the politicians, who thereafter withdrew from military matters, limiting themselves to bursts of support for increases in the size and the weaponry. The 1962 war led to the rearmament of India's forces, but without dramatic changes in military organization. Indeed, the war enshrined the implicit arrangement of the independence handover: that politicians would not interfere in the internal matters of the military, which was translated as operational freedom, in return for the Army accepting strategic direction from the elected government.

The demand for operational freedom became evident in next war against Pakistan in 1965. Faced with Pakistani attacks, the Indian Army sought to gain the initiative by attacking across a wide front in Punjab and Rajasthan. The strategy risked early commitment of reserves. Had Pakistani forces broken through to the Beas River, the road to Delhi might have been open. In the event, the Pakistan's 1 Armoured Division disintegrated at Khem Karan in the Battle of Asal Uttar. The Indian Army failed to press the advantage and it would suffer its own debacle in the Battle of Chawinda. Lieutenant-General Harbakhsh Singh (1991: 90–91), who led the Western Command during the war, later wrote how the commander of 54 Infantry Brigade lost touch with the spectacularly successful 3 Jat Regiment in the Amritsar sector, costing major gains. The mistakes—the lack of reconnaissance, command failure, little close support infantry, faulty concentration of forces, and inability to manœuver—were identical on both sides, which suggests not only weak national power, but also institutional inadequacy, especially in training. At the strategic level, Army chief General J.N. Chaudhuri asked for and received operational freedom, but without great impact on the outcome. Indeed, Chaudhuri advised Prime Minister Shastri to agree to a UN ceasefire based on a mistaken belief that the Army was running short on ammunition when in fact only 20 per cent of the stores had been expended (Palit 1991: 427).

Inability to read the battlefield also contributed to the debacle in Sri Lanka, where the Army sent the Indian Peacekeeping Force (IPKF) in 1987–90. The Tamil Tiger insurgency reportedly killed 1,200 Indian soldiers, more than any other external conflict. The experience has been called India's Vietnam (Taylor 2000). As in 1962, the political failure was massive, but the Army fell short as well. The first Indian troops sent into action were not from the counter-insurgency formations, but from a conventional air assault team located closest to the battlefield. The units sent to Sri Lanka were under-strength and lacked basic tools such as maps and proper weapons. Indian troops, for example, had no answer for the short-burst assault rifles used by the Tigers. This was eventually corrected when the government bought 70,000 AK-47 rifles from Eastern Europe and shipped them directly to the Indian Army in Sri Lanka. There were doctrinal and tactical failures. Infantry units patrolled in bunches, failed to practice basic fire and manœuver, and many collapsed when commanders died or were wounded. Half the total casualties of the war occurred in initial fighting in Jaffna, where the Tigers fought a positional battle, not a guerrilla one. J.N. Dixit, India's ambassador to Sri Lanka and one of the architects of the intervention, has criticized the rigidity of Army commanders. He was particularly peeved at the field commanders for not preventing the Sri Lankan forces from forcibly removing fifteen captured Tigers from Jaffna to Colombo (for completing versions of events, see Joseph 2000a). The Tigers committed suicide en masse, plunging the peacekeeping mission into combat.

Similar command failures contributed to the Kargil War in 1999, though public discourse remains tethered to the idea of intelligence failure rather than the misjudgments of the general officers on the scene. The Army discovered the extent of Pakistani incursions into Indian territory between 3 and 12 May 1999. It took another twelve days, until 25 May, to prepare a plan of action, which required assault teams to climb up hillsides swept from on top with machine-gun fire. Most of the 450 casualties of the war died early. It took another ten days to get air power and artillery to bring in dominating fire. Once the artillery found the mark, infantry assault teams were finally able to climb up the hills to capture the enemy positions on top. This began the reversal of the Pakistani incursion, culminating in victory that should never have been in question. The conflict occurred inside Indian territory and the intruders had little international support except that of Pakistan's. The intruders threatened India's road links to the Ladakh region of Jammu and Kashmir state, but they were not going to cut off the region without a full-fledged attack by the Pakistan Army. India enjoyed overwhelming superiority in the theatre and overall disposition. Yet the Army's initial approach showed lack of preparation and poor appreciation of the battlefield. Was it necessary to send troops up the hills into heavy fire before artillery had been brought in? Why did it take a war to work out air–land coordination? Local commanders waited crucial weeks to react, allowing the intruders to fortify. Reconnaissance continued to be poor even after Indian forces were arrayed. While much has been made of the intelligence failure that allowed the intrusions to occur, little attention has been paid to the command failures that transpired. The Army censured the division commander and removed the brigade commander, but no public effort drew out the causes of these rudimentary lapses to recruitment, promotion, and command training practice, which remain unchanged, at least as far as outsiders can tell.

Given these debacles, the real puzzle in Indian military history is the 1971 victory against Pakistan. What caused it? How did the Indian Army develop the 'lightning concept', a blitzkrieg doctrine that diverged so dramatically from the practice in the past and the future? Existing literature offers many answers. At the broadest, the outcome is believed to have resulted from favourable political circumstances: Pakistan's appalling handling of its Bengali-speaking eastern wing and incompetent national leadership, the presence of a robust local insurgency that had emerged with Indian help, and Soviet support that precluded American intervention on behalf of Pakistan. It is also attributed to the political sagacity of Prime Minister Indira Gandhi, who reportedly gave Army chief Sam Manekshaw specific but limited objectives to be won in the east along with sufficient time and resources to plan the campaign. Last, the military literature identifies the central role of Manekshaw and Lieutenant-General Jasjit Singh Aurora, the eastern theatre commander, in developing a new way of war in the subcontinent (Palit). Because these explanations are all true—a perfect constellation of factors—it raises the comparative question: can the Indian Army succeed only when everything goes right?

Certainly, the lessons of 1971 were not completely recognized. The western front saw another 1965-like draw (Menezes 1999: 501). Lieutenant-General K.P. Candeth, then Western Army commander, wrote later that had Pakistan struck preemptively, India might have had to move forces from the east to west, jeopardizing the success on the eastern front (Amin 2001). The reorganization of the Army in the 1980s was deeply influenced by the eastern victory in 1971. It created mobile armoured columns capable of striking deep inside Pakistani territory, only to have nuclear weapons neutralize this capability within a few years. The irony lay in the fact that while General Sundarji, the Army chief who led the reorganization, foresaw the coming nuclear age (evident later in his writing, see Sundarji [1993]), he still chose to develop armoured strike capability that would be useless. At the operational level, the poor performance of the reserve Territorial Army battalions in 1971, after six months of training, remained unaddressed. When called up for counter-insurgency duty in Kashmir in the 1990s, the units became infamous for their human rights violations. At the tactical level, Major-General D.K. Palit, who became a keen military historian after leaving the Army, writes with mirth about a young tank commander in 1971 bogged down in the bed of the Basantar River, but making so much noise in the retrieval that the enemy decamped mistaking his small force for a much larger one.[4] What should have led to reprimand for failing in basic reconnaissance

---

[4]The Battle of Basantar is seen as one of the greatest victories of Indian armour in which sixty-six Pakistani tanks were destroyed. The story of the tank commander, however, suggests that a closer look at the battle victories as well.

was seen as comedy of errors. On the other hand, Lieutenant-General Sagat Singh, the most successful corps commander in 1971, was not decorated or promoted. The incentives within the institution were wrong. It is little wonder that the Indian Army finds itself on a steep learning curve at the start of each new war, an increasingly costly place to be in as weapons become deadlier and wars shorter.

Internal Wars

The Indian state has fought long and bloody internal conflicts, typically, lasting twenty years and losing thousands of lives of civilians and soldiers alike.[5] The length of the insurgencies and the counter-insurgency campaigns is truly one of the remarkable facts of the Indian Army's internal war record. They suggest two dramatically different conclusions: one, that the Indian Army has displayed great tenacity by staying in the field; but equally, it has not been able to bring conflicts to a quick end. A government outlasting guerrillas is expected. Few insurgencies have succeeded against the power and organization of the modern state. It is also true that the longevity of internal wars in India is due to more political than military failure. National leaders are supposed to provide material, legal, and political resources for the Army to fulfil its goals. The government has used state elections to identify and empower local allies, but these efforts have usually come after the first phase of escalation and intensifying rebellion. Further, the Army has been limited to the use of minimum force, abjuring air power and artillery shelling, which is a rare restraint for a regular military force. But restraint and staying power alone are not good measures of military effectiveness, particularly because they emanate from political rather than military strategies. We have to look beyond at how the Army used available resources in internal conflict.

Though the Indian Army marched soon after independence to compel the princely states of Hyderabad and Junagadh to remain within the Indian Union, the real test of internal duty began in

---

[5]Based on Major-General Banerjee's presentation at the United States Institute of Peace in Washington, DC, on 5 June 2003. Summary at http://www.usip.org/ fellows/reports/2003/0605_ RPTbanerjee. html#summary. For good histories of the north-east rebellions and Indian response, see Baruah (1994) and Hazarika (1994).

1955–56 when New Delhi ordered the disarming of Naga rebels in India's north-eastern region. The conflict and the Army's campaign lasted three phases. The first started with the Army setting upon its objective in brutal earnestness: torching villages, forcing people to flee, taking men prisoners, and raping and molesting women (Hazarika 1994: 109–11). The insurgency only got worse until New Delhi worked out a ceasefire in 1963–64. The peace negotiations really went nowhere, but went on for years until 1971. In this second phase the Army held back, but developed local knowledge and infrastructure. In 1966 the Army established the College of Insurgency and Jungle Warfare for training incoming troops. The third phase began with the formal breakdown of talks in 1971. The Army returned to active counter-insurgency until New Delhi finally persuaded a section of the Nagas to settle. Though other factions continued to resist, the government and the Army thereafter considered the original Naga troubles resolved. Nagaland erupted in violence once more in the 1980s, but this time New Delhi had local allies willing to fight the rebels. This was the second Naga rising and ended with a ceasefire agreement in 1997.

Starting in the mid-1960, the Mizo insurgency saw a similar twenty-year three-phase trajectory. The first response of the national government was unique in its brutality. Responding to the insurgent takeover of the city, the Indian Air Force strafed the city—the only case in Indian history of the government using air power against the population. Following that initial burst of violence, the Army settled down to a more than decade of attrition, which was broken loose when the government began negotiations with the rebels in the early 1980s. The combination of military action and political negotiation defused two other regional insurgencies: the Assamese revolt and the ethnic Bodo uprising. In both cases a hardcore military wing continued to resist and the Indian Army launched two major clean-up operations against the remaining rebels. But the rebels were able to secure sanctuaries in Bhutan and Bangladesh. It was only in December 2003 that India finally persuaded the Bhutanese Army to launch a joint operation to smash the bases (Swami 2004). Assistance from Bangladesh continues to be a source of concern and the Indian Border Security Force is fencing the border between the two countries.

Across the country, the Kashmir insurgency is now edging toward the twenty-year mark in 2009. In the first four years military and paramilitary forces conducted their separate and often brutal counter-insurgency campaigns, resulting in human rights abuses, growing alienation, and increasing international pressure (for a good general history of Indian efforts in Kashmir see Joshi 1999; for a more academic treatment, see Ganguly 1997). In 1993 the state police mutinied, holding up the chief and other senior officers in the headquarters complex (BBC 1999). The Army had to break through police barricades to rescue the chief. The deteriorating situation compelled New Delhi to act, beginning the second phase of the insurgency. In 1994 the Army launched a counter-offensive with the hope of creating the conditions for new elections, the state's first in almost a decade. The Army made a number of organizational and operational changes. It raised a counter-insurgency formation in the state, pulling troops and officers from the underutilized non-infantry corps. With separate structures focusing on internal and external wars, the Army tried to alleviate its identity crisis and bring continuity to both constabulary and expeditionary roles. The Army also broke from the practice of border deployment to a grid system that assigned every inch of the state to a specific unit. Further, a new statewide unified command system brought all the agencies under a former army chief who was appointed state governor. Most importantly, however, the Army raised local militias—called Ikhawanis—from captured and surrendered rebels to take the fight to the insurgents (Hamid 2005). The militias became the strike arm of the state, helping eliminate rebels and supporters with great ruthlessness. Following the Army's successes, the rebellion passed into the hands of increasingly hardline leaders, who brought foreign fighters into the conflict, initiating the third phase in 1998–99. The foreign fighters, many of them veterans of the other Islamic wars in Afghanistan, Chechnya, and Bosnia, but also new recruits from the same Pakistani *madrassas* that supplied the Taliban forces, introduced suicide terrorism. The insurgency was also able to eliminate many of the militia leaders who had provided the basis for the Army's earlier successes—particularly since the government did not know what to do with after they had lived out their utility. The violence actually spread out of the Kashmir

Valley and in the south. The continuing conflict in Kashmir has soaked up ever-increasing numbers of military and paramilitary troops. By some accounts, a fourth of its entire strength of the Army is now in Kashmir, not to forget another 250,000 paramilitary and police forces. The Army's most intractable has been its inability to stop cross-border movement—though in early 2005 the combination of a new border fence and a more cooperative Pakistan seems to have led the Indian Army to conclude that infiltration had in fact reduced.

The Kashmir counter-insurgency was supposed to be modelled on the successful campaign conducted in Punjab in the mid-1990s. In Punjab, as elsewhere, the Army began on the wrong foot. In response to Sikh militants barricading themselves in the Golden Temple in Amritsar, the holiest shrine in the religion, the government ordered a frontal assault in 1984 (for a general history of the Sikh problem, see Gurharpal Singh 1996, Thandi 1996, Tully and Jacob 1985). The Army used tanks and artillery to force the militants out, but in the process severely damaged the temple, causing a popular uprising, a mutiny of Sikh soldiers in the Army, and Indira Gandhi's assassination by her Sikh bodyguards. Thereafter, efforts to reach a compromise failed as moderate leaders who wanted to negotiate with New Delhi were assassinated. The Army returned to Punjab in 1988 to remove the militants holed up in the Golden Temple, but this time held its fire and laid siege. The government ordered the first sustained Army deployment in the state in 1990 to cut off weapons supplies from Pakistan and restore order in the worst hit border districts. In May 1991 the government suspended military operations in hope of initiating peace talks, but resumed action in July after calls for negotiations failed. This began the third phase during which new elections were held and though the turnout was poor, a provincial government was put in place. The new government took ending the rebellion as its mandate and appointed as state police chief K.P.S. Gill, the man who is credited with finally defeating Sikh militancy.

Gill authored the Punjab model of counter-insurgency, a revision of the traditional policy of combining military and political action. Gill has been particularly critical of the political idea of ceasing counter-insurgency operations in the hope of starting negotiations. He advocated instead relentless offensives to contain and eliminate terrorists. His militaristic approach, however, was centred on the police rather than the Army. Whereas in the north-east and in Kashmir the Army operated as the primary counter-insurgency force, Gill demanded that as state police chief he have overall authority over deployment and operations. He later argued that the Army's strategy put pressure on the rebels, but failed to alter the course of the rebellion itself. In Punjab, in 1990–91, Army operations had effectively squeezed militancy out of the border districts and into the rest of the state (Gill 2001: 64). Instead, Gill wanted to isolate the militancy in the handful of border districts and thereafter seek its elimination. On his advice, the Army moved from amassing troops to dispersal methods, using small units split down to section level to saturate the entire state (ibid.). Gill deputed liaison officers from the corps to each battalion to ensure coordination (ibid.). These changes contained the problem to a smaller geographical space, within four border districts.

The Army's counter-insurgency experience generally shows that political negotiations preceded military success. In this, the Indian Army actually broke from the dominant theoretical construct that held military action as enabling political negotiations.[6] This recognition would be a major innovation had it not been for the fact that despite recognizing the political nature of insurgency, each new campaign has made the same mistakes as previous ones. The Army has gone in with blazing guns that has worsened rather than alleviated the problem. This is followed by years of trying to calibrate military action, which yields better results, but is almost always the outcome of political breakthroughs, whether in the form of negotiations with rebel factions or being able to install local allies in the state government. The analytical problem, of course, is that the decisions to use force and then back off are not that of the Army's. Though the military leadership bears responsibility for consenting to such policies and for negligence in failing to provide proper advice, the decisions are those of the political leadership. As such, then, errors of initial deployment are properly the domain of politicians.

---

[6]On whether politics enables counter-insurgency victory or vice versa, see Thompson (1966) and Kitson (1971).

The role of the military must be judged more narrowly with respect to how force was used once the decision to use force had already been made. Rajesh Rajagopalan (1998), one of the few scholars to examine Indian Army's counter-insurgency doctrine, concludes that the institution is predisposed toward conventional or positional warfare—which might explain the intial burst of overwhelming force. Though his analysis is based primarily on evidence from the Army's operations in Sri Lanka, they appear to be valid elsewhere at home as well. The initial phases of the Naga and Mizo campaigns were very much in the positional war tradition. In Punjab it took Gill's leadership to move the Army towards a small unit saturation policy. Only later, once political negotiations had advanced, was the Army able to use local groups for intelligence gathering and raised militias for counter-attacks. But there is no systematic analysis of the Army's militia policy. Rajagopalan, for example, does not even consider militias important enough for consideration in his examination of the Army's counter-insurgency doctrine. The reason for this neglect, arguably, is that the Army views policy in this regard as a political matter even though its operational commanders are responsible for the militias themselves. In Kashmir, for example, support for the Ikhwanis was withdrawn after they achieved some early successes, only to have deleterious consequences. On the one hand, the militias indulged in a modern form of forage and plunder to support themselves, and, on the other, they became targets of separatists. Not only did the Ikhwanis get a bad reputation and bring opprobrium on the government, they were in fact militarily neutralized.

REORGANIZATION AND MODERNIZATION

The military performance outlined in the previous section shows the Army making changes, but with a few exceptions these are not changes that bring the country winning advantages. We find reorganization efforts have been largely linear. Troop numbers have increased, new weapons have been added, and new commands have been created, but these efforts have not reached into the bowels of the Army to re-examine the fundamentals of its organization. In all but one case, the Army's reorganization efforts were also post-hoc—by definition, in preparation for the last war.

The creation of new commands has been the most visible form of military reorganization in India. The Western Command grew out of the Delhi and East Punjab Command, which was created to restore order during Partition, and followed the Punjab Boundary Force. The First Kashmir War was the impetus for creation of the Northern Command. The experience of the 1962 war led to the creation of a new Eastern Command in Calcutta. These reforms moved commanders closer to theatres, but did not alter the chain of command or decision-making system in any significant way. Regional commanders, for example, continued to report to the chief of army staff rather than directly to political authority such as a civilian commander-in-chief.[7] The objective was to preserve the military chain of command. In higher defence planning, a three-tier structure has continued from the colonial period to today through fifty years of combat experience: the apex tier of the cabinet, a second group managed by the defence minister, and a last tier of service chiefs on the military side and secretarial coordination committee on the civilian side. More recently, in the years following India's nuclear tests in 1998, more commands have been created. The full implications of these changes are yet to be seen. The Indian Air Force, for example, has been given control of the Strategic Air Command, but the country's missiles are under the Army's control. A joint force command was recently inaugurated at the Andaman Islands in the Bay of Bengal, but it is unclear how authority will run and how the capabilities of these command will develop. A new position of national security advisour was created to coordinate foreign policy and defence issues. A new National Security Council (NSC) and the National Security Advisory Board (NSAB) have also been mooted, though it is clear the larger political and bureaucratic structure limits the NSC to managerial rather than policy capacity and the NSAB is a public relations exercise.

A more substantive position creating exercise long proposed by the Army is a new position of chief of defence staff. The British had

---

[7]A new layer on this problem is the rise of paramilitary forces that do give political leaders control over armed forces outside the Army's chain of commands, but the rise of these forces have also given rise to problems of institutional competition that jeopardizes overall coordination (on military-paramilitary rivalry, see Rustamji 1992).

a commander-in-chief who functioned in that capacity, but the nationalist leadership made the civilian defence minister responsible for service coordination to reduce military influence. This arrangement did not work very well because the defence minister did not have an independent ability to evaluate competing demands. The civilian bureaucracy, with little capacity to make military judgements, appropriated this function, inflaming bureaucratic jealousy between the civilian and military bureaucratic bodies. The proposal for a new chief of defence staff has remained mired in this bureaucracy for over two decades. The smaller Indian Navy and the Indian Air Force, which expected to lose out in the new arrangement, stalled the idea as well. To expect a new defence chief to resolve the coordination problem, however, is unrealistic. No matter how brilliant or experienced an officer he may be, he cannot evaluate competing demands without independent analyses. The analyses cannot come from the services or, for that matter, the civilian bureaucracy. It has to come from private individuals working in an open forum, which demands a new culture of openness in defence matters. Without a new culture—a marketplace of ideas—arbitrating efficiently between competing demands is impossible. This is the change that is needed and this is the change that is most difficult to achieve—much more in fact than the creation of a new position of defence chief.

The second type of reorganization stemmed from weapons purchases. There have been three episodes of this kind of linear expansion. The first was triggered by India's collapse in 1962. The Indian Army more than doubled in size and budget as well as acquired a new range of weapons. In a few years it went from ten to twenty-five divisions, with new tanks, artillery pieces, and individual equipment from rifles to shoes. The Army raised specialized mountain divisions to deter future Chinese invasions from over the Himalayas. The country bought Soviet MiG-21 fighters to build a fighting air force. The modernization was mostly straightforward increase in size and firepower; its shape determined by what weapons were available. The second episode occurred in the mid-1980s when the country bought new tanks, artillery guns, aircraft, and ships. The Army chief, General Krishnaswamy Sundarji, used the new weapons to push slowly towards combined arms. To test the new organization and concepts, Sundarji ran Brasstacks, the biggest Indian military exercise until then and one of the largest non-NATO manœuvers ever. The movement nearly erupted in war with Pakistan (Bajpai et al. 1995). The general later wrote that Brasstacks was the last time India could expect to win a war against Pakistan (Sundarji 1993). Thereafter, Pakistan accelerated its nuclear programme and allegedly deterred an Indian attack in 1990 (Hagerty 1995).

Once nuclear deterrence came into play in South Asia, however, the premise of Sundarji's reorganization fell apart. The Indian Army has since not had to fight a war with tanks, but maintains large armoured forces. The Kargil War in 1999, which launched the third episode of military modernization, caught Sundarji's army unaware. India's defence budgets have been growing explosively in real terms, but remain less than 4 per cent of its GDP. Though it is unlikely that India will match China's defence budget, which is said to be around 6 per cent of a much larger GDP, Indian capabilities on most conventional measures does not lag significantly behind. After a hiatus of a decade, India inaugurated a new round of weapons purchases. Early orders have gone to Israel (fighter retrofit, radars, and missiles) and to Russia (major platforms including an aircraft carrier).[8] Incredibly, plans involve upgrading and buying new tanks even though Pakistan has said that it would use nuclear weapons if India made a deep armoured strike into the country (BBC 2001).

A third kind of reorganization that has been totally bypassed is changing the Army's social composition. The Army suffers from a severe shortage of junior officers but cannot bring itself to widen its recruitment, particularly from among enlisted ranks due to reasons of class and caste. The Army's failure in this regard is critical because junior leadership ranks account for the greater part of its military effectiveness. This high casualty rate shows that they lead from the front. The shortages, therefore, can be expected to have a magnified impact on performance. What makes the situation worse is that the Army has been unwilling, and perhaps unable, to devolve leadership down the chain to junior commissioned officers and non-commissioned

---

[8]The growing India–Israel defence relationship has been widely commented upon. See, for example, Kapila (2003). On India–Russia weapons deals, see CNN (2000).

soldiers. At the same time, the Army itself has grown older with most soldiers staying on for the full twenty years of service in order to become eligible for pension. It would make sense to promote from within or push command responsibility down the chain, but neither has happened.

No law prohibits enlisted men from seeking commission, but the practice is discouraged. An upper-class officer corps does not socially accept the few enlisted men who become officers.[9] Though fewer and decreasing, there are still social and economic obstacles for sons of junior commissioned officers and non-commissioned soldiers to enter the officer corps.[10] A defence of the status quo in the name of current effectiveness implies a misreading of the Army's record. It suggests that social classes that produce good *jawans* cannot produce officer material—an untenable position given the racial integration of the United States Army. The officer–men relationship in the Indian Army is reminiscent of a bygone era. Many officers use soldiers as servants in their homes despite prohibitions against the practice. This is not only a waste, but also precludes a promotion policy that could alleviate the officer shortage. The attitude reflects the caste, class, and ethnic consciousness of Indian society at large—and while the military is no place for social experiments, the Army loses out on having a full-strength officer corps because it is unable to make changes to its recruitment, training, and promotion practices.

CONCLUSION

This chapter has sought to relate the Indian Army's equivocal performance to the lack of basic reforms. Three sets of interrelated problems bedevil the institution. First, the Army lacks a clearly

---

[9]The evidence here is anecdotal and drawn significantly from personal interviews. Also, the contention here is not that the social origins of the officer class have remained unchanged. Rather, there has been a remarkable expansion of groups and communities entering the military, but the class differences still remain significant. The fact that there is a shortage of officers adds credence to the belief that the Indian Army is overly restrictive in its officer recruitment.

[10]On class and the Indian Army, see the writings of a junior commissioned officer, Kunju (1991, 1993).

defined role. The identity crisis that led to the Curzon–Kitchener dispute returned dramatically as the new national state has tried to consolidate itself. This is clearly a political rather than a military problem. The inability of the political leadership to manage rebellion cannot be blamed on the Army. Second, an inadequately structured relationship with the civilian leadership has meant that the political leadership has not developed interest in and understanding of military issues, with the result that size and firepower expansion have substituted for real reform. Here the blame must be shared by political and military leaders. Burnt by the defeat of 1962 and buoyed by the success of 1971, politicians have turned away from active involvement in defence issues. When asked to provide security, they have sought linear expansion. The military leadership has failed in this respect because it has successfully kept the political leadership—and by extension the public at large—from being able to legitimately and competently comment on national security matters, except in the abstract as part of a larger foreign policy analysis. Third, the Army's insistence on its internal autonomy has come at a cost. In this case the Indian Army's leadership is fully culpable. Their choice of operational freedom over military change has been deliberate and neglectful. The inability to fill the officer billets, devolve command responsibility, and promote the right officers indicates serious organizational weaknesses. These weaknesses will loom large as India proceeds on the path to developing a nuclear arsenal and undertake other modernization efforts. This is not a problem that can be overcome easily. Currently, the Army does not even recognize these weaknesses and outsiders do not have the credibility to push for reform. The best chance of change, as Rosen (1991) points out, lies in the emergence of an internal candidate for reform.

The description of India's wars shows the Army's persisting identity crisis between constabulary and expeditionary roles. The Indian government and the military leadership have tried to alleviate the problem through growth. In the last four decades the Indian Army has grown exponentially to a million men, the third largest in the world. India's paramilitary forces, which are not institutionally a part of the Army though they are a complement of the internal security apparatus, number another million. The Army itself is a three-in-one:

a counter-insurgency force, a defensive infantry for holding off invasion, and an armoured force of limited value in the nuclear era. The problem of divided armies usually is that no part of them becomes truly effective. Samuel Huntington (1962: 22), for example, wrote that countries could ill-afford multiple armies not only because of resource constraints, but also because the logics of their organization were contradictory. Whereas external security forces brought to bear maximum force against an enemy, internal security forces used political–military strategies, often involving greater emphasis on intelligence than on the use of force itself. In the competition between constabulary and expeditionary elements, one side usually dominated the other. In the Indian Army positional warfare has dominated the mindset even though the force has undergone an overall infantry-ization resulting from growing internal duties.

In a democratic country, elected politicians restructure the system, but India's civil–military arrangement has kept political leaders away from developing interests in military reform. According to the implicit post-independence balance, the military could preserve its internal structure provided it submitted to the higher direction of the nationalist government. This worked when the security environment was benign. The political leadership, however, made a miserable effort to take the initiative against China, resulting in a humiliating defeat. Thereafter, political leaders swore off interfering in internal military matters while remaining suspicious of military ascendancy. The 1971 victory further consolidated the post-independence civil–military arrangement. The Army has enjoyed its operational and institutional freedom precluding political interference. The political class—with the civilian bureaucracy—has excluded the military from national security planning. The lack of political–military integration resulted in military reform falling between the two distinct spheres of policy. The political leadership, which should have demanded military reform, did not even see any need for it. The military leadership, which was not part of the higher planning, had no incentive to connect internal structural weaknesses to war performance. Though it would be wrong to expect bureaucratic agencies in democratic societies to change directions without political support, the Army's acquiescence in the civil–military arrangement implies a degree of complicity. The Army's leadership has not even held itself responsible for effectiveness. The one proposal that the Army has long forwarded, a new chief of defence staff, preferably from its own ranks, cannot be expected to resolve the real problems. What is lacking is not a position, but independent military expertise that would help evaluate competing claims and offer alternative ways of doing things. The Army has done itself a disservice by failing to foster an open culture that would have resulted in a flowering of civilian expertise on the military. Inability to recognize that the police might be a more effective lead agency, for example, has resulted in the military serving that role in Kashmir and the north-east, exacerbating the identity crisis between being a constabulary and an expeditionary force. There are many who see a loss of India's security following the nuclear tests. Kargil and the high level of cross-border terrorism are an example of the 'stability–instability paradox', which raises the prospect of conflict at the sub-nuclear level between nuclear rivals. The Indian Army has responded with a limited war doctrine that can be equally destabilizing.

Meanwhile, the Army's practices in recruitment, training, and promotion have not changed since the colonial period, except perhaps to accommodate the demands of new weapons technology. The Indian Army is hard pressed to find a full complement of officers in its battalions, but remains unwilling to devolve command responsibility down the ranks to junior commissioned officers. Further up the chain, the conduct of war by commanders has been suspect. Evidence from the Army's last tank battles in 1971 show terrible failures that went unrecognized. Similar mistakes of command occurred in Kargil in 1999 in an entirely different type of war, indicating that the persisting shortcomings in the training of commanding officers.

At a time when military strength may be one of the determinants of India's rise to great power status, this analysis has grave implications. India faces three external threats (Pakistan, China, and international terrorism) and some less serious infiltration problems (Nepal, Sri Lanka, and Bangladesh). It continues to be rife with internal unrest. Even if there is no war, a strong and capable Army will give the country confidence to pursue its national interests. The Indian Army's success or failure will also prove whether developing nations can become great powers in the same way as European states, by generating economic and military strength. While the nuclear tests themselves broke the pattern of war-initiated reforms, the Army's past record is ambiguous. In the future the costs of mid-course corrections in blood and treasure will only increase as weapons become deadlier and wars shorten. Without a culture of peacetime innovation, the Indian Army can only serve as an uncertain instrument of national power.

BIBLIOGRAPHY

Akbar, M.J. (1985). *India: The Siege Within.* New Delhi: Penguin.

Amin, A.H. (2001). The Anatomy of Indo–Pak Wars: A Strategic and Operational Analysis. *Defence Journal* (Pakistan), http://www.defencejournal.com/2001/august/anatomy.htm

Bajpai, Kanti P., P.R. Chari, Pervaiz I. Cheema, Stephen P. Cohen, and Sumit Ganguly (1995). *Brasstacks and Beyond: Perception and Management of Crisis in South Asia.* New Delhi: Manohar.

Baruah, Sanjib (1994). The State and Separatist Militancy in Assam: Winning a Battle and Losing a War. *Asian Survey* 34 (10) (October): 863–77.

BBC (1999). Six Policemen Killed in Kashmir Attack. http://news.bbc.co.uk/1/hi/world/south_asia/563018.stm

BBC (2001). India to Buy Russian Tanks. 15 February, http:/news.bbc.co.uk/1/hi/world/south_asia/1171405.stm

Biddle, Stephen (2003). Afghanistan and the Future of Warfare. *Foreign Affairs*, 82(2), pp. 31–46.

Bloch, Marc (1949). *Strange Defeat: A Statement of Evidence Written in 1940,* Translated from the French by Gerard Hopkins. London: Oxford University Press.

CNN (2000). Defense Contracts Expected to Dominate India–Russia Talks. 2 October, http://www.cnn.com/2000/ASIANOW/south/10/01/india.putin.advancer

Cohen, Stephen P. (1988). The Military and Indian Democracy. In Atul Kohli, ed., *India's Democracy: An Analysis of Changing State–Society Relations.* Princeton: Princeton University Press. pp. 99–143.

——— (1971 [1990]). *The Indian Army: Its Contribution to the Development of a Nation.* Berkeley: University of California Press.

Dasgupta, Sunil (2001). India: The New Militaries. In Muthiah Alagappa, ed., *Coercion and Governance: The Declining Political Role of the Military in Asia.* Stanford: Stanford University Press. pp. 92–120.

Feaver, Peter D. (1996). The Civil–Military Problematique: Huntington, Janowitz, and the Question of Control. *Armed Forces and Society*, 23(2), pp. 149–78.

Finer, Samuel E. (1976). *The Man on Horseback: The Role of the Military in Politics.* New York: Penguin Books.

Ganguly, Sumit (1991). From the Defense of the Nation to Aid to the Civil: The Army in Contemporary India. *Journal of Asian and African Studies*, 26(1–2), pp. 11–26.

———— (1994). *The Origins of War in South Asia: Indo-Pakistani Conflicts Since 1947.* Boulder, Co: Westview.

———— (1997). *The Crisis in Kashmir: Portents of War, Hopes of Peace.* New York: Cambridge University Press.

Gill, K.P.S. (2001). *Terror and Containment: Perspectives on India's Internal Security.* New Delhi: Gyan Publishing House.

Hagerty, Devin T. (1995). Nuclear Deterrence in South Asia: The 1990 Indo-Pakistani Crisis. *International Security*, 20(3), pp. 79–114.

Hamid, Peerzada Arshad (2005). In the Line of Fire. *Mid Day*. http://www.midday.com/news/nation/2005/apri/108139.htm

Hazarika, Sanjoy (1994). *Strangers of the Mist: Tales of War and Peace from India's Northeast.* New Delhi: Penguin.

Huntington, Samuel P. (1957). *The Soldier and the State: The Theory and Politics of Civil–Military Relations.* Cambridge: Belknap Press.

———— (1962). Patterns of Violence in World Politics. In Samuel P. Huntington, ed., *Changing Patterns of Military Politics.* Glencoe: Free Press, pp. 17–50.

———— (1968). *Political Order in Changing Societies.* New Haven: Yale University Press.

IDR Team (1990). Afghanistan and Sri Lanka: Comparison of Operational Style. *Indian Defence Review*, pp. 78–87.

Jeffrey, Keith (1981). An English Barrack in the Oriental Seas? India in the Aftermath of the First World War. *Modern Asian Studies*, 15(3), pp. 369–86.

Joseph, Josy (2000a). Interview with J.N. Dixit, 'The intelligence agencies said, "Don't worry about the LTTE, they are our boys, they will not fight us,"' Rediff.com series, India's Vietnam. The IPKF in Sri Lanka: 10 Years On. http://www.rediff.com/news/2000/mar/24 lanka.htm.

———— (2000b). Interview with Major-General Harkirat Singh, 'Till the LTTE get Eelam, they won't stop, and shoot Prabhakaran, shoot Mahathiah!' Rediff.com series, India's Vietnam. The IPKF in Sri Lanka: 10 Years On. http://www.rediff.com/news/2000/IPKF in Sri Lanka: 10 Years On. http://www.rediff.com/new/2000/mar/30 lanka.htm and http://www.rediff.com.news/2000/mar/ 31 lanka.htm.

Joshi, Manoj (1999). *Lost Rebellion: Kashmir in the Nineties.* New Delhi: Penguin.

Kapila, Subhash (2003). Israel–India Strategic Cooperation and Prime Minister Sharon's visit. South Asia Analysis Group Paper 777. http://www.saag.org/paper 777. html.

Karl, Terry Lynn (1990). Dilemmas of Democratization in Latin America. *Comparative Politics*, pp. 1–26.

Kier, Elizabeth (1997). Culture and French Military Doctrine Before World War II. In Peter Katzenstein, ed., *The Culture of National Security: Norms and Identity in World Politics.* New York: Columbia University Press, pp. 186–215. http://www.ciaonet.org/book/katzenstein/katz06.html

Khalidi. Omar (2003). *Khaki and Ethnic Violence in India.* New Delhi: Three Essays Collective.

Kitson, Frank (1971). *Low Intensity Operations.* London: Faber and Faber.

Kukreja, Veena (1991). *Civil–Military Relations in South Asia.* New Delhi: Sage Publications.

Kundu, Apurba (1991). The Indian Army's Continued Overdependence on Martial Races Officers. *Indian Defence Review*, pp. 69–84.

———— (1996). The Indian Armed Forces, Sikh and Non-Sikh Officers Opinions of Operation Blue Star. *Pacific Affairs*, 67(1) (Spring), pp. 46–69.

———— (1998). *Militarism in India: The Civil and Military in Consensus*. London: Tauris Academic Studies.

Kunju, N. (1991). *Indian Army: A Grassroots Review*. New Delhi: Reliance.

———— (1993). *Olive Green Home Truths: How the Army Suffers from a Colonial Hangover*. New Delhi: Reliance.

Lynn, John A. (2003). *Battle: A History of Combat and Culture*. Boulder, Co: Westview.

Mason, Philip (1974). *A Matter of Honour*. New York: Holt, Reinhart, and Winston.

Maxwell, Neville (1970). *India's China War*. New York: Pantheon.

———— (2004). How the East Was Lost? Parts I, II, and III). http://www.rediff.com/news/2001/may/23spec.htm

Menezes, S.L. (1999). *Fidelity and Honour: The Indian Army from the Seventeenth to the Twenty-first Century*. New Delhi: Oxford University Press.

Millet, Allan R., Williamson Murray, and Kenneth H. Watman (1998). The Effectiveness of Military Organizations. In Allan R. Millett and Williamson Murray, eds., *Military Effectiveness, Vol 1*. Boston: Allen & Unwin pp. 1–30.

Nibedon, Nirmal (1981). *The Ethnic Explosion: North East India*. New Delhi: Lancer.

Palit, D.K.. (2005). The Lightning Concept. http://www.bharat-rakshak.com/LAND-FORCES/Army/History/1971War/Palit.html

Palit, D.K. (1991). *War in the High Himalaya: The Indian Army in Crisis, 1962*. New Delhi: Lancer.

Phadnis, Urmila (1989). *Ethnicity and Nation-Building in South Asia*. New Delhi: Sage Publications.

Pion-Berlin, David (1997). *Through Corridors of Power: Institutions and Civil–Military Relations in Argentina*. University Park: Pennsylvania State University Press.

Praval, K.C. (1990). Indian Army After Independence in Major Shankar Bhaduri ed., *The Sri Lankan Crisis*. New Delhi: Lancer International.

Rajagopalan, Rajesh (1998). Explaining Anomalous Outcomes In War: The Indian Army In Sri Lanka. Ph.D. Dissertation, Graduate Faculty in Political Science, City University of New York.

Rosen, Stephen Peter (1991). *Winning the Next War*. Ithaca, NY: Cornell University Press.

———— (1996). *Societies and Military Power: India and its Armies*. Ithaca, NY: Cornell University Press.

Roy, Kaushik (2001). Coercion through Leniency: British Manipulation of the Courts-Martial System in the Post-Mutiny Indian Army, 1859–1913. *Journal of Military History* 65(4), pp. 937–64.

Rustamji, Khusro F. (1992). The Paramilitary–Army Interface. *Indian Defence Review*.

Sardeshpande, S.C. (1992). *Assignment Jaffna*. New Delhi: Lancer International.

Singh, Gurharpal (1996). Punjab Since 1984: Disorder, Order, and Legitimacy. *Asian Survey*, 36(4), pp. 410–21.

Singh, Harbakhsh (1991). *War Despatches: Indo–Pak Conflict, 1965*. New Delhi: Lancer.

Singh, Jaswant (1999). *Defending India*. New York: St. Martin's Press.

Singh, Nagendra (1969). *The Theory of Force and Organization of Defence in Indian Constitutional History*. London: Asia Publishing House.

Stepan, Alfred C. (1973). The New Professionalism of Internal Warfare and Military Role Expansion. In Alfred Stepan, ed., *Authoritarian Brazil*, pp. 47–65. New Haven, CT: Yale.

Sundarji, Krishnaswami (1993). *Blind Men of Hindoostan: Indo–Pak Nuclear War*. New Delhi: UBS Publishers and Distributors.

Swami, Praveen (2004). The View from New Delhi. *Frontline*, 21(1), http://www.frontlineonnet.com/fl2101/stories/20040116005101500.htm

Swami, Praveen (1997). Jallianwala Bagh Revisited. *Frontline*, 14(22), http://www.flonnet.com/fl1422/14220500.htm

Tanham, George K. (1992). *Indian Strategic Thought: An Interpretive Essay*. Santa Monica: RAND.

———— (1995). *The Indian Air Force: Trends and Prospects*. Santa Monica: RAND.

Taylor, John (2000). Totally unprepared and ill-equipped, that was the IPKF. Rediff.com series India's Vietnam. The IPKF in Sri Lanka: 10 Years On. http://www.rediff.com/news/2000/mar/23 lanka.htm

Tellis, Ashley (2001). *India's Emerging Nuclear Posture: Between Recessed Deterrent and Ready Arsenal*. Santa Monica: RAND.

Thandi, Shinder S. (1996). Governance and Peripheral Regions in South Asia: Fighting Sikh Militancy: Counterinsurgency Operations in Punjab (India) 1980–1994. Paper presented at the Conference of the Political Studies Association, http://www.psa.ac.uk/cps/1996/than.pdf

Thompson, Robert (1966). *Defeating Communist Insurgency*. London: Chatto & Windus.

Tully, Mark and Satish Jacob (1985). *Amritsar: Mrs. Gandhi's Last Battle*. London: Jonathan Cape.

Same as it Ever Was? India's Arms Production Efforts

Amit Gupta

One of the central concerns of Stephen Cohen's academic work has been to examine how a state's military capability impacts on its international behaviour. This chapter examines one part of India's military capability—its indigenous arms industry. India today has a comprehensive arms industry comprising fifty-one defence research laboratories, forty ordnance factories, and eight defence public sector undertakings (as of August 2004). These defence production establishments both license produce and independently develop a range of weapons systems for the three branches of India's armed forces. The indigenous production efforts include the Tejas Light Combat Aircraft (LCA), the Arjun Main Battle Tank (MBT), the Integrated Guided Missile Development Programme (IGMDP), as well as a nuclear submarine programme. Further, the Indian space programme, with its increasingly impressive record of launches, allows India to both improve its surveillance and missile delivery capabilities.

Despite such progress, however, the Indian arms industry remains constrained by some of the problems that have beset it since independence. There is a continued reliance on external suppliers both for technological components and complete systems. There are lengthy delays in the production of indigenously developed systems and, consequently, the arms industry is unable to secure some of the basic needs of the Indian armed services. In times of war India has had to look elsewhere for ammunition and has had to undertake expensive imports of less advanced systems that could have been produced at home.

This chapter argues that despite positive changes in the past decade, the Indian arms industry continues to display patterns for selecting weapons production programmes that come from the country's economic strategy during the era of state-sponsored socialism. Consequently, not only is the country's defence preparedness affected, but so too is the viability of the nation's defence industries. While recent Indian arms production policy has sought to remove some of these deficiencies, the government will have to take steps to move the arms industry away from wasteful and lengthy projects to ones that can not only be successfully completed but will also find a ready market among the country's armed services—as the Agni and Prithvi ballistic missiles from the IGMDP have.

This may require giving up some of the expensive and prestigious projects that are ongoing and, instead, focus on producing what cannot be acquired from external suppliers. Further, the pursuit of joint ventures and the development of non-competitive systems will help the Indian arms industry be competitive and satisfy the country's defence requirements.

PAST ARMS PRODUCTION POLICY

After India attained independence, the Indian government invited the British scientist P.M.S. Blackett to write a report on Indian defence requirements including any future attempts to initiate indigenous weapons production efforts. Blackett's most important suggestion, taking into account the state of Indian defence science and the general level of Indian industrialization, was that India develop non-competitive weapons systems. These were weapons that would not become obsolete because of the development of competing and more advanced systems in the industrialized world and ones where the relative quality of the system did not matter. Blackett recommended that India develop anti-aircraft guns, transport vehicles, and set the grounds for an aircraft industry by designing and developing trainer aircraft (Gupta 1997: 33).

Indian defence production, however, did not take this path. In the 1950s Jawaharlal Nehru took the decision to both cut back military expenditure and use existing defence production facilities to encourage broad-based industrialization in the country. Indian ordnance factories used surplus capacity to produce coffee percolators and sewing machines. At the same time, the Nehru government authorized the development of a supersonic combat aircraft, the HF-24 Marut, the logic being that it would help India develop a modern aircraft industry.

Indian arms production efforts, therefore, followed the country's broader economic strategy. Arms production was state owned, and directed and aimed not only at achieving autonomy in military policy, but also in helping to further national economic development. The result was that the country followed a two-fold path to weapons development. Ignoring Blackett's advice, the Indian government sought to develop expensive and ambitious projects like the HF-24 Marut. It also invested in the licensed production of conventional weaponry, taking the decision in the early 1960s to license-produce the Soviet MiG-21 and later the Vickers Vijayanta tank.

DEVELOPMENTAL CONSTRAINTS

Indian defence production efforts were constrained, however, by developmental delays, the existence of threats that needed to be countered, and the bureaucratic agendas of the military and the arms production units. As a late-industrializing country, India found it difficult to develop weapons in a reasonable time frame or to match the superior systems produced in industrialized countries. The Marut programme, for instance, was started at a time when India lacked both the industrial infrastructure and the scientific personnel to carry out such an ambitious programme. The emphasis on self-reliance and indigenization, which was integral to Nehru's strategy of state-driven industrialization, led to India wasting scarce resources on reinventing the wheel. Thus, Indian weapons programmes were marked by lengthy delays and outright failures or, when weapons finally became available, they were considered obsolescent and the armed forces preferred to import better and more reliable systems—as was the fate of the Marut (Graham 1984: 170).

The immediacy of threats has also forced India to import weapons rather than permit the lengthy developmental periods required for indigenously developed weaponry to reach production. In the modern day context, for example, Indian Air Force requirements have led to the purchase of Sukhoi-30 and Mirage 2000 fighters while the indigenously designed Tejas continues to go through flight tests. In the 1980s, India purchased the Bofors howitzer because it found that Pakistan had out-gunned it by buying Pakistani 155mm howitzers. (Rikhye 1990: 38)

Similarly, the Arjun MBT, that took nearly three decades to develop, became a lower priority because of the purchase of Russian T-72 and T-90 tanks. In 2004 the Indian Army received its first batch of Arjun tanks that were to undergo trials. The Army wants to reduce the imported components in the tanks from 50 per cent to 20 per cent. This will not be easy to achieve. Further, Army chief General N.C. Vij admitted that the Arjun cost more than the imported Russian T-90, but saw the 124 tanks the Army had ordered as a suitable replacement for its aging T-55 and T-72 tanks (*Hindu* 2004). Such a small order of tanks may, however, make the programme economically not feasible, and with the more attractive and cheaper T-90 available, the option to import instead of indigenously produce may well be adopted.

India is now negotiating the purchase of Scorpene conventional submarines from France and Amur class submarines from Russia. There have also been reports that the Indian government is seeking to lease Akula class nuclear submarines from Russia. Press reports state that purchase of the Admiral Gorshkov carrier was the precondition for negotiations on the sale of the Akula and Backfire bombers. Both Indian and Russian sources have officially denied this, but the Russians did claim that anything was for sale if the 'price was right.'[1] This may further slow down progress on the indigenous nuclear submarine programme.

---

[1]Unconfirmed reports suggest that India has already entered into an agreement to lease two Akula class nuclear powered submarines from Russia. See Bedi (2004).

From an Indian perspective, the purchase of Russian naval equipment fits nicely into the plan to develop a strategic navy by 2010. Such a navy would be able to project power around the Indian Ocean littoral and deter Chinese expansion into the area. Given the problems domestic programmes have run into, the procurement of Russian nuclear submarines and long-range bombers would give India a quick and ready nuclear strike force. In fact, India's Navy chief Admiral Arun Prakash has called for the country to quickly firm up the Scorpene deal with France and also reiterated the Navy's 'desperate desire to acquire nuclear submarines but said it was for the government to take decisions' (*Times of India* 2004).

While threats have constrained the indigenous development of weapons systems, bureaucratic agendas have pushed the Indian government to agree to continue funding programmes both to keep scientists employed as well as to help in the overall development of the economy—the old argument of defence aiding development. This resulted in the 1980s in several major programmes getting government funding—the IGMDP, the Dhruv advanced light helicopter (ALH), the Tejas LCA, and the Arjun tank (Gupta 1997: 54–55).

The Indian armed services, however, were operating in a global military environment and, therefore, comparing their weapons requirements and doctrines to those of Western militaries. In the 1960s the Indian Navy, for example, drew up a requirement for four aircraft carriers because it wanted to assume the role recently relinquished by the Royal Navy in the Indian Ocean (Gupta 1995: 445). The Indian Air Force, in the 1980s, while drawing up requirements for the LCA, based them to a large extent on the 1970s' US Light Weight Fighter programme that produced the F-16.

The armed forces, therefore, came up with technological requirements that, given the state of Indian technological development, were difficult to achieve. They also changed requirements midway through a programme—as was the case with the original LCA programme and with the earlier Ajeet fighter programme (Chengappa 1988; Prabhu 1987). This made the task of bringing the programme to fruition even more difficult since changes in specifications led to design and developmental delays. Moreover, when it became possible to purchase weapons from abroad, the armed services preferred to acquire proven imported systems rather than rely on untested indigenous weaponry.

The Indian government, however, has been committed to creating and sustaining a defence science base within the country and this led India's defence scientists to propose that state-of-the-art weapons systems be designed as opposed to realistic programmes that are easily deliverable and do not tend towards obsolescence. Thus, in the 1980s the Indian government, at the insistence of the defence science establishment, agreed to fund the development of the LCA and an MBT. At that point of time the Indian Air Force was pressing for a new trainer aircraft for its fleet and the plane it wanted was to be imported from Britain. When I asked V.S. Arunachalam, the then head of India's Defence Research and Development Organization, why the country was building an LCA that was technologically ambitious and prone to obsolescence rather than build a technologically feasible jet trainer, he replied that building a jet trainer was subjecting the country to technological colonialism.[2] In the broader context of national technological development, Arunachalam's objection made sense. But the arms industry did not have a track record of delivering such systems.

Further, recent reports about the LCA have been pessimistic about the plane's chances of entering squadron service on time and in significant numbers. It has been argued that the prototypes have not been tested with radars, have not had pylons, drop tanks, and ordnance mounted to them, and have not carried out manoeuvers that would test the full capability of the aircraft (Sharma 2005). Moreover, the indigenously built Kaveri engine remains in the developmental stage and, therefore, cannot be tested on the aircraft. The Air Force would like to have one squadron in service by 2010, but, given the time taken to produce the aircraft, it will take Hindustan Aeronautics Limited up till 2027 to deliver the complete set of 200 aircraft required. The plane, as I have argued elsewhere, will be obsolescent by the time it enters service.

At the same time, the lure of purchasing foreign aircraft will further hurt the LCA's chances of becoming a mass-produced and

---

[2]Interview with V.S. Arunachalam, New Delhi, 9 August 1991.

successful frontline combat aircraft. India is already set to license produce the Sukhoi-30MKI—a far more capable aircraft. The Indian Air Force would like to purchase the Mirage 2000 as an 'interim fighter' (although nowadays, given the cost and length of service of any aircraft, the word interim is an incorrect label) and the United States has offered India the rights to manufacture F-16 or F-18 fighters.

The F-16 would be especially suited to India's long-term commercial interests since dozens of air forces around the world operate it and lack the financial resources to buy the follow-on American aircraft—the F-22 Raptor and F-35 Joint Strike Fighter. The F-16 would be a good and affordable alternative. India would then be able to sell new F-16s around the world much in the same way as Brazil built and sold the Volkswagen Beetle for years after the production line was closed down in Germany. The Tejas LCA may, therefore, face an uphill battle in being mass-produced and entering service.

Instead, there were definite advantages to producing an Advanced Jet Trainer. The plane was an advanced trainer that did not require the expensive avionics package and powerful engine that the LCA needed. It would, therefore, be easier to design and develop. Nor would it be obsolescent by the time it entered service since its mission was to train advanced pilots. It would have led to multi-billion-dollar savings in hard currency as the 2004 decision to purchase the British Aerospace Hawk would not permit. It would have given the Indian aeronautical community a proven aircraft to show their political masters.

Almost two decades later, the arms industry agreed to make an Intermediate Jet Trainer (IJT) for the Air Force, and the technological path chosen as well as the progress made on the programme were instructive. The decision was taken to use as many off-the-shelf components as possible to facilitate rapid development. To integrate the plane with the training and missions of the Indian Air Force, the plane's mission computer is the same one that has been fitted in the Su-30 MKI and the Tejas. A realistic appraisal of technological capabilities and mission requirements led to the IJT being developed in three years—a heartening development for the arms industry that has had few indigenous successes (Reddy 2002).

What makes it difficult for the arms industries to indigenously develop weapons systems is the attitude of the government to such programmes once initiated. While supporting their development, the government has not provided the monetary support to make Indian weapons systems economically viable and internationally marketable. When it does, the success of a programme is more likely. A good case in point is the Dhruv helicopter. The Dhruv was built as a multi-mission helicopter that would fulfil the requirements of the Army, Navy, Air Force, and Coast Guard for its medium lift requirements. It was also seen as being used in a civilian market. The Dhruv programme has been successfully completed and Hindustan Aeronautics Limited has produced a working helicopter that, while not technologically advanced, can carry out a range of missions for the armed forces and find a civilian market. The Indian government is making the Dhruv into a commercially viable product by helping sell it to the domestic civil aviation industry and use it for both the central and state governments. This will make it an attractive product for foreign customers.

In the country's arms production efforts, the Indian government has in fact allowed financial imperatives to override considerations of technological advancement and national security. In that context, its approach has been similar to that of West European governments that have repeatedly cut weapons programmes when they have been viewed as being financially exorbitant or when, quite rightly, the threat environment has changed.

The fate of these programmes shows the course Indian arms production has taken and the factors that have constrained it. The missile programme succeeded in delivering a series of ballistic missiles that made India's nuclear deterrent a credible one because sanctions prevented the import of comparable systems. On the other hand, the LCA and the Arjun both suffered from developmental delays and, in the case of the Arjun, the Indian Army's reluctance to accept the system into service. The LCA now is slated to enter significant service sometime towards 2015 with an engine and avionics suite from the late 1980s, thus making the plane obsolescent by the time it is inducted into the Air Force. The Indian Air Force may well decide, therefore, to commit its resources to the more versatile Sukhoi-30 MKI that is to be licence produced in India.

Indian arms production policy has at times adversely affected the country's defence preparedness and its long-term military capability.

The emphasis on major projects has led to the more basic requirements of the armed forces being ignored. During the 1999 Kargil conflict with Pakistan, for instance, India, despite its large defence production base, was unable to supply artillery and mortar shells to the army. The Indian government had to make an emergency purchase of 40,000 artillery shells and 30,000 mortar shells from Israel so as continue the bombardment of Pakistani positions in Indian Kashmir (Bedi 2003). Thus, one of the major shifts in arms production may be to develop what is appropriate rather than what is advanced. For Indian soldiers fighting in the mountainous terrain of Kashmir, it is important that they have suitable light weapons, night vision equipment, and adequate supplies of ammunition to combat both insurgency and the Pakistani armed forces.

While conventional systems have faced opposition from domestic constituencies as well as subsequent delays, non-conventional systems have been successfully brought to production and induction in the Indian armed services. The development and production of the Prithvi and Agni missiles was possible because there was a need for nuclear capable delivery systems and these systems could not be purchased from external suppliers. Coupled with the unavailability of external suppliers was the fact that the missiles were not prone to technological obsolescence. Further, neither of India's rivals—Pakistan and China—had (or are likely to have) ballistic missile defences. Thus, a combination of existing threats, the inability to purchase systems externally, and continued technological relevance made it possible to shield the Agni and Prithvi programmes from bureaucratic pressure that might otherwise have led to their termination. From the perspective of Indian defence industries what is required, therefore, is a greater governmental commitment to programmes that can be pursued without fear of termination or of being hindered by constant organizational infighting.

CURRENT STRATEGY

In the past decade, India's arms production policy has shifted towards a multi-pronged strategy for weapons production. While the government continues to support big-ticket items and licensed production, it has cautiously moved to allow private Indian companies to produce weaponry. It has also invested in joint ventures and decided to produce non-competitive weapons systems. Joint ventures are currently being pursued with Israel and Russia (and potentially the United States), and these collaborative efforts reflect the changed international environment.

India established diplomatic relations with Israel in 1992 and since then has forged a mutually beneficial military relationship. Israel has now become India's second largest supplier of military hardware, and New Delhi has worked the new relationship to its advantage in several ways. India has gained access to advanced technologies and has been able to modify its existing weapons systems as well as newly purchased ones with improved Israeli systems. Thus, India's MIG-21 fleet is being upgraded with Israeli assistance and its Russian Sukhoi-30 MKI has Russian, French, Israeli, and Indian avionics and computers integrated into it. Israel has now agreed to help market the ALH, thus providing the marketing skills of its aircraft industry to India. It has made the helicopter more competitive by incorporating Israeli avionics into it.

The linkage with Israel also serves an important political function as some analysts view it as forging an alliance between two democracies that is aimed at achieving complementary foreign policy goals. For the Israelis, India has emerged as a lucrative market that helps sustain Jerusalem's military–industrial complex. Israel will be selling India the Phalcon airborne warning and control system. India would also like to purchase the Israeli Arrow 2 anti-ballistic missile to help establish a missile defence grid (the United States, however, has reportedly vetoed the sale). The ties with India are also viewed as lessening Israeli isolation in the non-western world (as well as moving an important country away from what, till the 1990s, was a very pro-Arab foreign policy).

THE MILITARY RELATIONSHIP WITH RUSSIA

The Indo-Russian arms production relationship has been revived because Moscow recognized its economic and strategic value. After the fall of the Soviet Union, Russia followed a pro-Western policy and terminated most of its old links with India. In the early 1990s India found it difficult to find spare parts for its large inventory of Soviet weapons. By the mid-1990s, however, the Russian leadership, strapped for hard currency and facing the rapid implosion of the country's military–industrial complex, renewed its arms sales relationship with India.[3] Russia, disappointed with its initial overtures to the West, also viewed India as an important strategic partner. It once again threw open the arms cupboard and New Delhi is now negotiating the purchase of aircraft carriers, long-range bombers, and the leasing of nuclear submarines. In return, India helped fund the development of the Sukhoi-30 and has invested in the joint production and development of a supersonic cruise missile, the Brahmos company's PJ-10. The two countries have also proposed the joint development of a fifth-generation fighter aircraft and Hindustan Aeronautics Limited was reportedly considering investing in the Irkutsk Aviation Production Organization.

Concerned about the quality of Russian equipment, as well as Moscow's tardiness as a supplier of spares, the Indian Parliament recommended that the government move away from its dependence on Russian arms and, instead, increase imports from other, more reliable suppliers. Given India's ambitious military plans, however, it is unlikely that the country can reduce its military dependence on Russian systems. For political and security reasons, the West will not provide the type of strategic systems India requires. Supplier restrictions remain on providing India with the dual-use and military technologies that it requires. Further, the broader Western concern about India's growing nuclear capability has also lead to restrictions on the transfer of sensitive Western technologies.

ENTER THE UNITED STATES

This may change, however, with the new agreement signed by Prime Minister Manmohan Singh and President Bush for the transfer of conventional weapons systems and, more importantly, permitting the

---

[3]For a discussion of the ongoing problems of the Russian military–industrial complex see Gidadhubli (2003).

sale of civilian nuclear technology to India. The decision to do so has
been hailed as a pragmatic one since it accepts India as a de facto
nuclear weapons state and allows it to separate its civil and military
nuclear programmes and place only the former under international
safeguards.[4] Further, as part of the new Indo–US defence agreement,
both countries have agreed that:

> In the context of our strategic relationship, expand two-way
> defence trade between our countries. The United States and
> India will work to conclude defence transactions, not solely
> as ends in and of themselves, but as a means to strengthen
> our countries' security, reinforce our strategic partnership,
> achieve greater interaction between our armed forces, and
> build greater understanding between our defence
> establishments.[5]

Thus, it seems likely that there will greater US-Indian military
cooperation in the future because the agreement discusses the possibility
of joint military operations, enhancing the capability to prevent the
proliferation of weapons of mass destruction, and to promote the
capabilities of both militaries to enhance security and defeat terrorism.
Such coordinated efforts will require a greater integration of Indian
and American weapons systems and communications technologies,
leading the United States to build up India's military capability.
Former US Ambassador to India, Robert Blackwill, explained the
American rationale for seeking to build up India's military capability:

> Of course we should sell advanced weaponry to India. The
> million-man Indian army actually fights, unlike the post-
> modern militaries of many of our European allies. Given
> the strategic challenges ahead, the United States should want

---

[4]For an opinion on how the new nuclear deal benefits India see Raja Mohan (2005).
For criticisms of the agreement by India's political parties see, Cherian (2005).
[5]See: 'New Framework For The US-INDIA Defense Relationship,' Washington,
DC, 28 June 2005, available at the Embassy of India, Washington, DC, Website,
http://www.indianembassy.org/press_release/2005/June/31.htm.

the Indian armed forces to be equipped with the best weapons systems, and that often means buying American. To make this happen, the United States must become a reliable long-term supplier through co-production and licensed-manufacture arrangements and end its previous inclination to interrupt defence supplies to India in a crisis (National Interest 2005: 11).

From a broader perspective, joint ventures, such as those proposed to be undertaken with the United States, have worked to India's advantage because they made Indian arms procurement and production more efficient and cost effective, they have helped India gain access to a range of new technologies, and they have helped firm up relationships with strategically important countries. The use of private corporations and universities to develop weapons systems has worked quite well, particularly in the case of the IGMDP.

NON-COMPETITIVE SYSTEMS

Finally, the Indian government has also gone in for the production of non-competitive systems that will not be obsolescent and will, therefore, find markets at home and potentially abroad. Two such systems are the ALH and the IJT. The ALH was designed and developed with German assistance and its components come from both France and Germany. The aircraft was never meant to be a state-of-the-art helicopter, but, instead, was meant to be a workhorse that could be used in the civilian and military sectors.

This emphasis on building a reliable and workable helicopter has led to the Hindustan Aeronautics Limited getting orders from the Indian military and civilian sectors for 300 aircraft. By installing a more powerful engine, India may be able to sell the helicopter to Colombia and Thailand. Given the needs of the various Indian state governments and those of its paramilitaries to conduct border patrols and surveillance, the ALH should be a genuine commercial success for the Indian arms industry.

The IJT, similarly, is on the right track since it fulfils a need of the Air Force and could potentially save the Indian exchequer the cost of importing comparable systems. The IJT was commissioned in 1999 and the first flight took place in 2003—a timely completion that will help the plane's domestic marketability. The IJT will replace the Air Force's Kiran basic trainer and, Indian aerospace analysts claim, a version with a more powerful engine could serve the need for an AJT.

The shift in arms production strategy has produced definite benefits for India, but in the long run it will have to forgo the development of expensive state-of-the-art weaponry, increase joint ventures, and make more non-competitive systems. The Arjun tank, for example, is an expensive project that will not fulfil the requirements of the Indian Army, which is also purchasing Russian T-90 tanks. The proposed plan to develop a Medium Combat Aircraft as a follow-on to the Tejas is also ambitious given that the developmental costs will be prohibitive and India will be licence producing the versatile Su-30 that can have its avionics modernized much more cheaply than initiating a new project. Further, such projects, where the armed forces have the alternative to buy abroad, will always flounder because they have lengthy developmental processes that do not fit the immediate needs of the armed services, and the question of matching the quality of imported systems will pose an additional stumbling block.

Further, while projects are being delayed, technology continues to develop. Thus, by the time a system is available, it may be obsolete or the armed service might want a technological upgrade. This further delays weapons induction and condemns it to failure. India should, therefore, not build such systems, but instead focus on the development of systems that cannot be procured externally because of technological restrictions. A case in point is the successful development of the Prithvi and the Agni series of missiles that took place only because sanctions prevented the purchase of such missiles from external suppliers.

One could even argue that a light aircraft carrier should be developed indigenously (and in fact a project to do so has been cleared) since Indian requirements cannot be met abroad easily and the carrier would have a long service life. While India has purchased the Gorshkov, an expensive and time-consuming retrofit is to follow that will not make the carrier available until 2008. Further, the principal strike aircraft aboard the carrier, the MiG-29K has yet to be tested and India no longer has pilots who have catapult take-off and landing experience. Thus, development of restricted systems would not only fulfil Indian defence requirements, but also ensure that indigenous effort could not be replaced by an imported system.

The production of non-competitive weaponry must also be expanded to meet the most basic needs of the military. Light arms, ammunition, and field artillery are some examples of non-competitive weapons that can be produced domestically. In conventional wars and low-level conflicts it is precisely such weaponry that sees the most use. Domestic production, therefore, ensures a steady supply of such hardware in wars and removes the need to seek emergency suppliers who may not always be as generous and prompt as the Israelis were during the Kargil conflict.

In an era of globalization the Indian arms industry has shifted to successfully integrate some of the key elements of transnational weapons production. What is now needed is a realistic appraisal of ongoing projects that will actually survive and prosper in a global arms market where new avenues have opened to India and put pressure on the Indian arms industry to change its production policies. To sum up, you cannot go it alone in a globalized world.

BIBLIOGRAPHY

Bedi, Rahul (2003). Moving Closer to Israel. *Frontline*, 20(4).
———— (2004). A New Doctrine for the Navy. *Frontline*, 21(14).
Chengappa, Raj (1988). LCA Project: A Testing Time. *India Today*, 31 August.
Cherian, John (2005). Deals and Doubts. *Frontline*, 22(16).
Gidadhubli, R.G. (2003). Refurbishing the Military–Industrial Complex. *Economic and Political Weekly*, 23 August, pp. 3546–50.
Graham, Thomas, W. (1984). India. In James Everett Katz, ed., *Arms Production in the Third World*. Lexington: Lexington Books.
Gupta, Amit (1995). Determining India's Force Structure and Military Doctrine: I Want My M-i-G. *Asian Survey*, 35 (5), pp. 441–58.
————— (1997). *Building an Arsenal: The Evolution of Regional Power Force Structures*. Westport, CT, and London: Praeger.
Hindu (2004). Arjun Induction: Move to Support Indigenization Process. 8 August.
National Interest (2005). The India Imperative: A Conversation with Robert D. Blackwill. 80, pp. 11.
Prabhu, Rajendra (1987). Misgivings Over LCA Plan Changes. *Hindustan Times*, 24 January.

Raja Mohan, C. (2005). Ending Our Nuclear Winter. *Indian Express*, 26 July.
Reddy, C. Manmohan (2002). Making Haste Slowly. *Hindu*, 26 December.
Rikhye, Ravi (1990). *The Militarisation of Mother India*. New Delhi: Chanakya.
Sharma, Ravi (2005). The LCA Puzzle. *Frontline*, 22(15).
Subramanian, T.S. (2004). The Seventh Flight of BrahMos. *Frontline*, 21(13).
Times of India (2004). Seal Scorpene Deal Fast: Navy Chief. 12 August.

Ideas, Technology Policy, and India's Helicopter, Combat Aircraft, and Lunar Orbiter Programs

Dinshaw Mistry

A state's technological prowess is closely linked with its economic prosperity and national security. On economic grounds technological advances sustain economic growth and development. On military grounds, technological superiority enables states to defend against rivals having better economic and military capacities. Accordingly, national technology policies are infused with economic and strategic objectives. Yet these objectives do not always lead states to acquire the best technologies. Instead, influential ideas about self-reliance and international prestige sway states to seek technologies that may have limited economic and strategic utility. This chapter shows the impact of these ideas on three high-profile projects pursued by India— a mission to the moon, a light combat aircraft (LCA) program, and an advanced light helicopter (ALH) program.

India's light helicopter program required an investment of several hundred million dollars, and has moved from research to production. The light combat aircraft project, which involved an investment of several hundred million dollars for initial research and development, is just completing its prototype and testing phase. India has built and flown four LCA demonstrators, but much more financing will be required before the LCA goes into large-scale production. The moon mission, costing some $100 million has been given government approval and is planned for 2008. These three projects did not involve the best technologies, nor did they bring substantial economic or military benefits, but the ideas of self-reliance and international prestige influenced Indian policy makers to press ahead with their development.

This chapter begins by summarizing India's science and technology policy, and its links with the ideas of self-reliance and prestige. It then reviews India's moon mission and its light combat aircraft and light helicopter programs. It concludes by noting that two new ideas—those of competitiveness and international collaboration—may offset the still influential ideas of self-sufficiency and prestige. If India's public sector technology enclaves can embrace these new ideas, they are more likely to produce better technological outputs with more substantial security and economic benefits.

SELF-RELIANCE AND PRESTIGE IN INDIA'S TECHNOLOGY POLICY

The idea of self-reliance and indigenous production is found in India's science and technology policies and its industrial policy. India's Scientific Policy Resolution of 1958 noted, 'The key to national prosperity, apart from the spirit of the people, lies, in the modern age, in the effective combination of three factors, *technology*, raw materials and capital, of which the first is perhaps the most important' (Government of India 1958). Emphasizing that technology should also be linked to *self-reliance*, India's 1983 Technology Policy said:

Political freedom must lead to economic independence ….
We have regarded science and technology as the basis of economic progress… In a country of India's size and endowments, self-reliance is inescapable and must be at the very heart of technological development.…[India must] attain technological competence and self-reliance, to reduce vulnerability, particularly in strategic and critical areas, making the maximum use of indigenous resources.' (Government of India 1983)

These arguments gave rise to an emphasis on self-reliance, self sufficiency, and indigenous development in Indian technology policy.[1]

While India's early policies emphasized technology for economic development, the links of technology with security became prominent after the 1962 Sino-Indian war (Gupta 1997; Thomas 1986). Well before this war, however, India established a number of technological enclaves such as the Department of Atomic Energy (DAE), the Defence Research and Development Organization (DRDO), and an arms industry (Cohen 2001; CSIR 1988; Nayar 1977), and it later also established the Indian Space Research Organization (ISRO). India's arms industry includes thirty-nine production entities and eight defence public sector undertakings (DPSUs)—one of which is the Hindustan Aeronautics Limited (HAL), which is under the defence ministry's department of defence production and supplies (Arnett 1994; Matthews 1989).[2] These enclaves undertook India's nuclear and space programs and oversaw India's aircraft production.

Prestige is another influential idea behind the indigenous development of technology (Government of India 1983). Policy elites are often enamoured by high technology, which is viewed as increasing a state's prestige and symbolizing its attainment of modernity and major power status—these themes of technological grandeur are found in major Western states and in Asian states such as Japan and China (Feigenbaum 2003; Gill and Kim 1995; Samuels 1994). Similar themes are found in India (and Pakistan), where the attainment of nuclear and missile capabilities are viewed as evidence of the greatness of their countries and cultures; these technical feats are lauded in the press

---

[1]Self-reliance (hedging against the disruption of the supply of materials and parts) is a more modest goal than self-sufficiency (autarky). Other literature on self-reliance and indigenous production includes the literature on autarky and the infant-industry argument. Another economic argument for local production is that it helps the balance of payments, saves foreign exchange, and provides employment for persons with scientific and technical skills. On security grounds, the strategic industry argument is that some industries are vital for national security, and, therefore, even if they are not competitive, they must be maintained.

[2]Besides HAL, the other DPSUs include Bharat Dynamics which makes missiles, Bharat Electronics Limited, which makes defence and civilian electronics items, several shipyards, and Bharat Earth Movers, which mainly produces civilian products and railway coaches.

and by politicians, and the scientists behind them receive the highest national awards (Chari et al.; Cohen 2003). This international prestige argument, of viewing high technology as a way of joining a 'club' or 'elite group' and gaining global recognition, influenced public and elite support for India's LCA project and moon mission. Illustrating this, Indian press commentary noted that India 'entered a select class of countries when the Light Combat Aircraft (LCA) took to the skies' (*Times of India* 2001b), while a headline on the first launch of India's geostationary satellite launch vehicle (GSLV) echoed similar themes: 'GSLV Launches India Into Elite Space Club' (ibid.: 2001a).

INDIA'S MISSION TO THE MOON

India's Space Programme

India's moon mission is the latest venture for its space program, a program that has produced some useful applied outputs. It traditionally focused on two major activities—building satellites used for remote-sensing, meteorology, and communications, and constructing rockets to launch its satellites (Mistry 2001). ISRO has built two generations of rockets; the less powerful SLV-3 and its upgrade, the augmented satellite launch vehicle (ASLV); and the more powerful polar satellite launch vehicle (PSLV) and its upgrade, the GSLV. The 17 ton SLV-3 (centred around a 9 ton solid fuel first stage) flew four times between 1979 and 1983, while the 41 ton ASLV (which used three of the SLV-3's 9-ton boosters) flew four times between 1987 and 1994. These satellite launchers were powerful enough only to launch a light payload (typically, a scientific satellite) to a 300–450 km altitude low earth orbit (LEO). Such lightweight low-orbit satellites did not have significant military or commercial capabilities. However, the SLV-3 could still be used as an intermediate-range ballistic missile, and its first stage was used in the Agni missile.

India's more powerful PSLV (which flew nine times between 1993 and 2005) and GSLV (which flew three times between 2001 and 2004) can launch heavier and more capable satellites into the optimal higher altitude orbits. The 270 ton PSLV can launch a 1,000 kg payload (the Indian Remote Sensing [IRS] satellites) to a 800–900 km altitude polar orbit. The approximately 430 ton GSLV can carry a heavier 1,500–2,000 kg communications satellite—it was actually designed to carry the 2,000–2,500 kg Indian National Satellite (INSAT)—to the required higher 36,000 km geostationary earth orbit (GEO). Having perfected basic satellite launch capabilities through the PSLV and GSLV programmes, ISRO sought new missions in the late 1990s—it planned a recoverable satellite experiment (whereby a satellite would splash down into the sea),[3] and conceived of a moon mission.

A Lunar Orbiter

International interest in exploring the moon revived after a twenty-five-year hiatus when a 1998 Lunar Prospector mission discovered the possibility of water on the moon. In this context, ISRO and other space agencies began conceptualizing moon missions.[4] In October 1999, at the annual meeting of the Indian Academy of Scientists, ISRO presented a paper on its capability for a lunar mission (Motta 2000). Thereafter, Indian scientists prepared a feasibility report for a moon mission. In a July 2000 interview, ISRO chairman K. Kasturirangan publicly outlined plans for a moon mission by 2005. ISRO planned to send a 350 kg lunar vehicle with cameras and scientific experiments to orbit the moon. Over the next two years, ISRO sought domestic consensus and governmental approval. Soon

---

[3]The only new technology required was that of re-entry (and even this was already available from India's missile programme) and splashdown. The project otherwise relied on existing systems such as the PSLV. It would carry experiments such as growing crystals and developing pharmaceutical products in the micro-gravity ambience of space (Subramanian 2003).

[4]The European Space Agency's SMART-1, weighing 366 kg, was launched on 28 September 2003. Japan's 520 kg Lunar Orbiter (Lunar-A) is proposed for launch in August 2007. It will have a high-resolution camera and two instrumented torpedo probes capable of penetrating 2 m into the lunar surface. Japan's SELENE (Selenological and Engineering Explorer), planned for launch in 2007, is a 1,600 kg spacecraft with spectrometers, imagers, laser altimeters, radar sounders and magnetometers. It aims to study the moon's origin and evolution by collecting detailed information on the moon's topography, the elemental and mineral content of its surface, and magnetism and gravity. China's Chang'e-1, planned for launch by 2007–08, aims at obtaining a three-dimensional map of the lunar surface and at analysing soil composition and material distribution.

after Kasturirangan's interview, an Indian embassy spokesperson clarified that ISRO's lunar plans would be submitted to India's space council and would then require approval from the prime minister and parliament (Sorid 2000). In April 2003 ISRO sought a peer review of its lunar mission during a presentation to some sixty scientists at a meeting in Bangalore (Chengappa 2003). The scientists approved, and in May, the Indian government's space commission also approved the project. In July the proposal was sent for cabinet approval, and Prime Minister Vajpayee took a personal interest in the file, with his office renaming the project Chandrayan (which means journey to the moon). Vajpayee then declared, during his 15 August independence day address, 'I am pleased to announce that India will send her own spacecraft to the moon by 2008. It is being named Chandrayan-1.'

Thus, by the time of Prime Minister Vajpayee's 2003 announcement, the dates of the moon mission had moved back from 2005 to 2007–08, but the basic technological contours remained much the same as those envisaged in 2000. India would launch a 525 kg orbiter (slightly heavier than the 350 kg orbiter proposed in 2000). The vehicle would carry 80 kg of payload—a terrain-mapping camera with 5 m resolution to generate three-dimensional images; a hyperspectral imager with 80 m resolution for mineral mapping; a laser ranging instrument; X-ray spectrometers to map minerals and radioactive nuclides; and approximately 10 kg of instruments for international partners. In 2005, ISRO signed an agreement with the European Space Agency to include three European instrument—a low-energy X-ray spectrometer, a near infrared spectrometer, and an atom reflecting analyzer—to augment the Indian instruments. Further, ISRO was considering having a miniature synthetic aperture radar (a lightweight low-power imaging radar on the lunar orbiter).

The Rationale for a Moon Mission

India's moon mission had weak scientific and technological objectives, but prestige reasons influenced decisions to move ahead with this mission. In scientific terms, the moon mission aimed to carry out high-resolution mapping of the moon's surface. Yet this did not significantly add to scientific knowledge about the moon because 97 per cent of the moon's surface has already been mapped. The moon mission's broader technological purposes were perhaps slightly more important, as Indian scientists anticipated that the mission would provide ISRO with the expertise for further interplanetary expeditions. Yet even here, ISRO was not undertaking a new technologically challenging venture. It had settled for the simplest possible moon mission in the form of a lunar orbiter, and had rejected more challenging alternative missions (Chengappa 2000). Partly because it used simple technologies and an existing proven launcher (the PSLV), the moon mission was affordable and feasible.[5] Yet, while affordable, it only had limited scientific and technological value. Domestic and international prestige explain why the Indian elite still pursued this mission.

Domestically, the moon mission dovetailed with a broader need for new missions for Indian scientists. By the late 1990s India had not been able to make major breakthroughs in building civilian aircraft or increasing the speed of railway engines, and India's science enclave was seeking missions that would generate 'excitement and confidence' (ibid.). Such exciting missions would boost domestic prestige: 'as a motivator, it will electrify the nation' (ibid.). Internationally, the mission would ensure Indian participation in a new frontier that other nations were also exploring. ISRO chairman Kasturirangan noted in his 2000 interview that

> The 21st century is going to be the century for planetary exploration....There is no way humans are going to be satisfied with just building satellites for communications, remote sensing, navigation or a space station. There is going to be a deeper outreach into the cosmos. Many countries would subsequently be thinking of colonizing the celestial bodies' (ibid.)

Similarly, the mission would enhance India's international prestige: it 'will demonstrate to the world that India is capable of taking up a complex mission that is at the cutting edge of space' (ibid.).

---

[5]ISRO scientists noted that the PSLV could be modified to send a 530 kg spacecraft on a flyby mission or a 350 kg spacecraft to orbit the moon, while the GSLV could launch an 850–950 kg spacecraft as a flyby mission or a 600 kg orbiter (Rao 2000).

In summary, prestige was perhaps the strongest motivator for India's moon mission. India's prime minister was arguably ahead of Indian scientists in the enthusiasm for a moon mission, primarily for its prestige value, despite the fact that it brought in few tangible benefits.[6] A thorough cost–benefit analysis of this mission is beyond the scope of this article, but the costs of approximately $100 million are much smaller than the several hundred million dollars invested in India's helicopter and combat aircraft programs. Beyond the idea of prestige, the notion of self-reliance has swayed decisions on these projects.

THE LIGHT COMBAT AIRCRAFT

Aircraft Production in India

Hindustan Aeronautics Limited (HAL) is India's main aircraft manufacturer.[7] It maintains sixteen production units and nine research and design centres (each focusing on areas such as aircraft, helicopters, transport aircraft, electronics, and engines). Since the 1950s, HAL has manufactured over 3,300 aircraft and 3,400 aero-engines (largely licence-produced versions of British, Russian, and French aircraft), and has overhauled over 7,700 aircraft and 26,000 engines. It initially produced low-tech light aircraft and then went on to build or license produce more capable aircraft. Thus, in the early 1950s, HAL designed and produced a two-seat piston engine HT-2 basic trainer aircraft. It then produced light aircraft and trainers for flying clubs, army air observation duties, and agricultural spraying. It also developed Kiran basic jet trainers, HPT-32 aerobatic trainers, and

---

[6]Echoing this criticism, Dr. H.S. Mukunda, chairman of the Aerospace Department of the Indian Institute of Science in Bangalore, noted: 'Why don't we work on something pathbreaking? Why do we need to do something that has already been done 30 years ago and many times over' (Rao 2000).

[7]Other Indian organizations that have developed and designed aircraft include the National Aerospace Laboratory (which falls under the Ministry of Science and Technology), which designed and developed the Saras light transport aircraft (which first flew in 2004, and can carry up to fourteen passengers) and the two-seat Hansa trainer.

HTT-34 turboprop trainers. It went on to build, with a German design team, the airframe of a supersonic ground attack fighter, the HF-24 or Marut. It could not find an appropriate engine for the fighter and the Maruts entered IAF service with underpowered engines in the 1960s. Thereafter, HAL manufactured hundreds of MiG-21, MiG-27, and Jaguar combat aircraft, and HS-748 and Dornier-228 transport aircraft under licence from Russia, the UK, Germany, and France. In the 2000s HAL plans to licence produce some 140 Su-30 aircraft, and to build several hundred helicopters, the intermediate jet trainer, and the light combat aircraft that is also called Tejas. The LCA was actually designed and developed by an ad hoc bureau, the Aeronautical Development Agency (ADA).

The Evolution of the LCA

In 1969 the Government of India approved a recommendation from an aeronautics committee for HAL to design and develop an advanced technology fighter aircraft (Wollen 2001). Based on Indian Air Force (IAF) technical papers, HAL then completed design studies for a tactical air support aircraft in 1975. Yet it could not procure an engine and the project fell through, but the IAF's need for a fighter continued. Accordingly, in July 1983, the LCA was given the go-ahead by the Indian government. It was conceived as an indigenously-built fighter that would replace the MiG-21s, MiG-23s, and MiG-27s. It was supported by V.S. Arunachalam, scientific adviser to the defence minister, and by defence minister R. Venkataraman. The project was undertaken by the newly created ad hoc body, the Aeronautical Development Agency. The ADA borrowed over a hundred designers and personnel from HAL to design and develop the LCA. In terms of organizational structure, the ADA is an autonomous body set up as a registered society managed by the DRDO (and thus falling under the Department of Defence's Research & Development wing). HAL is the principal partner of the LCA program, while the DRDO and CSIR laboratories and public and private industries provide additional support to the program.

The LCA project was delayed in the mid-1980s when its management team changed—in 1985, the science advisor to the Indian government sought and obtained the removal of the LCA's main design expert, Raj Mahindra, and, as a result, ADA director-general S.R. Valluri also resigned (Valluri 2001, 2005). Thereafter, Indian scientists worked with a French consultant, Dassault Aviation, on the first major LCA task of project definition (definition is vital for the design and development of aircraft as it provides detailed information on design, construction, and maintenance costs). This task commenced in October 1987 and was completed in September 1988. Upon examining the project definition, the IAF felt that the risks were too high to proceed further. Yet a review committee formed in May 1989 noted that the project's infrastructure, facilities, and technology had advanced in most areas. It, therefore, recommended proceeding in two phases, each estimated to cost some $500 million.[8] Phase 1 involved building and flight-testing two technology demonstrator aircraft (TD-1 and -2); two prototype vehicles (PV-1 and -2); and an infrastructure and test facilities. Phase 2 would involve three more PVs (PV-3, -4, and -5) with the last, PV-5, being a trainer. The first phase commenced in 1990, but the project was substantially delayed from 1988 to 1993 due to governmental indecision over financing (India also faced a financial crisis in 1991). In April 1993 the government granted formal and financial sanction for Phase 1, which resulted in an upsurge in work. The first mock LCA model rolled out, in the presence of Prime Minister P.V. Narasimha Rao, in November 1995 (Sharma 2001b).

The LCA first flew on 3 January 2001, and completed its first phase of testing with its twelfth flight on 1 June 2001. It achieved a subsonic maximum speed of approximately Mach 0.5–0.6 (610 km/h) and a height of 8 km, and also conducted 2 g turns at 60 degree banks. The first TD-2 flight was planned for October 2001, but only

---

[8]The estimated cost of Phase 1 was Rs. 21.88 billion and that of Phase 2 was Rs. 23.40 billion, which are $480–510 million at 2003 exchange rates, but which were $1,200 million at the 1990 exchange rates. In total, since the mid-1980s India has spent some Rs. 55 billion (approximately $1,200 million at 2005 exchange rates) on the LCA project. In the first meeting of the ADA general body in July 1984, involving then defence minister P.V. Narasimha Rao and finance minister V.P. Singh, the ADA director-general S.R. Valluri estimated lower costs. Valluri noted that if the first LCA flight took place by 1991 as planned, total expenditures from 1984–91 would be Rs. 12.50 billion, and that any delays would cost Rs. 15 billion to Rs. 17.5 billion each year (Valluri 2001).

took place on 6 June 2002. The TD-2's main feature was its reduced weight—the fuselage was made of composite materials such as advanced carbon fibre rather than of metal. During 2002 only TD-2 flew, completing thirty-six flights and attaining a maximum altitude of 12 km and a maximum speed of Mach 0.8. In 2003 the complexity and number of LCA test flights increased. The TD-1 made its first supersonic flight on 1 August and the TD-2 crossed the sound barrier on 27 November—by then, both aircraft had logged approximately sixty flights each. The third LCA, PV-1, first flew on 25 November 2003, and crossed the sound barrier in February 2004. By March 2004 the three LCAs had logged 200 flights with some 124 hours of flying. By 1 December 2005, the three aircraft had completed 474 flights (166 for TD-1, 199 for TD-2, and 109 for PV-1) with over 200 hours of flying. The fourth LCA, PV-2, first flew on 1 December 2005. It was intended to have the configuration of the series production aircraft, and had two new features—a high percentage of composites that reduced its structural weights, and new avionics and cockpit displays. It did not have features such as a multi-mode radar and R 73 missiles as originally planned. Further it borrowed its Engine Driven Pump from PV-1, with the result that this aircraft could not then fly. ADA next intends to fly the fifth and sixth proto types in 2006– 07 (one of which may be a two seat trainer), followed by a seventh prototype, and to then build two naval prototypes. Overall, the LCA would require some 1,200 flights before receiving Initial Operation Clearance (IOC) to be handed over to the Indian Air Force.

Indigenous and Imported Content

The ADA recognized at the outset that the LCA required five critical technologies: a carbon composite wing, flight control system, glass cockpit, high-performance multi-mode radar, and propulsion system (Reddy 2003). It succeeded in the design, fabrication, and testing of a fly-by-wire flight control system. Further, the long delay in the LCA project allowed the parallel development and indigenization of many smaller systems and components—such as an auxiliary gearbox developed by India's Combat Vehicles Research and Development Establishment (CVRDE) that was nearly 60 per cent cheaper than an imported one (ibid.). While Indian scientists also developed advanced carbon composites, these were not used in the wings for the initial LCAs, which were instead built from imported composites. Overall, India imported major sections of the three main components—engine, airframe, and avionic systems (*Indian Express* 2001). Most avionic systems such as radars, electronic warfare equipment, altimeter, ground-mapping system, and other pilot support systems were imported from Israel, France, and Sweden. The pulse doppler multi-mode radar to track and deliver beyond-visual range weapons, being developed by HAL, had run into problems as of 2005 (and it had only been installed and tested on an Avro HS-748M but not on the LCA). India may, therefore, consider Israel's Elta radar or Lockheed Martin's AN/APG-67 radar for the LCA. Parts of the airframe were not entirely Indian as the composite wings were imported from Italy. And the engine was an 18,000 lb thrust American General Electric GE-F404-F2J3 (the F-404 also powers Sweden's Gripen, the American F-18, Singapore's A-4, and South Korea's planned KTX-2 advanced trainer/light combat aircraft).

In 1998, after General Electric had supplied eight engines, Washington blocked further deliveries under US non-proliferation sanctions. India's Gas Turbine Research Establishment (GTRE) at Bangalore then continued development of the 20,200 lb thrust Kaveri engine—similar in configuration to the GE-F404—which it had to send to Russia for high-altitude tests.[9] In late 2001 Washington lifted sanctions and subsequently allowed the transfer of forty GE engines and advanced avionics. The IAF expects the first two squadrons of LCAs (forty aircraft) to use GE engines, while later LCAs could use Kaveri engines—the GTRE was preparing to test a completed prototype Kaveri engine in 2005–6, and anticipated that it could integrate this engine with an LCA prototype in 2007. However, an April 2005

---

[9]The GTRE began working on the Kaveri project in 1986, but the project stalled for much of the 1990s. By 2001 three Kaveri engines had been put through the test bed, with four more to be built in the next three years. Although the engine went through over 900 hours of bench tests and was sent to Russia by the end of 2001 for high-altitude tests, it was still years away from being integrated on to to a flying platform. A Kaveri engine had exploded on the test bed in Bangalore, impeding progress (Sharma 2001b). By 2005 India had spent Rs. 113 billion ($300 million) on the Kaveri's development.

report by the Indian Parliament's Standing Committee on Defence projected that the Kaveri would only be installed on the operational LCAs by 2012, by when its development would have cost Rs. 28 billion ($650 million at present exchange rates). In mid-2005, recognizing the difficulty of indigenously developing the Kaveri, GTRE sought international partners to jointly develop and produce either a modified Kaveri or a new engine. By late 2005, four companies—General Electric, Pratt and Whitney, Sneema Moteurs, and NPO Saturn—had submitted bids for this project.

Future Prospects

On 6 June 2002 the ADA and HAL signed a memorandum of understanding for producing a small number of LCAs. In 2005 the IAF stated that it would order 40 LCAs with GE engines for $1 billion though by the end of 2005, it had not officially placed this order. The same year, India's defence minister announced that India was investing $2.2 billion in three projects—the LCA, the Kaveri engine to power the LCA, and early warning systems. Yet to produce several hundred LCAs, HAL would require massive investments for tooling and machining facilities. It may seek private sector collaboration for such investment, especially since India's government may not be able to afford yet another aircraft project (Sharma 2001c; Srikanth 2001). India's government had already authorized $3 billion for the licensed production of 140 Su-30s (the first of which were delivered in March 2005); it was also purchasing the advanced jet trainers and airborne early warning systems, costing over $1 billion each; and it intended to spend perhaps $3 billion on 125 multi-role combat aircraft (to be selected from among Sweden's KAS-39 Gripen, Russia's MiG-29M/M2, France's Mirage 2000-5-Mk 2, and the US F-16). Would private investors or India's government support further development of the LCA? Factors such as price and combat capability would have a bearing on whether the LCA is worth the investment.

In terms of price, HAL estimated that the LCA would cost $20–25 million apiece, which, it argued, was far cheaper than the Mirage 2000 ($30–35 million), Mirage 2000-5 ($55 million), the French Rafale ($65 million), the US F-16 ($35 million), the F-22 ($150 million), and the Euro Fighter ($90 million). Others note that the LCA could eventually cost $35–40 million, which, however, was still favourable compared to US or European or Russian aircraft (Sharma 2001a). Most of these aircraft, while more expensive, are also more powerful than the LCA. In terms of comparative data, the LCA weighs 5.5 tons when empty or 8.5 tons when loaded, and carries an additional 4 tons of payload. It is described as the world's smallest, lightest, supersonic multi-role fighter, and is probably closest in weight and dimensions to Sweden's 12–14 ton Gripen. The LCA is also probably somewhat cheaper than the Gripen. Thus, the LCA could be cheaper than imported fighters, but questions remain as to whether it is well-suited for major militarily missions.

In terms of military capabilities, the 'software' or electronic warfare abilities and the 'hardware' or general capabilities of the LCA are worth clarifying. On software, proponents argue that the LCA's avionics, configured around a powerful computer with three MIL-STD-1553B digital data buses, are based on open system architecture and software extension capabilities to ensure that it stays abreast of the latest technology (Sharma 2001b). Yet in terms of general capabilities—speed, range, manœuvrability–the LCA (with a maximum speed of Mach 1.4–1.7, range of 850 km, and payload of 4 tons) would probably be outperformed by its European, Russian, or US counterparts.

Ultimately, the LCA's combat capabilities are best assessed according to its missions. Combat aircraft are used for three types of missions—establishing air superiority; strategic bombing and deep strikes into enemy territory; or short-range missions and close air support of army operations (Harkavy and Neuman 2001). The LCA may not be ideal for the first two missions, and may be confined to the third mission. Here, especially if its costs can be kept down, it may be worth the investment compared to foreign aircraft. But for their major requirements of air superiority and deep strikes, the Indian Air Force would still rely on superior imported aircraft.

In short, even though India will import large numbers of Russian, European, or American aircraft for other missions, the norm of self-sufficiency has influenced India's decisions to embark on the LCA project. If this norm remains influential, India could continue mass production of the LCA venture rather than end it after limited procurement, just as it has continued the advanced light helicopter project.

THE ADVANCED LIGHT HELICOPTER

India's Helicopter Industry

HAL's involvement with helicopters dates back to June 1962, when the Indian government signed an agreement with France's Sud-Aviation (now Eurocopter) for the licensed production of French helicopters. HAL's helicopter division then built two light helicopters—the 1.2 ton Chetak (a licence-produced Alouette-II) with a maximum take-off weight of 2.2 tons, and the 1.1 ton Cheetah (a licence-produced Aerospatiale Lama SA-315) with a maximum take-off weight of 1.9 tons. The Cheetah is powered by a 550 shp Artouste-IIIB engine, which is also manufactured at HAL under licence from France's Turbomeca. HAL produced 336 Chetak and 246 Cheetah helicopters for India's armed forces and civilian users. The Chetak and Cheetah can typically carry five to seven persons. The 2.6 ton ALH with a maximum take-off weight of 5.5 tons and carrying twelve to fourteen persons was intended to replace the Chetaks and Cheetahs.

The Evolution of the ALH

HAL began working on the ALH in July 1984 in consultation with Germany's MBB (now Eurocopter Deutschland). An ALH prototype first flew on 20 August 1992, followed by a skid-gear version for the Indian Army and Air Force in May 1994, and a wheeled-gear version for the Indian Navy in December 1995. On 18 March 2002 India's Coast Guard became the first user to induct the ALH. By early 2005 HAL had manufactured and delivered over thirty of these helicopters to the Indian armed forces, and had also exported two to Nepal and one on lease to Israel. In 2005, HAL was also negotiating an agreement to export twenty to thirty ALH helicopters to Chile. Eventually, HAL plans to produce over 300 ALHs, including 120 for the Indian Army, 120 for the Navy, sixty for the Air Force, and seven for the Coast Guard, over a fifteen-year period. It is expected to progressively increase production from about ten to fifteen helicopters annually during 2003–5 to over twenty annually in the future.

Indigenous and Imported Content

The ALH relies on significant foreign content, particularly for propulsion and avionics. Avionics for the initial ALHs were built in India, but later ALHs will use a package supplied by the Lahav divison of the Israel Aircraft Industries (IAI)—in February 2004, HAL and IAI signed a $33 million contract for initial deliveries of the avionics package. France's Turbomeca supplies the ALH propulsion. Initial prototype ALH's had a pair of Turbomeca TM333-2B engines with a power of 746 kw (1000 shp). HAL then sought the Allied Signal (now Honeywell) LHTEC CTS800-4N engine developing 970 kw (1300 shp). It fitted one in a prototype ALH, and sought an option for an even more powerful CTS800-54 engine developing 1235 kw (1656 shp). In 1998 US sanctions blocked the delivery of these engines. HAL then had to re-certify the ALH (with 1,300 hours of flying in desert and high altitude conditions) with two less powerful Turbomeca TM333-2B engines, delaying its entry into service (India Defense Consultants 2002).

In 1999 the Indian Army tested the ALH and sought more out of the TM333-2B engine. Subsequently, in September 2000, HAL and Turbomeca agreed to develop a more powerful engine, the TM333-2B2, also called Shakti in India and Ardiden-1H in France. This engine was rated at 825 kw (1100 shp) at take-off, and had the potential to be upgraded to 900 kw (1200 shp). In February 2004 Turbomeca and HAL signed a contract for 318 TM333-2B2 engines, which will propel all future ALHs, perhaps from 2006 onward. All prior ALHs with the original TM333-2B engine will also be retrofitted with the new TM333-2B2 engine.

Future Prospects

Over the next decade, the world's helicopter manufacturers will build perhaps 400 military and 900 civil helicopters annually; India will build about twenty to thirty of these through its ALH program (Jaworowski and Dane 2003). The ALH (renamed the Dhruv) will be deployed with India's armed forces and civilian users for transportation, search and rescue, and patrolling functions. Some ALHs will also be used for combat missions. In particular, a Navy version will carry torpedoes, depth charges, and anti-ship missiles. Further, India's Air Force seeks a gunship version called the light combat helicopter (LCH). India's Air Force chief allocated Rs. 3 billion in 2003 for the development of this gunship, but a prototype was not completed as planned by 2005.

The ALH is, as the name suggests, a light helicopter. India's military and civilian users will still rely on Russia, the US, or Europe for medium and heavy helicopters, which have better range and payload capabilities, and will mainly use the ALH for missions that do not require heavy lifting. Even for these, the ALH may not be the most competitive helicopter. It cannot operate at very high altitudes, and only has a ceiling of 4,400–4,500 m (though in November 2004, when it was not carrying passengers and payload, an Air Force Dhruv broke the world record for the highest cruise by a medium-class helicopter by flying at 27,000 feet or 8,230 m). The IAF may still have to rely on Cheetahs and Chetaks (that have a ceiling of 5,400 m) for missions on the Siachen glacier. In terms of price, the ALH is probably competitive. Priced at $4–6 million, depending on the configuration and variant, it is perhaps somewhat cheaper than other helicopters of its class (Sharma 2001c).

In summary, the ALH project is another example of how the norm of self-sufficiency influences technology policy decisions. This norm influenced the original decision to develop the helicopter. Once the development decision was taken, the project was sustained by bureaucratic support. As a result, India will build several hundred ALHs even though Indian military and civilian users could probably have imported a better and not much more expensive light helicopter from foreign suppliers.

ASSESSING INDIA'S INDIGENOUS PROGRAMS

Table 5.1 shows the time of development, indigenous and imported content, costs, and strategic and economic utllity of India's lunar orbiter, LCA, and ALH programs. The moon mission will cost perhaps $100 million; it is a largely indigenous venture (since it relies on the existing PSLV launcher); it will provide no substantive scientific or economic benefits. The LCA and ALH each cost a few hundred million dollars in research and development over five to ten years. They rely on many imported components. They could eventually satisfy India's requirements for 'work horse'-type light combat aircraft and light helicopters, but India could have fulfilled these requirements by importing better-performing combat aircraft and helicopters at only slightly higher prices. Yet, influenced by norms of self-sufficiency and prestige, India's policy planners pressed ahead with these projects.

Table 5.1: India's Lunar Orbiter, LCA, and ALH Programs

	Lunar Orbiter	LCA	ALH
Time of development			
Idea conceived research & development	c.1999–2000	c.1983–85 Design 1987–88; First prototype flown in 2001	c.1984 First prototype flown in 1992
Entry into service	2007–8	2010–2012	2002
Indigenous and imported content	Mostly indigenous	Engines, airframe, and avionics imported	Engines and avionics imported
Costs	$100 million	Approx. $500 million for Phase 1 (four prototypes and infrastructure and tests facilities); approx. $500 million for Phase 2 (additional prototypes); 40 ordered at $20–25 million apiece thereafter	Approx. 300 ordered at $5 million apiece

contd...

	Lunar Orbiter	LCA	ALH
Cost efficiency	--	Somewhat cheaper than alternatives	Possibly cheaper than alternatives
Strategic/ economic utility	--	Useful for short range air support operations; not optimal for deep strikes and long-range air patrols	Useful for light transport and patrol operations, not capable of heavy lifting
International prestige	High	--	--
Self-reliance	--	High	High

In the end, India's experience with the ALH and LCA projects is not very different from its more general experience with defence production—although India has not realized significant benefits from indigenous or licensed production, policy makers have continued to invest hundreds of millions of dollars in indigenous projects. Raju Thomas (1997) explains some reasons for India's lacklustre performance in building its own defence hardware. Thomas notes that India faced a basic dilemma: seeking technological independence would mean relying on indigenous low-technology armaments that fell short of military needs, while satisfying the demand for high-technology weapons would mean foregoing an indigenous armaments capability. To counter this dilemma, the industry often adopted an imitative approach (relying on licensed production of complete items and the imports of major components) that, however, was not conducive to developing a mature technology base. At the same time, the resources necessary for fully exploiting better imported technology were taken up by the less advanced indigenous program. As a result, India neither realized the full benefits of licensed production nor those of a capable indigenous program. Pointing out the poor record of indigenous production, a retired Indian Air Force officer notes: 'HAL has been termed as a white elephant...the armed forces are perennially on the look out for their operational requirements of aircraft and aviation equipment from the suppliers abroad' (Pant

2000). Similarly, Eric Arnet (1997) describes Indian indigenous arms production as a case of 'rhetorical self-sufficiency and feigned self-reliance', noting that despite an energetic drive for technological self-reliance, India is a significant importer of arms and components. Despite this poor record, India's public sector organizations persisted with and obtained governmental approval for the ALH and LCA projects.

In reforming Indian technology policy, two competing ideas could counter those of prestige and self-reliance—the idea of competitiveness, and the notion of international collaboration and global partnerships. Competitiveness can be implemented by privatizing firms such as HAL. Analysts note:

> It will indeed be a bold step in the right direction if the nation's large and reputable industrial houses are afforded the opportunity to own a sizeable portion of HAL's share holding. This will infuse not only much needed funds for design and production of new aircraft for civil and military use but the company will also be able to tap the best brains in the field of management and technology in order to lead it towards greater heights in performance and growth. (Pant 2000)

In an era of globalization, India's elite themselves have recognized the value of competition—India's 2003 technology policy mentions the new norm of competitiveness, in contrast to the 1958 and 1983 policies that emphasized self-reliance.[10] India's recent successes in information technology and business process outsourcing are another example of how the idea of competitiveness positively influences industrial sectors (Kapur 2002). To the extent that these norms spill over to the government sector, they will influence Indian public sector firms to be more competitive.

International collaboration is another norm that can lead to better production by Indian public sector firms. India has begun pursuing

---

[10]The 2003 statement advocates technology policy reforms for India, noting, 'This [reform] will enable it to be competitive, achieve greater self-reliance and self-confidence, and fulfil national goals' (Government of India 2003).

limited collaboration in the defence industry. The Brahmos cruise missile project between Indian and Russian firms is perhaps the best recent example of such a collaborative venture. Another area of collaboration could be through tie-ups with American industry—at US–India Defence Policy Group meetings, the two sides included collaborative production as a potential area of cooperation (Embassy of India 2001, 2002). Both the light combat aircraft program and the moon mission could also benefit from international partners. In short, embracing the ideas of competitiveness and collaboration could positively influence technology decisions in India, and lead to the production of better technological outputs that bring more substantive security and economic benefits.

BIBLIOGRAPHY

Arnett, Eric (1995). Military Technology: The Case of India. *SIPRI Yearbook*: 343–66. London: Oxford University Press.

———— (1997). Military Research and Development in Southern Asia: Limited Capabilities Despite Impressive Resources. In Eric Arnett, ed., *Military Capacity and the Risk of War: China, India, Pakistan, and Iran*. Oxford: Oxford University Press, pp. 243–76.

Chari, P.R, Pervaiz Cheema, and Stephen Cohen (2003). *Perception, Politics and Security in South Asia: The Compound Crisis of 1990*. New York: Routledge Curzon.

Chengappa, Raj (2000). India's Moon Mission. *India Today*, 3 July, pp. 27–32.

———— (2003). Lunar Mission: Reaching For The Moon. *India Today*, 1 September, 2003.

Cohen, Stephen (2001). *India: Emerging Power*. Washington, DC: Brookings.

Council on Scientific and Industrial Research (CSIR). 1988. *Status Report on Science and Technology in India: 1988*. New Delhi: CSIR.

Embassy of India (2001). Joint Statement of the India–US Defence Policy Group. 4 December, Washington, DC.

———— (2002). Joint Statement on US–India Defence Policy Group Meeting. 23 May Washington, DC.

Feigenbaum, Evan (2003). *China's Techno-Warriors: National Security and Strategic Competition from the Nuclear to the Information Age*. Stanford: Stanford University Press.

Gill, Bates and Taeho Kim (1995). *China's Arms Acquisitions from Abroad: A Quest for Superb and Secret*. Oxford: Oxford University Press.

Government of India (1958). Scientific Policy Resolution. 4 March. New Delhi.

———— (1983). Technology Policy Statement. New Delhi.

———— (2003). Science and Technology Policy. New Delhi

Gupta, Amit (1997). *Building an Arsenal: The Evolution of Regional Power Force Structures*. Westport, CT: Praeger.

Harkavy, Robert and Stephanie Neuman (2001). *Warfare and the Third World.* New York: Palgrave.

India Defence Consultants (2002). *The Advanced Light Helicopter Story.*

Indian Express (2001). Swadeshi LCA has US Engine, Israeli, Swedish Avionics, Italian Wings. 8 February.

Jaworowski, Raymond and William Dane (2003). The World Rotorcraft Market 2003–2012. *Vertiflite,* 49(1), p. 17.

Kapur, Devesh (2002). The Causes and Consequences of India's IT Boom. *India Review,* 1(2), pp. 91–110.

Matthews, R.G. (1989). The Development of India's Defence–Industrial Base. *Journal of Strategic Studies,* 12(4), 405–30.

Mistry, Dinshaw (2001). The Geostrategic Implications of India's Space Program. *Asian Survey,* 41(6), pp. 1023–43.

Motta, Mary (2000). India Moon Mission Update. http://www.space.com/news/spaceagencies/indian_moon_000717.html

Nayar, Baldev Raj (1977). *India's Quest for Technological Independence.* New Delhi: Lancer.

Pant, N.K. (2000). Aircraft Industry in India: An Appraisal. *Institute of Peace and Conflict Studies,* article no. 444.

Rao, Radhakrishna (2000) India Sets its Sights on Moon. *Tribune,* 24 August.

Reddy, C. Manmohan (2003). The LCA Success. *Frontline,* 20(5).

Samuels, Richard J. (1994). *Rich Nation, Strong Army: National Security and the Technological Transformation of Japan.* Ithaca: Cornell University Press.

Sharma, Ravi (2001a). Airborne at Last. *Frontline,* 18(2).

———— (2001b). The Stumbling Blocks. *Frontline,* 18(2).

———— (2001c). Soaring Hopes. *Frontline,* 18(14).

Srikanth, B.R. (2001). Flights of Hope and Anxiety. *Outlook,* 15 January.

Sorid, Daniel (2000). India Plans to Send Spacecraft to Moon. http://www.space.com/missionlaunches/missions/india_moon_000629.html

Subramanian, T.S. (2003). Future Space Missions. *Frontline,* 20(22).

Thomas, Raju (1986). *Indian Security Policy.* Princeton: Princeton University Press.

———— (1997). Arms Procurement in India: Military Self-Reliance versus Technological Self-Sufficiency. In Eric Arnett, ed., *Military Capacity and the Risk of War: China, India, Pakistan, and Iran,* Oxford: Oxford University Press, pp. 110–29.

Times of India (2001a). GSLV Launches India into Elite Space Club. 18 April.

———— (2001b). Light Combat Craft Takes India into Club Class. 30 April.

Valluri, S.R. (2001). Developing the LCA. *The Hindu.* 3 March.

———— (2005). LCA and Project Management. *Deccan Herald,* 3 August.

Wollen, M.S.D. (2001). The Light Combat Aircraft Story. *Bharat Rakshak Monitor,* 3(5).

Diaspora Populations, the Internet, and Political Mobilization

Kavita R. Khory

Scholars and policy makers alike are grappling to better understand and explain the revolutionary potential of new information technologies for global politics. In a post-9/11 world, information technologies, specifically those associated with the Internet and the World Wide Web, are often depicted in one of two ways. First, the Internet is believed to be among the most important weapons in terrorists' arsenals for exchanging information, disseminating propaganda, fund-raising, and recruitment (Sageman 2004; Weimann 2004). 'Cyberterrorism,' aimed at disrupting communications and computer networks, is now routinely cited as a significant threat to national and international security. On the opposite end of the global politics spectrum, the Internet is hailed as a powerful liberating force that can dramatically expand opportunities for political participation, build and sustain transnational advocacy networks, challenge state power and sovereignty, and render territorial boundaries meaningless. The relationship between evolving information technologies and global politics, needless to say, is more complex and multifaceted than popular conceptions of it would suggest.

Interactive and operating in real-time, the Internet and the World Wide Web serve as powerful—largely unregulated—media for shaping the production and consumption of information and knowledge, constituting and reconfiguring identities and interests, and promoting political mobilization and activism. This chapter examines how the Internet and related technologies influence, facilitate, or inhibit transnational political mobilization by focusing on two comparative examples drawn from South Asia—Sikhs, principally from the Indian state of Punjab, and Tamils from Sri Lanka—who use the Internet and the World Wide Web to construct cultural and political identities, pursue self-determination projects, and, most importantly, communicate with globally dispersed diaspora populations.

Both Sikhs and Tamils are linked to specific geographical areas that, as symbols of contested sovereignty, inspire collective action at home and abroad. Neither Sikh nor Sri Lankan Tamil migration to Europe, North America, South-east Asia, or Australia is of recent origin; however, since the early 1980s, Sikh and Tamil political organizations operating outside India and Sri Lanka have come under extensive international scrutiny—more so after 9/11—for ostensibly promoting and sustaining nationalist movements and violent insurgencies in Punjab and the north-east region of Sri Lanka. Whereas conflict and violence in Punjab have waned over time, the civil war in Sri Lanka continues, with intermittent ceasefires and several attempts, previously by India, and more recently Norway, to control the violence and fashion a political settlement.

We are especially interested in analysing the use of digital and electronic media by diaspora populations for whom advanced communications technologies are indispensable tools for forging and sustaining ties with their country of origin and networking among widely scattered members. First, diaspora organizations, operating in transnational contexts, are by no means a new feature of world politics; however, their visibility, networking capabilities, and likely impact on the policies of home and host states are enhanced significantly by the contemporary forces of globalization, particularly technology and capital flows (Shain and Sherman 2004). Political, cultural, and financial flows between and among diaspora organizations and homelands, however, are neither unidirectional nor linear. Diaspora populations frequently mirror homeland conflicts and depend on homeland governments and organizations for political support, economic resources, and cultural sustenance.

Second, diaspora organizations can inspire, motivate, and sustain nationalist movements and insurgency groups in home states by providing valuable moral, political, and financial support using faster, cheaper, and more reliable information and transportation technologies. Scholars and practitioners of international relations, therefore, are focusing special attention on the role of diaspora organizations in constituting communal identities and, in some cases, actively encouraging or even engaging in political violence in home states and host societies (Kaldor-Robinson 2002; Mills 2002; Sheffer 2003).

Finally, the primacy of the state in international relations today is routinely challenged in both theory and practice, as is the flawed assumption that domestic politics is somehow disconnected from the practice of foreign policy. Diaspora politics, located at the intersection of comparative politics and international relations, is an important example of a vital, but thus far neglected, area of study that is benefiting from the analytical perspectives offered by alternative approaches such as constructivsm, with its emphasis on ideas and norms in international relations and the formation of social networks and information exchange among non-state actors.

We will not present an exhaustive survey of numerous Websites devoted to Sikh and Tamil politics or organizations, nor will we analyse sketchy data on audience, access, and usage of informational technology and audio-visual media among relevant populations. Rather, we treat texts and images created and circulated by Sikhs and Tamils on the Internet and the World Wide Web as rich and complex sources for studying, among other things, dynamic forms of cultural and political identities, strategies for mobilizing multiple constituencies, and fostering pubic attention and sympathy for nationalist causes. What do select Websites and discussion groups, for example, reveal about the histories, motives, and goals of nationalist movements and diaspora organizations? How are nationalist ideologies represented via texts and visual imagery? What are the major tropes that help shape political narratives and nationalist visions at home and abroad? How do the two cases expose the intrinsic tensions of collective projects in the nationalist vein? More broadly, what can we learn from these examples about the functions and limitations of digital and electronic media in transnational conflicts, which have significant implications for international security?

Sikh and Tamil nationalist movements and diaspora populations, like others, encompass numerous formal and informal transnational organizations and networks devoted to a broad range of issues and objectives. Although many of the organizations are located in the cities and towns of Europe and North America, their electronic networks extend globally. We explore the use of the Internet and the World Wide Web by selecting examples from two types of non-state actors and organizations involved in nationalist movements and diaspora politics, both of whom are engaged in transnational advocacy and mobilization but represent distinctly different goals, values, and discourses. Broadly, sympathizers, activists, and leaders form the first category, for example, organizations like the Council of Khalistan or insurgency groups such as the Liberation Tamil Tigers of Eelam (LTTE), who assert a distinct ethnic identity as the basis for political action; claim they are the victims of an exclusionary national ideology, discriminatory political institutions and economic policies, and systematic violence perpetrated by the Indian and Sri Lankan states; and advocate for political autonomy—even separation—for Sikh- and Tamil-dominated areas in India and Sri Lanka respectively.

The second category consists of organizations such as Ensaaf[1] and the Sri Lanka Democracy Forum whose organizational identities and interests, on the one hand, are closely linked with the politics of the Punjab and Sri Lanka, specifically in the area of human rights. On the other hand, Ensaaf and the Sri Lanka Democracy Forum, among others, largely reject monolithic and exclusive conceptions of ethnic identity; critique the coercive and violent politics of both states and nationalist movements; and argue for a different understanding of community, one that is exemplified by transnational organizations and networks devoted to two missions—publicizing and addressing human rights violations and promoting the reconciliation and reconstruction of war-torn societies. These categories, like ethnic and national identities, are by no means static or mutually exclusive. Rather, they reflect complex histories, political processes, and social relations among

---

[1] 'Ensaaf,' which means 'justice' in many South Asian languages, is a US-based organization devoted to exposing human rights violations in Punjab and advocating for victims of human rights abuses.

heterogeneous populations. Analysing Internet use and representation by several different as well as similar organizations, especially those based in the diaspora, is more likely to offer deeper insights into the highly contested arena of diaspora politics that is all too often subsumed within a monolithic formulation of ethnic identity and nationalism.

The human rights organizations and ethno-nationalist movements covered in the two cases espouse distinctive ideologies and goals, but oftentimes their strategies and tactics are shaped by the incentives and constraints of a common political opportunity structure (Esman 1994: 31–32). First, they are likely to target some of the same audiences dispersed among diaspora members, home states, host societies, international organizations, and non-governmental agencies. By using the Internet, however, organizations can tailor their message to each audience cheaply and expeditiously so as to build and sustain support for their cause.

Second, activists and leaders of movements and organizations might lobby for a single issue at first, but quickly find that it is almost impossible to limit the agenda if sustained political mobilization is to occur. Given the linkages between domestic and international politics and policy making, ethnic groups dispersed across territorial borders often compel diaspora organizations to tackle particular local issues, sometimes far removed from the organization's own territorial or ideological objectives. The Internet and the World Wide Web allow diaspora organizations to express moral support in the spirit of transnational solidarity, without necessarily addressing the problem itself or dealing with the consequences of flawed actions and policies.

Third, liberal democratic political structures and institutions in host states afford opportunities for nationalist movements and affiliated organizations to engage in fund-raising, lobbying, and recruitment in locales far removed from the primary sites of conflict and violence. 'Long-distance nationalism', Benedict Anderson argues, is a 'radically unaccountable' form of politics. For the participant in long-distance politics, 'that same metropole which marginalizes and stigmatizes him simultaneously enables him to play, in a flash, on the other side of the planet, national hero' (1994: 327). The immunity offered by long-distance nationalism, however, can no longer be taken for granted, especially in host states. In the wake of 9/11 and the bombings in

London in July 2005, the United States, Canada, and a number of European countries are cracking down on advocates for Khalistan and organizations like the LTTE, which increasingly are seen as serious threats to societal and state security (Dogra 2003). Proposed anti-terror legislation in Britain, for example, targets Websites and political activity conducted over the Internet in addition to more traditional forms of organization and activism (*Guardian* 2005).

SIKH DIASPORA: IDENTITY AND THE INTERNET

The political mobilization of a distinct Sikh identity and its culmination in a nationalist movement in India in the 1980s is well known and thoroughly analysed by scholars of Indian history and politics (Kapur 1986; Nayar and Singh 1984; Tully and Jacob 1985). Our purpose is not to re-examine the origins of political violence in Punjab or to study the role of the Indian state in precipitating the conflict, but to explore the production and representation of Sikh identities on the Internet, especially in relation to Punjab's politics and the search for statehood. How effective is the Internet for projecting Sikh grievances onto an international stage, soliciting funds, and generating support for key objectives, particularly among diaspora members and host states? How is the relationship between and among a globally dispersed, highly segmented Sikh diaspora and the 'homeland', in this case Punjab, shaped and mediated by the use of Internet technology?

Before analysing specific Websites, two caveats are in order. First, Sikh migration is not of recent origin but can be traced to colonial practices of recruiting and transporting Sikhs for labour and military service throughout the British Empire. After decolonization, large numbers of South Asians, including Sikhs, sought economic and educational opportunities in the United Kingdom, Canada, and the United States, among other destinations. Riven by political factions and competing religious traditions and institutions, however, few could claim a self-conscious, cohesive Sikh diapsora identity, even in the wake of the Indian government's attack on the Golden Temple in 1984. Moreover, as some scholars have argued, it is unlikely that a single event like the storming of the Golden Temple could instantly forge a singular Sikh identity traversing territorial boundaries or produce a coherent political agenda (Singh 1999b). As such, the Websites examined are largely snapshots of a much longer, multifaceted process of identity formation and political mobilization among Sikhs located outside of India.

Second, there is still some debate over the precise role of diaspora members in spearheading the quest for Khalistan. Some observers of Sikh diaspora politics believe that the demand for Khalistan originated outside of India and diaspora support was crucial for both launching and sustaining the insurgency in Punjab. Others, however, remain more sceptical of the diaspora's ideological independence or its leadership claims toward articulating Sikh grievances and pursuing territorial sovereignty (ibid.: 305). Without discounting the significance of diaspora support for the insurgency, it is important to note the largely reactive politics, before and after 1984, of Sikh groups and organizations operating in the diaspora. Although the diaspora, with a few exceptions, can provide sites, opportunities, and even leadership for fashioning a politics of resistance outside the purview of the Indian state, it generally reflects and reinforces major trends in Punjab's politics.

The Demand for Khalistan

The Council of Khalistan Website is among the many devoted to Sikh politics in India and abroad.[2] Funded largely by Dr. Gurmat Sikh Aulakh, the self-designated president of the Council of Khalistan, the organization, according to its Website, operates out of Washington, DC as a representative of the Council of Khalistan, ostensibly located in the Golden Temple in Amritsar, Punjab. Sikh grievances, chiefly those against the Indian state, are tracked and highlighted on the site. Advocating principally for self-determination and the 'liberation of Khalistan from Indian occupation', the Council of Khalistan, however, urges its supporters to pursue and protect globally the fundamental rights of the 'Sikh nation' regardless of citizenship. Protests against the French government's restrictions on Sikhs wearing turbans in public institutions or an assessment of India's human rights record at Congressional hearings are profiled under the 'latest news on the struggle for a free Khalistan', as are news items culled from small

---

[2]See http://www.khalistan.com

towns in the United States, for example, Sikh individuals or community organizations protesting hate crimes against minority populations.

The Council of Khalistan seeks to build support for a 'sovereign, independent Khalistan', but the Website presents few concrete strategies or tactics for 'liberating' Khalistan. It does, however, rely heavily on posting and circulating open letters and petitions to US Congressional representatives, members of the administration, and government officials in countries like Canada and England, calling on them to pressure the Indian government to address Sikh grievances including outstanding human rights violations and resource allocation. Although the Council of Khalistan continues to propagate the creation of an independent Sikh state, its Website's coverage of a much broader range of issues suggests that there is some recognition of the negligible support remaining for Khalistan among Sikhs within and outside of Punjab and India (Singh 1999a). The Council of Khalistan claims to speak for the collective Sikh nation, but provides no information on the level or extent of support among Sikhs for continuing the struggle for Khalistan. More importantly, a closer reading of the text-based Website cautions us against ascribing group characteristics or collective identity to an organization that professes to represent a 'community', but in reality draws for the most part on the beliefs and actions of an individual such as Aulakh.

Unlike the Council of Khalistan Website, which in its present form stresses current events and activism, 'Sikh Underground,' the Website 'dedicated to the saint soldiers', is oriented towards a historical narrative of the persecution suffered by Sikhs from the sixteenth century to the present.[3] As the Website's title suggests, militancy, violence, and martyrdom are the dominant themes of the multimedia site, carrying audio recordings and videos along with conventional written texts. Melding political rhetoric with religious metaphors and imagery, the Website presents a chronicle of the violence against Sikhs in India, specifically the 'invasion' of the Golden Temple in 1984 and the riots in New Delhi following the assassination of Indira Gandhi.

Graphic depictions—in written texts and photographic and video images—of torture, as a particular form of violence, remind a global

---

[3]See http://www.sikhunderground.com

audience of the Indian state's atrocities and its failure to prosecute the instigators of the riots and massacres. Portraits of militants, designated as 'Sikh martyrs', are displayed and circulated on the site, among others, as well as in *gurdwaras* and community centres. These portraits, as Axel (2002) explains, serve as a unifying symbol for diaspora Sikhs, many of whom are far removed from the violence itself. The gallery of portraits is recreated at multiple venues to memorialize Sikh martyrs so as to inspire individual sacrifice and collective action for preserving and defending the Sikh nation. Video clips of Bhindranwale's speeches and short documentaries spliced from largely unknown sources augment visual and aural cues on the Website. Granted the power of visual cues, online portraits and videos are more likely to capture the imagination of a larger audience who might not otherwise be exposed to the images.

Neither the Council of Khalistan nor the 'Sikh Underground' Website, which does not claim affiliation with a specific organization, presents an explicit condemnation or instigation of violence, although by glorifying martyrs, 'Sikh Underground,' it seems, tacitly endorses militancy as a response to state-sponsored acts of violence. Targeting an audience that includes state and non-state actors, the Council of Khalistan has had some success in drawing international attention to Sikh grievances, although popularizing coverage of the conflict has not translated into a commensurate degree of support for a sovereign Khalistan. The 'Sikh Underground', on the other hand, appears to focus largely on mobilizing Sikhs within India and abroad and less on lobbying IGOs or host states.

Diaspora and Human Rights: Seeking Justice

More recently, in light of the twentieth anniversary of the Indian government's attack on the Golden Temple and the massacre of Sikhs in New Delhi following Prime Minister Indira Gandhi's assassination, Sikh organizations in Europe, the United States, and Canada are lobbying for justice and compensation for the victims of human rights violations in Punjab. While the desire for accountability and justice cuts across different generations, a major impetus for documenting the narratives of survivors of human rights abuses in Punjab comes from second- and third-generation Sikhs in Europe and North America.

'Ensaaf,' a relatively new US-based organization, is compiling testimonies of survivors living in the United States—and publishing them on the Internet—in order to draw international attention to the failure of successive Indian governments to provide some measure of justice for the victims of extra-judicial executions in Punjab and the violence that followed Indira Gandhi's assassination. Set up in 2003 by two human rights lawyers, Sukhman Dhami and Jaskaran Kaur, 'Ensaaf' represents a new, technologically sophisticated, and politically savvier generation of American-born activists seeking justice for human rights victims in Punjab.

While advocating for Sikh victims, Dhami and Kaur link their efforts with those of a number of US-based human rights organizations working with victims of communal violence throughout India. Rather than advance their cause through ethnic or identity politics, Dhami and Kaur seek to inform, educate, and mobilize an international audience by appealing to the principles of human rights and international law. Argentina and Chile's Truth and Reconciliation commissions, among others, are cited as examples of how the Indian state could adjudicate the claims of victims of human rights abuses. Individual testimonies are solicited in English and Punjabi with the final version posted in English. Dhami and Kaur's aim is not only to address past human rights violations but also to push for institutional safeguards against future abuses (*Ensaaf Dispatch* 2004).

Within a year, 'Ensaaf' succeeded in widely publicizing the failure of several government commissions and judicial process over two decades, to hold accountable the state and Congress Party officials who encouraged violent attacks on Sikhs in New Delhi. Barbara Crossette, the former *New York Times* bureau chief in New Delhi, interviewed Kaur and cited 'Ensaaf's' work in a story entitled 'India's Sikhs: Waiting for Justice', published in the *World Policy Journal*, which is widely circulated among US scholars and policy makers.[4] Dhani and Kaur, in turn, cite Crossette's article on 'Ensaaf's' Website to build their case against the Indian government and the Akali Dal

---

[4]See Crossette (2004). The journal can be accessed via the World Policy Institute's home page at www.worldpolicy.org, which provides the full text, plus an online discussion forum for each article published in the journal.

leadership, raise the organization's profile among international human rights agencies, and legitimize its initiatives.

In this instance, the Web serves at least two important functions. First, it facilitates information sharing and dissemination among individuals and organizations with common goals—to uncover and document human rights abuses, advocate for victims of violence, and pressure governments to acknowledge and accept responsibility for human rights violations. Although relevant information would eventually reach its target audience through more traditional forms of communication like community bulletins, newspapers, and relevant journals, it is unlikely that, in the absence of the Web, an organization like 'Ensaaf,' operated by a very small number of activists with limited resources, could garner a commensurate level of publicity and support under similar time constraints. Second, instantaneous circulation of first-person accounts of human rights abuses and detailed information about the organization's goals and activities, locally and globally, advances one of 'Ensaaf's' chief objectives: to bring together families in North America who, as survivors of human rights abuses in Punjab, can challenge more effectively the Indian government's record on accountability and justice in Punjab and elsewhere.

Recognizing the limitations of the Web, however, Kaur and Dhami have advocated for the survivors of Punjab's human rights abuses at international fora in the United States, Europe, and India, and engaged in outreach programmes at *gurdwaras* in California where the organization is located. Given that much of the campaigning for Punjab's autonomy as well as for Khalistan occurred within *gurdwaras* throughout the diaspora, Kaur and Dhami, channelled their efforts through existing community institutions as well. Their strategies and tactics reinforce the point that information exchange and mobilization via the Internet and the Web do not take place in a political or cultural vacuum. Rather, such processes are deeply affected by cultural practices, social exchanges, and the political opportunities and constraints that exist outside of the electronic media.

THE HOMELAND MOTIF

Scholars, like Brian Axel, argue that conceptions of Sikh identity, especially outside of India, rely more upon images and narratives of violence and resistance than on a conception of the 'homeland' and a desire to return to it (2002: 423–24). Others, for instance, Darshan Singh Tatla (1999), privilege place and location—specifically the 'idea' of Punjab as a homeland—in forming Sikh identity. The three Websites, in many ways, reflect the different interpretations of Sikh identity formation. The Council of Khalistan promotes the idea of a homeland with territorial boundaries and political sovereignty. The 'Sikh Underground' Website, in contrast, draws upon religious symbols, traditions, and rituals to remind Sikhs of the 'sacrifice of our martyrs' in the struggle for fundamental rights. Khalistan, though, is never explicitly mentioned. Although religious symbols play a powerful role in shaping and asserting Sikh identity, the political significance of religion varies for Sikhs in Punjab and the diaspora. 'Ensaaf's' activism, for example, is rooted in a language of universal human rights rather than a singular religious identity. While the organization is concerned for the most part with Sikh victims of state violence, it does not promote political autonomy or self-determination as a panacea for Sikh grievances. In fact, Dhami and Kaur are highly critical of both the Indian state and the Akali Dal government in Punjab. Justice, for them, means addressing first the claims of Sikh victims living in the diaspora, and ineffectual Sikh leadership in Punjab is hardly the solution to the deeper problems of restitution and reconciliation.

The Websites show, too, that many formulations of Sikh identity draw upon particular symbols or sites in Punjab such as the Golden Temple, but Khalistan is only one among several points of reference for Sikhs living in North America or Europe. The Indian government's attack on the Golden Temple in 1984, for example, has become a major trope in Sikh narratives aimed at forging a common, cross-generational identity. The initial impetus for Khalistan came from a small number of Sikhs within and outside of Punjab; it became both a popular symbol and a key demand among many Sikhs in Punjab and in the diaspora only after the Indian government launched Operation Blue Star, followed soon thereafter by the involvement of some of its members in the brutal attacks on Sikhs in New Delhi in October 1984. While the support for an independent Sikh state in Punjab has declined over time, the memory, experience, and narratives of violence continue to play a powerful role in shaping and sustaining different facets of Sikh political identity in the diaspora.

Websites of organizations like 'Ensaaf' or the Council of Khalistan are devoted to a specific political agenda and are fairly limited in scope. Other sites, for instance, 'Sikhsangat.org' and 'UKSikhs.com,' combine political content with a broader range of material and exchanges devoted to popular culture. By incorporating news items, discussion lists, Web logs (blogs), and links connecting globally dispersed individuals and organizations, both sites envision and promote a Sikh identity grounded mainly in cultural symbols and practices, social relations, and religious traditions and rituals. Reviving and popularizing the study of the Punjabi language and literature, for example, is seen as way to create and sustain—especially among Sikh youth—a shared cultural identity that is not specific to a particular location.

The Websites also host active fora where historical narratives and religious idioms function as devices for interpreting contemporary politics in India and abroad, and framing appropriate responses. Thus, the Sikh tradition of '*sevadars*' or volunteerism—embedded in a historical and religious context—serves as a rallying cry for educated and skilled individuals in the twenty-first century to help community members, particularly students, develop technological knowledge and expertise. Aimed at second- and third-generation Sikhs in the United States and the United Kingdom, Websites like 'UKSikhs.com' simultaneously carry diatribes against 'Western influence among youth' as well as paeans to high-tech tools and skills for collectively achieving material progress and political power. Among some second- and third-generation Sikhs in the UK and elsewhere, a common identity forged through shared religious and cultural symbols holds some appeal, it seems, even when there is no indication of a desire to return permanently to the 'homeland' in Punjab or to influence its politics significantly. 'Home', in this instance, is 'less experienced than imagined, and imagined through a complex of mediations and representations', (Anderson 1994: 319). As Gurharpal Singh (1999b: 229) points out, Sikh youth are more attracted to a 'romanticized' Punjab, imagined through a hybrid popular culture, than a strictly ideological or religious agenda.

SRI LANKAN TAMILS, CIVIL WAR AND MIGRATION

In the early 1980s a combination of long-standing political and economic grievances stemming from exclusivist conceptions of national identity and discriminatory state policies vis-à-vis Tamils in Sri Lanka culminated in a violent insurgency movement. Whereas the idea of an independent Tamil state, located in the Tamil majority areas of northern and eastern Sri Lanka, was not a new one, it became a key demand and objective of Tamil political parties and organizations after the massive anti-Tamil riots in Colombo in 1983.

Several scholars attribute the long duration of the Tamil insurgency, especially the LTTE's resilience over the last two decades, to the sustained moral, political, and, most critically, financial, support of Tamil diaspora networks (Wayland 2004: 405). Although it is difficult to gauge the precise level and extent of financial support from abroad and its impact on the conflict in Sri Lanka, a number of sources corroborate the dynamic role of Tamil diaspora organizations and networks in sustaining the insurgency over the long term, particularly after the Indian government withdrew its support from Tamil insurgents and staged a deeply flawed intervention to end the civil war in Sri Lanka in 1987 (Byman et al. 2001: 41–60).

Like many others, the Sri Lankan Tamil diaspora, too, is widely dispersed and heterogeneous, formed by distinct historical conditions, distinguished by class and gender, and differentiated along generational lines. Tamils residing in Western Europe or North America may share a common language, cultural practices, or the experiences of exile, but they are not immune from the homeland's conflicts and violence that are reproduced in the diaspora, or new sets of tensions arising from socio-economic and political conditions encountered in the diaspora.

Tamils began leaving Sri Lanka in large numbers following the violent attacks on Tamils in 1983, moving first to Tamil Nadu in south India and thereafter in increasing numbers to Western Europe, Canada, and Australia. Fleeing state violence and, in many cases, the LTTE's coercive and violent politics as well, Tamil émigrés from Sri Lanka gravitated toward states like Australia and Canada with relatively liberal asylum laws. Migration from Sri Lanka, motivated by the lure of economic and educational opportunities abroad, had long preceded the violent phase of the conflict. Consequently, the more recent Tamil asylum-seekers with limited income and resources received at times a lukewarm reception from an earlier generation of Tamils who saw asylum-seekers as interlopers, posing a special set of problems for the more prosperous and established members of the Tamil community (Fugelrud 2001: 205).

Notwithstanding the complexity of the conflict in Sri Lanka and the challenge of negotiating different transnational social and political spaces, the divisions between those Tamils who support the LTTE and those who do not are reconstituted in the diaspora, where many Tamils are reluctant to confront directly the LTTE's monolithic vision of Tamil identity and nationalism, its militancy and violence at home and abroad, and its tight control over Tamil media and cultural and political organizations in the diaspora (Fugelrud 1999: 85; McDowell 1996: 35). Sinhalese émigrés, although much smaller in number than Tamils, are developing a public and media profile in Canada, the United Kingdom, and Italy, among other countries, by actively promoting a Sinhala Buddhist identity to underscore their support for the Sri Lankan state's campaign against Tamil 'separatists' and 'terrorists'. (Cheran 2004: 9). Despite the contested vision of homeland politics, there is little evidence of Tamil–Sinhalese tensions erupting into violence in the diaspora.

A new generation of Tamils who are born and educated outside of Sri Lanka, however, seems less inclined to affiliate with a singular Tamil identity, even in the face of pressure by LTTE sympathizers to do so (ibid.: 12). Identifying more often as Tamil–Canadians or Tamil–Norwegians, or even Sri Lankans and South Asians, second-generation Tamils are challenging in subtle ways the imposition of an exclusive identity, without necessarily diminishing their connections to the 'homeland' in South Asia.[5]

---

[5]One example is 'Diaspora Flow', a Minnesota-based 'Sri Lankan American' non-profit arts organization seeking collaboration between young Tamil and Sinhalese Sri Lankan artists who are committed to 'building solidarity along political and aesthetic lines'. Jeevamanoharan and Wanduragla (2001). The South Asia Citizens Web emphasizes a regional identity to 'promote exchange of information between and about citizens initiatives from South Asia (and its diasporic communities' (http://www.sacw.net).

Our analysis of the use of the Internet for advancing transnational connections in the service of political mobilization focuses on four Websites: (a) 'Eelam.com'; (b) 'Tamilnet.com'; (c) 'Lankademocracy. org' (Sri Lanka Democracy Forum); and (d) 'Lacnet.org' (Lanka Academic Network).

Tamil Eelam on the Internet

Among the numerous Websites dedicated to Tamil politics, 'Eelam.com' and 'Tamilnet.com' largely reflect the LTTE's perspective on the conflict in Sri Lanka. Operated by the LTTE, which identifies itself as a 'military and political organization representing the aspirations and hopes of the Tamil people', 'Eelam.com' is designated as the 'official' Website of the Tamil nation—Eelam. Aimed at audiences within and outside of Sri Lanka, 'Eelam.com' serves several functions: first, it outlines the LTTE's conception of the Tamil nation and lays out its strategies and tactics for achieving self-determination; second, it conveys news and information about Tamils in Sri Lanka to a transnational audience; third, it facilitates communication between and among Tamils in Sri Lanka and those in the diaspora; and last, it is a vehicle for fund-raising and organizing at the grassroots level.

A map of Sri Lanka on the Website's home page displays Eelam's territorial boundaries, which are carved out of the northern and eastern regions of Sri Lanka. Eelam, as depicted on the Website, represents both a unitary nationalist movement as well as a specific territory embodying the quest for self-governance and sovereignty. A distinct Sri Lankan Tamil identity, according to 'Eelam.com,' is formed by a common language, culture, and understanding of history. The impetus for collective action, however, comes from a common set of grievances fuelled by systematic ethnic discrimination and persecution by the state. Having eliminated most of its rival organizations, the LTTE claims the exclusive right to represent Tamils in Sri Lanka and abroad. Tamil and English language statements, as well as speeches and communiqués posted on the site, for example, assert the LTTE's status and power as the sole representative of Tamils and present the LTTE's leader, Velupillai Prabhakaran, as the leader of the Tamil nation and Eelam. Drawing analogies with Palestinian nationalists and anti-apartheid South Africans, the LTTE sees itself as waging a struggle for the 'national liberation' of the Tamil people's 'traditional homeland' (Gourevitch 2005: 59).

Eelam.com functions as a highly effective tool for conveying up-to-the-minute news and information about the LTTE and affiliated organizations such as the Tamil Rehabilitation Organization (TRO).[6] Detailed accounts of the full range of the LTTE's activities in Sri Lanka, which run the gamut from military operations and refugee rehabilitation programmes to educational and cultural initiatives and judicial institutions, are juxtaposed with descriptions of the LTTE's international offices and activities. As some reports suggest, widespread publicity of the LTTE's 'victories' against the Sri Lankan armed forces has in the past strengthened diaspora support for the LTTE and produced a commensurate increase in financial contributions to the cause (Fair 2005: 141; Sengupta 2000). Although the LTTE relies on numerous sources and mechanisms for raising money,[7] Internet technology allows a growing number of individuals and organizations to transfer funds rapidly via credit card transactions, and provides an alternative to the informal, paperless moneylending systems prevalent in many developing states.

'Tamilnet.com,' one of the most comprehensive and technologically advanced Websites dedicated to Tamil affairs, projects a transnational Tamil identity, although the Website's coverage focuses almost exclusively on Tamils in Sri Lanka and those of Sri Lankan origin residing in the diaspora. 'Tamilnet.com' combines both news reports and longer feature articles on the political and socio-economic conditions facing Tamils in the north and east of Sri Lanka as they engage in an 'armed struggle' against the Sri Lankan state and military forces. Text and photographs are interspersed throughout the Website, which also contains a small archive of photographs dating back to 1997. A number

---

[6]The Tamil Rehabilitation Organization was set up by the LTTE in 1985 to assist Sri Lankan Tamil refugees in Tamil Nadu, India. Subsequently, TRO turned its attention to humanitarian relief operations in the north and east of Sri Lanka. The TRO claims to be a humanitarian non-governmental organization, though it is widely acknowledged to be closely linked to the LTTE (Source: Human Rights Watch, http://hrw.org/reports/2004/srilanka).

[7]For a summary of LTTE's funding sources and operations, see Byman et al. (2001: 49–54).

of photographs display stark images of victims of violence and the almost routine chaos of daily life in a war zone. The state's atrocities against Tamils and the violence perpetrated by Sinhalese nationalists are catalogued extensively on the Website, but there are no references to the LTTE's brutal tactics employed against political rivals and fellow Tamils, including the practice of recruiting child soldiers.

In an attempt to be 'fair and balanced', 'Tamilnet.com' includes reports on ceremonial occasions, for example, independence day celebrations in Colombo, as well as events or issues pertaining to Sinhalese organizations in Sri Lanka and abroad. Such reports, however, invariably focus on extremist agendas and polemics, while giving short shrift to civil society organizations engaged in peace-building initiatives on both sides of the conflict.

'Eelam.com' and 'Tamilnet.com,' nominally located outside of Sri Lanka, reflect the LTTE's transnational organizational structure and the broad scope of its operations in the Jaffna peninsula where the LTTE functions as a de facto government. The LTTE's network covers five continents, with representatives, offices, and front organizations located in several dozen countries (Jeganathan 1998: 525). Given the variations in the LTTE's organizational capacity—especially in light of the crackdown on the LTTE and affiliated groups in North America and Europe after 9/11—the Internet remains an efficient medium for connecting diaspora Tamils with the 'homeland' and creating a shared cultural and political space that is defined by the LTTE's nationalist ideology and sustained by its narrative of violence, sacrifice, and mourning.

Tamils, who commemorate LTTE 'freedom fighters' on 'National Heroes Day' or 'Black Tigers Day,' are likely to find descriptions and photographs of these events, held at multiple locations, posted on the Web, together with speeches delivered by Prabhakaran and LTTE cadres to mark the occasion, and portraits of LTTE fighters dressed in military fatigues who gave their lives for 'the freedom of the Tamil nation'. The Internet connects diverse—and dispersed accounts—of 'Heroes Day' rituals to form a common narrative among Sri Lankan Tamils, many of whom support the nationalist struggle but do not necessarily endorse the LTTE's leadership or its protracted involvement in political violence (Gunaratna 2003).

By establishing a significant Internet presence, the LTTE has been quite successful in both circumventing the Sri Lankan state's monopoly of information and countering its media strategies aimed at weakening the LTTE's power and support at home and abroad. One measure of the LTTE's successful Web-based communications strategy is that major news agencies, for example, the BBC or *The Hindu* newspaper published in Chennai, India, frequently cite 'Tamilnet.com' or 'Eelam.com' sources in their reports (Ranganathan 2003). Reliance on the LTTE's Internet sources, however, is more likely a function of foreign correspondents' limited access to conflict areas rather than an endorsement of the LTTE's politics and perspectives.

The LTTE and TRO used the Internet effectively to solicit aid and assistance from the Tamil diaspora in the aftermath of the tsunami that devastated South Asia in December 2004. LTTE and TRO Websites functioned as conduits for exchanging information about tsunami victims and their families, the destruction of infrastructure and economic livelihood, and the relief efforts of the Sri Lankan government and international agencies. Bypassing traditional media channels and the Sri Lankan government, the LTTE and TRO directly appealed to ethnic bonds and the international community for disaster relief, rehabilitation, and reconstruction aid for Tamil areas in the north and east in Sri Lanka.[8] Against a backdrop of severe conflict, the politics of allocating relief and reconstruction aid, too, was played out on the Internet where principally the Sri Lankan government, its coalition partners, and the LTTE sought international support and legitimacy for their goals, which at times seemed to be at odds with the chief objective of addressing the needs of tsunami victims.

NGOs and the Net: Challenging Political Violence

Using formal and informal organizations and communication networks, non-governmental organizations, committed to human rights and humanitarian assistance, challenge the exclusivist ideologies and violent tactics of the Sri Lankan state and the LTTE. Transnational

---

[8] www.eelam.com

in origin and operations, organizations like the Sri Lanka Democracy Forum (SLDF) identify with a human rights 'community that shares a commitment to democratic and pluralistic values'.[9] Presenting itself as a 'global network of activists', the SLDF's principal objective is to focus international attention on the human rights abuses committed by the Sri Lankan government, its security forces, and the LTTE. Working to promote 'inter-ethnic co-existence', and strengthen civil society, the SLDF draws upon the strategic and tactical resources of non-governmental organizations in South Asia, Great Britain, Canada, and the United States to pursue initiatives—for example, 'conflict-sensitive' rebuilding after the tsunami, campaigning against the LTTE's recruitment of child soldiers, and lobbying for minority rights—that require sustained, long-term commitment of resources and personnel.

The SLDF's Website is linked to Human Rights Watch, Amnesty International, and UNICEF, as well as local NGOs such as University Teachers for Human Rights based in Jaffna, among others. For Human Rights Watch and Amnesty International, Web-based advocacy is crucial for advancing their mandate to investigate, monitor, and address human rights violations in all regions of the world. Combining a transnational knowledge base with local activism, Human Rights Watch, for instance, has collaborated on several initiatives aimed at exposing human rights abuses, securing individual and group rights in Sri Lanka, and limiting overseas funding of insurgency groups.

Using the Internet to publicize human rights violations or persuade sceptics among non-state and state actors, however, can sometimes produce unintended consequences and risks, as Human Rights Watch discovered in December 2004, when it organized fora in Toronto and London to present its report on the recruitment and use of child soldiers by the LTTE in Sri Lanka. Specifically for Sri Lankan Tamils, both events were disrupted by presumed LTTE supporters who threatened to expose the identities of local Tamils working with Human Rights Watch, which published the report on its Website, condemning in particular the LTTE's coercive tactics. The LTTE and its sympathizers, in turn, posted on the Web the names and addresses

---

[9]www.lankademocracy.org

of Tamil activists and participants in the events in Toronto and London to intimidate their critics and stifle public dissent.[10]

Diaspora and Development

As the examples illustrate, state and non-state actors alike, seek to harness the knowledge-base, material resources, and technical skills of diaspora populations in order to achieve their goals. The rhetoric, strategies, and tactics adopted by the LTTE, the Sri Lankan state, and the SLDF are explicitly political. The Lanka Academic Network (LACNET), in contrast, seemingly eschews an overtly political message or agenda.[11] Evolving from an 'electronic gathering of people from and/or interested in Sri Lanka', LACNET's Website is located at the University of Western Ontario in Canada, while its financial officer operates out of Silver Spring, Maryland. Supervised by a board of directors drawn from the academy and industry in the United States, Canada, and the United Kingdom, LACNET's objectives, according to the Website, are two-fold: one, to develop worldwide electronic networks for disseminating news and information about Sri Lanka; and two, to turn Sri Lanka into a 'technologically advanced society' by promoting the use of computers and the Internet, especially among students in rural areas and in urban communities lacking resources and infrastructure.

Formed in 1991, LACNET solicits over the Internet financial contributions, material support, and volunteers in Sri Lanka and abroad to set up its projects for computer and Internet literacy, which, it claims, traverse ethnic lines and areas of conflict. It has ostensibly secured funding from the Sri Lankan government via the University Grants Commission as well as hardware from the World Bank to set up information technology centres in Sri Lanka.

From what appears to have been a series of relatively small information technology and education projects, LACNET quickly expanded its Internet operations to launch a 'tsunami relief effort' designed to raise and coordinate donations, medical supplies, and

---

[10]See http://hrw.org/English/docs/2004/12/20/Canada
[11]See http://www.lacnet.org

volunteer networks for rebuilding tsunami-devastated areas in 2005. Detailed reports of donor contributions and disbursement of funds are posted on LACNET's Website, although in the absence of corroborating evidence it is almost impossible to verify the accuracy of the numbers.[12] Through volunteers' blogs and videos circulated on the Internet, LACNET chronicles its relief efforts in Sri Lanka.

Strikingly apolitical in tone and content, individual blogs and LACNET's mission statement completely ignore the contentious politics of reconstruction involving Tamils, the Sri Lankan government, and Muslim communities residing largely in the eastern part of the state, not to mention the challenges facing non-governmental organizations when providing humanitarian assistance and disaster relief in the context of a civil war. Whether the omission of politics in this instance is aimed at striking a 'non-partisan' posture, believing that it would facilitate LACNET's operations in a conflict zone, is unclear. In the absence of more detailed information and analysis, however, it is difficult to gauge the efficacy of LACNET's approach toward achieving its objectives. Nonetheless, the examples of LACNET—and similar diaspora-funded projects and organizations— remind us of how technology, capital, and diaspora activism are intersecting in powerful ways in contemporary politics. First, by funding and organizing projects to promote computer literacy in Sri Lanka and elsewhere, diaspora organizations like this are both widening and deepening the communications processes and networks that form the nexus between diaspora populations and homelands.

Second, relatively inexpensive and readily accessible information communications technology helped LACNET to advance swiftly from a loosely based diaspora network interested in developing Sri Lankan students' computer skills to an organization involved in a far more complicated disaster relief operation. Finally, the Sri Lankan diaspora's long-standing engagement with homeland politics—and its vital role in tsunami relief operations—has refocused international attention on how diaspora members and organizations could play a more active role, politically and economically, in conflict transformation initiatives

---

[12]See http://www.lacnet.org/payment/budget.html

and post-conflict reconstruction (Zunzer 2004: 11–15, 22–26, 29–30). The 2002 ceasefire agreement between the LTTE and the Sri Lankan government, though rather tenuous, provides opportunities for increasing diaspora involvement and investment in rebuilding infrastructure, educational institutions, and health care facilities in the north-east. Despite the financial support and active participation of a growing number of diaspora members in reconstruction projects, there is little evidence to suggest that permanent return ranks high on their list of priorities.

CONCLUSION

The two cases demonstrate how non-state actors with few traditional sources of information or funding can make use of the Internet and the World Wide Web to amplify their message and command a global audience. Combining text, graphics, and sound, the World Wide Web is a cost-effective, versatile tool for communications, sharing vast quantities of information, and for political organization. Advanced information technology allows individuals and organizations, like the LTTE and its front organizations, to craft sophisticated multimedia campaigns for promoting a semblance—at least online—of political legitimacy. Both after the ceasefire of 2002 and following the tsunami in 2004, for example, the LTTE's media strategy aimed at casting the organization as an equal partner in multilateral fora, especially with international donor agencies. At the same time, local civil society organizations, many with limited resources, depend on the Internet and Web for informing international public opinion, rapidly mobilizing transnational organizational support, and gaining legitimacy in a complex international environment, where state sovereignty and security are vigorously asserted and defended in the face of multiple challenges from within and outside of territorial boundaries.

Generally, a ubiquitous Web presence and visibility alone is unlikely to translate into a commensurate degree of influence and political power. Each of the non-state actors and organizations we have examined employ multiple strategies and tactics for political mobilization. The Internet, though a crucial instrument for sustaining political identities, activating international responses to humanitarian crises, and fund-raising, cannot fully replace grassroots organizing and advocacy. As we see, community centres, *gurdwaras*, forums, and conventions provide vital spaces and opportunities for building coalitions and promoting activism at the local and transnational level.

Political identities are formed and mobilized through a long, complex process that is dynamic and responsive to changing threats and opportunities. The Internet, as a medium for information gathering and communication, can help ethnic entrepreneurs or leaders of social movements articulate collective interests and present goals, strategies, and tactics to varied audiences. However, the Internet is rarely the chief venue or mechanism for shaping new or dramatically different identities; rather, the Websites of nationalist movements, diaspora groups, or civil society organizations largely reflect and reinforce identities that are conceived of and formed in offline social and political contexts.

Although diaspora members rely heavily on the Internet for a wide range of cultural, social, and political interactions and services, it is often unclear how these connections are transformed into specific forms of political participation or collective action on- or offline. Except for anecdotal evidence, there is little systematic analysis available on the efficacy of Web-based political organization. Even though accessing and using the Internet has become relatively uncomplicated and inexpensive, especially with wireless connections and a combining of Internet and cellphone technology, it is important, nonetheless, to note that the Internet may well privilege the views of individuals and organizations with the resources and wherewithal to acquire and utilize information technologies.

By seizing the opportunities created by contemporary processes and mechanisms of globalization, specifically capital, technology, and communications, Sikh and Sri Lankan Tamil transnational organizations have shown how diaspora members can participate in and impact the politics of home countries. The technological innovations of the current phase of globalization, moreover, have made it possible for nationalist movements to adopt decentralized organizational structures that complicate international efforts aimed at disrupting networks of political and financial support for insurgency groups involved in armed conflicts.

The rapid mobility and flow of capital, technology, and information has encouraged the belief that state authority and control over its territory is eroding and that its boundaries have become increasingly porous, perhaps even irrelevant. A closer examination of international security discourse and policies after 9/11 suggests a somewhat different reality. Passports and visas, two of the primary forms of state control of citizens and borders, have been invested with new powers to control the free movement of peoples, as host states have become increasingly reluctant to allow foreign nationalist movements to operate on their territories. Simultaneously, fearing the lethal power of 'cyber sanctuaries' (Wolfowitz 2004) that seemingly allow terrorist organizations to operate with impunity, governments everywhere are seeking to monitor and control information and communication technologies, especially those associated with the Internet. Whereas threats to societal and state security are manifold, diverse, and genuine, surveillance and censorship of Internet use and content does not even begin to address the underlying sources of insecurity in world politics today, nor is it likely to bring about a significant reduction in incidents of political violence. It will, however, seriously limit opportunities for progressive politics and democratic empowerment—popular panaceas for armed conflicts, especially when terrorism is the weapon of choice.

BIBLIOGRAPHY

Anderson, Benedict (1994). *Exodus. Critical Inquiry*, 20(2), pp. 327.

Axel, Brian Keith (2002). The Diasporic Imaginary. *Public Culture*, 14(2), pp. 414.

Byman, Daniel, Peter Chalk, Bruce Hoffman, William Rosenau, and David Brannan (2001). *Trends in Outside Support for Insurgent Movements*. Santa Monica, CA: RAND.

Cheran, R. (2004). Diaspora Circulation and Transnationalism as Agents for Change in the Postconflict Zones of Sri Lanka. Policy paper submitted to the Berghoff Foundation for Conflict Management, Berlin.

Crossette, Barbara (2004). India's Sikhs: Waiting for Justice. *World Policy Journal*, 21(2), pp. 76–77.

Dogra, Chander Suta (2004). The Idea in Repose. *Outlook*, 26 May.

Ensaaf Dispatch (2004). August, http://www.ensaaf.org

Esman, Milton J. (1994). *Ethnic Politics*. Ithaca, NY: Cornell University Press.

Fair, C. Christine (2005). Diaspora Involvement in Insurgencies: Insights from the Khalistan and Tamil Eelam Movements. *Nationalism and Ethnic Politics*, 11, pp. 141.

Fugelrud, Oivind (1999). *Life on the Outside: The Tamil Diaspora and Long Distance Nationalism*. London: Pluto Press.

———— (2001), Time and Space in the Sri Lanka–Tamil Diaspora. *Nations and Nationalism*, 7(2), pp. 205.

Gourevitch, Philip (2005). Tides of War. *New Yorker*, 1 August.

Guardian (2005). Full Text: The Prime Minister's Statement on Anti-Terror Measures. 5 August, http://politics.guardian.co.uk/terrorism/story

Gunaratna, Rohan (2003). Sri Lanka: Feeding the Tamil Tigers. In Karen Ballentine and Jake Sherman, eds., *Political Economy of Armed Conflict: Beyond Greed and Grievance*, pp. 201–2. Boulder, CO: Lynne Rienner.

Jeevamanoharan, Pradeepa and Chamindika Wanduragla (2001). *Samar*, No. 14, Fall/Winter 2001.

Jeganathan, P. (1998. eelam.com: Place, Nation, and Imagi-Nation in Cyberspace. *Public Culture*, 10(3), pp. 525.

Kaldor-Robinson, Joshua (2002). The Virtual and the Imaginary: The Role of Diasporic New Media in the Construction of a National Identity during the Break-up of Yugoslavia, *Oxford Development Studies*, 30(2).

Kapur, Rajiv A. (1986). *Sikh Separatism: The Politics of Faith*. London: Allen and Unwin.

McDowell, Christopher (1996). *A Tamil Asylum Diaspora: Sri Lanka Migration, Settlement, and Politics in Switzerland*. Providence, RI: Berghahn Books.

Mills, Kurt (2002). Cybernations: Identity, Self-determination, Democracy and the 'Internet Effect' in the Emerging Information Order. *Global Studies*, 16(1), pp. 69–87.

Nayar, Kuldip and Khushwant Singh (1984). *Tragedy of Punjab: Operation Bluestar and After*. New Delhi: Vision Books.

Ranganathan, Maya (2003). Potential of the Net to Construct and Convey Ethnic and National Identities: Comparison of the Use in the Sri Lankan Tamil and Kashmir Situations. *Asian Ethnicity*, 4(2), pp. 276.

Sageman, Marc (2004). *Understanding Terror Networks*. Philadelphia, PA: University of Pennsylvania Press.

Sengupta, Somini (2000). Canada's Tamils Work for a Homeland From Afar. *New York Times*, 16 July.

Shain, Yossi and Martin Sherman (2001). Diasporic Transnational Financial Flows and their Impact on National Identity. *Nationalism and Ethnic Politics*, 7(4), pp. 1–36.

Sheffer, Gabriel (2003). *Diaspora Politics: At Home Abroad*. New York: Cambridge University Press.

Singh, Amardeep (1999a). Sovereign Cybernation of Sikh Diaspora@K300. *Samar*, 12, http://www.samarmagazine.com

Singh, Gurharpal (1999b). A Victim Diaspora? The Case of the Sikhs. *Diaspora*, 8(3), pp. 301–4.

Tatla, Darshan Singh (1999). *The Sikh Diaspora: The Search for Statehood*. Seattle: University of Seattle Press.

Tully, Mark and Satish Jacob (1985). *Amritsar: Mrs. Gandhi's Last Battle*. London: Jonathan Cape.

Wayland, Sarah (2004). Ethnonational Networks and Transnational Opportunities: The Sri Lankan Tamil Diaspora. *Review of International Studies*, 30(3), pp. 405–26.

Weimann, Gabriel (2004). www.terror.net: How Modern Terrorism Uses the Internet. Special Report No. 116, United States Institute of Peace, Washington, DC, March.

Wolfowitz, Paul (2004). Prepared Statement for the House Armed Services Committee. Washington, DC, August, http://www.dod.mil/faq/comment.html

Zunzer, Wolfram (2004). Diaspora Communities and the Civil Conflict Transformation. Berghoff Occasional Paper NO. 26, September http://www.berghoff-center.org

Citizens' Initiatives in South Asia: Lessons from the Indo–Pak Conflict

CHETAN KUMAR*

INTRODUCTION

Citizens' initiatives for peace—also referred to as Track II diplomacy—as well as commentary and analyses on such initiatives have seen tremendous growth in South Asia over the past fifteen years. Both the initiatives and the commentaries have varied significantly in terms of quality and impact.

In Nepal citizens' initiatives have had little impact on the obdurate determination of the royal government and the Maoist insurgency to resolve differences through violent civil conflict and to continue to abort repeated attempts towards a ceasefire. Nepal is now on the verge of becoming a failed state (*Economist* 2004). In Sri Lanka the Norway-supported diplomatic peace track has not been underpinned by a wider foundation for peace among a larger group of actors and stakeholders, and the fragile *entente* between the government and the LTTE has recently appeared shaky at best, some valiant efforts by citizens' groups notwithstanding. More so than recent efforts by human

*The author works with an agency of the United Nations. The views expressed in this article are strictly his own, and do not reflect any official positions of a UN department or agency.

agents, the tsunami of 2004 could unblock an otherwise deadlocked peace process (Balachanddran 2005).

Arguably, the most prominent impact of citizens' diplomacy has been on the Indo–Pak dispute over Kashmir, with a number of highly visible initiatives making waves in the global media. However, progress in this area has also coincided with the aftermath of the terrorist attacks on the US in 2001, the rapid expansion of the Indian economy—including as a factor in US politics and economics—over the past five years, and the fortuitous and simultaneous ascendancy of technocrats as prime ministers in both countries. Hence, while increased and visible citizens' diplomacy correlates with better Indo–Pak relations, it is difficult to draw precise causal links among a number of these contiguous phenomena, and to identify such diplomacy as a significant factor.

In light of this, this article will offer a brief analysis of some of the achievements and drawbacks of citizen's initiatives between India and Pakistan, and then identify therein some pointers for the future prospects for such initiatives. Pointers will also be provided for improving the prospects of such initiatives for the consolidation of peace in both Sri Lanka and Nepal.

TAXONOMY

The terms 'citizens' initiatives' and 'Track II diplomacy', often used interchangeably, have been used to refer to at least three types of related but distinct phenomena:

1. attempts by citizens' groups to forge links and relationships across the borders of states or groups in mutual conflict;
2. attempts by analysts and scholars from across various borders to develop—via a network of think-thanks or research institutions supported by counterparts in the developed world—common policy prescriptions and proposals for building and consolidating peace; and
3. attempts by non-governmental or international entities to develop, often with the backing of state parties and the informal cognizance of parties to conflict, 'back channels' to negotiation where official processes are deadlocked.

While representing different objectives and formats for action, various manifestations of these phenomena have all shared two common elements: first, they have often been catalysed by the very same individuals, often journalists or scholars of some repute; second, they have, until recently, had very little access to the jealously guarded bastions of foreign or domestic policy making, where terms such as 'non-governmental organizations' or 'civil society' continued to be viewed with suspicion. This has often limited their effectiveness. In fact, the recent successes of all three types of initiatives may owe more to changes in the global context than to their otherwise considerable intrinsic worth. The concluding section of this article will offer some suggestions as to how these types of initiatives could work closer together in effecting change, and the degree to which a certain type of initiative may be more relevant in a particular situation.

One type of initiative that has not been seen in South Asia with same frequency involves what has been generically referred to as 'multi-stakeholder dialogue'. In this process different groups and sectors across or within borders of countries attempt to build consensus on divisive issues through a series of steps involving mutual learning and confidence building. Official actors are often represented by duly empowered proxies in such processes, the results of which constitute a national template or for further reform action. Such processes played a critical role in the democratic transitions in Latin America, and in the ending of civil wars in that region (World Bank 2000). Among the more notable dialogue processes in recent experience are the Gran Dialogo Nacional that accompanied the Guatemalan peace process, the constitutional dialogue that yielded post-apartheid South Africa in 1994, the national conference that led to Benin's surprisingly resilient democracy in 1990, and the Afghan *loya jirga* that led to the recent return of constitutional order—however shakily—in that country.

Neither of the two major situations of internal conflict in South Asia—Nepal and Sri Lanka—have seen multi-stakeholder dialogues or systematic attempts thereof. In fact, attempts towards ceasefires and peace talks have repeatedly involved only the government and the Maoists, and pointedly left out both the political parties as well as organized civil society (Bose 2004). Similarly, while the prime minister's office in Sri Lanka and a select group in the LTTE have provided the primary basis for the Norwegian-supported peace process, no commensurate process has engaged a wider group of stakeholders who are in a significant position to affect the prospects for peace, including political parties, Buddhist religious organizations, and the Muslim communities of the north-east.

While the backdrop to the recent progress in Indo–Pak talks includes several sustained dialogue efforts, these have involved particular groups or actors—businessmen, scholars, retired government officials, parliamentarians, media persons, etc.—as opposed to being multi-stakeholder dialogues. One factor that has limited the possibility of wider dialogue, especially among those within and outside officialdom, is the lack of common tools, aptitudes, skills, and a shared epistemology for such efforts.

PROGRESS IN INDO–PAK TALKS: BRIEF REPRISE OF CITIZENS' INITIATIVES

To the extent that a number of exhaustive accounts of Indo–Pak citizens' initiatives already exist (Waslekar 1995), this article will not attempt to repeat them. Some highlights, however, are provided.

The most sustained Track II initiative—and the one best approximating a sustained multi-stakeholder dialogue—has been the Neemrana Initiative, which was launched in 1991 with the support of the Ford Foundation and other private contributors, and has involved Indian and Pakistani scholars as well as retired military officers and diplomats. In the strained South Asian environment, it is a tribute to this effort that it has in fact managed to continue and outlast major downturns, such as the tensions leading to and resulting from the Kargil conflict. The core group of participants has constituted a community referred to as the Neemrana Group that meets twice a year to offer shared perspectives to Indian and Pakistani policy-makers on common peace and security challenges. In the aftermath of the relaunch of the Indo–Pak dialogue between Prime Minister Manmohan Singh and President Musharraf, the Neemrana Group met in New Delhi in October 2004 to discuss options for the resolution of the Kashmir issue, and proposed Andorra as a model, where France and Spain—who have traditionally both claimed the principality—jointly guarantee its defence and finances, but allow it autonomy on internal matters (Mustafa).

While the Neemrana Initiative has promoted contacts at the elite level, similar dialogue efforts have also occurred at other levels. The Pakistan–India Peoples' Forum for Peace and Democracy remains the most significant, as well as the best known among these, having systematically promoted cross-border visits by groups of activists, parliamentarians, business and media persons, and common people. Established in 1994, the Forum held its most recent meeting in Lahore in Pakistan in 2004, which was attended by a typically-sized group of about seventy-five delegates. Most meetings have focused on a range of issues, from strategic questions concerning the resolution of the Kashmir imbroglio to day-to-day concerns of common citizens unable to easily visit relatives on either side of the border. While recent meetings have been held with greater ease given the thaw in Indo–Pak relations, earlier meetings of the Forum encountered far greater obstacles from hostile governments and radical nationalists on each side. For instance, a radical nationalist had filed an unsuccessful 'public interest' lawsuit against a meeting of the Forum in Bangalore in 2000, claiming that the presence of individuals from Pakistan would disrupt civic peace. In persisting against these obstacles, the Forum has caught the public imagination and that of the regional and international media (its chairpersons have been awarded the prestigious Magsaysay Award), and has been essential in demonstrating that the demand for a resolution of outstanding Indo–Pak disputes is not limited to an elite intellectual community.

The launch of the Forum had been preceded by a candlelight vigil at the India–Pakistan border near Wagah, on the forty-seventh anniversary of the two countries' independence, which brought together an estimated 10,000 people on both sides of the border to send a message of friendship. Similar border vigils have become more common over the past decade, helping send a strong message to both governments that peacemaking might be a safe political proposition.

A similar role has been played by the Women's Initiative for Peace in South Asia, whose leadership and membership includes prominent women from several walks of public life from a number of South Asian countries (Dev Rai 2000). Other noteworthy initiatives include the Indian Pakistani Soldiers' Initiative for Peace, which has been formed by retired military officers, often drawing on a shared educational heritage at locations such as St. Stephen's College in New Delhi, Kinnaird College in Lahore, or the Doon School in Dehradun during pre-partition days (Chadha Behera 2003), and the well-publicized cross-border visits by Indian and Pakistani parliamentarians in June 2003. Anti-nuclear activists on both sides have also formed cross-border coalitions. For instance, the Coalition on Nuclear Disarmament and Peace (CNDP) was launched at a convention in New Delhi in 2000 that brought together Indian and Pakistani activists. Together with the Pakistan Peace Coalition (formed in 1999), the CNDP subsequently organized the Pakistan India Peoples' Solidarity Conference in New Delhi in July 2001. The declaration of the Conference was endorsed by nearly 250 similar organizations and coalitions from both countries, thus providing a concrete pointer of a growing acceptance of the idea of lasting peace between both countries (Bidwai 2004). Indeed, contrary to the charged atmosphere of the early 1990s, the revival of cricket matches between the two countries in 2004 (Economist.com 2004) was met with widespread public acclaim, and immediately followed by a plethora of 'friendship' matches, many involving schools and children from both sides of the border.

Track II efforts have not been limited to India and Pakistan alone. A number of sub-regional associations linking media persons, writers, businessmen, and scholars have been formed, with prominent think-tanks such as the Regional Centre for Strategic Studies in Colombo, the Bangladesh Institute for International and Strategic Studies in Dhaka, the Centre for Policy Research in New Delhi, and the International Institute for Strategic Studies serving as focal points for these associations and networks. While they have taken significant strides towards the creation of a sub-regional discourse on peace and security issues, these networks and associations have had very limited impact on the lasting resolution of actual internal conflicts. On a wider scale (barring a small left-oriented intelligentsia), the growing Indian middle class has not, for instance, evinced the same degree of enthusiasm for addressing the suppurating conflicts in the country's north-east, or addressing more systematically the needs of the aboriginal and tribal populations in parts of the country whose marginalization leads to sporadic outbreaks of violence, as they have for nuclear disarmament or Indo–Pak peace. All of a sudden, due to a profound confluence of geopolitical, sociological, economic, and political factors, being anti-nukes and pro-peace is 'cool' in a way that being pro-*dalit* or pro-*adivasi* might not yet be.

ANALYSIS

The brief reprise offered leads to the central question: is the efflorescence and visibility of citizens' initiatives, as well as a greater official tolerance for them, a function of the wider changes in the Indo–Pak relationship, or has it played a role in bringing about these changes? In order to better understand this issue, a number of key elements of context should be mentioned. In this regard, the article also proposes a number of tentative observations that, if further developed by students of this issue, could yield greater insights into the phenomenon of citizen diplomacy in South Asia.

Both India and Pakistan have experienced significant paradigm shifts in foreign and international policy during the past decade and a half. India's shifts have arguably been precipitated by its burgeoning economy and Pakistan's by the impact of the aftermath of the terrorist attacks on the US in 2001. The relationship between economic growth and greater public demands for peace might not, however, be as straightforward as some might assume.

Analysts have traditionally assumed that countries with higher economic stakes are less likely to wage war, given the greater risk of ensuing economic loss. Historically, however, economic growth and surpluses have increased states' ability to aggressively pursue or defend their interests, including through military means if necessary. Indian nationalists have repeatedly pointed out that India's growing foreign exchange reserves should permit it to easily outspend Pakistan into bankruptcy in the case of a prolonged war (an argument partially borne out by the fact that the Kargil conflict, while costly in human lives, did not significantly affect the Indian stock markets or the overall state of the Indian economy).

Economic growth does, however, affect the prospects for peace and war in other, indirect, ways. Four possible factors pertaining to India are presented below for further research.

First, rapid economic growth, resulting to a significant extent from the explosion of the information technology industry, has both increased the ranks of the upper and middle classes, as well as the degree to which their attitudes and perceptions—especially those of the younger generation—are shaped by an 'Internetworked' global culture. For the MTV generation in particular, support for causes such as nuclear disarmament and Indo–Pak peace might constitute, somewhat anachronistically, elements of the same packaged 'hip' lifestyle that also includes patronage of fast food restaurants and rap music (this might explain why young Indian activists who march for nuclear disarmament are far less likely to be aware of the several violent insurgencies in the country's north-east). While the 'heavy lifting' on border vigils and other forms of activism might still be done by left-oriented organizations, the latter are now more likely to find support from the urban *nouveau riche* than in the 1980s.

Second, the Indian middle class has witnessed an explosion of a phenomenon generic to its counterparts in other 'middle-income' countries, that is, the small-scale family mutual fund account. While returns on these accounts are not affected by sporadic outbursts of Indo–Pak conflict, the government's macro-economic policies, especially large current and trade account deficits, are likely to affect flows of foreign investment into Indian markets, and hence returns on shares and other investments. Voters are, therefore, more likely to support governments that pursue better macro-economic policies, as well as the policies themselves. Given the degree to which this issue has been commented upon in the Indian media, many middle-class voters are likely to be aware that a reduction in India's disproportionately large defense expenditures could certainly contribute to more balanced finances.

Third, the economic self-confidence created by an expanding economy is likely to cause the business and political elite to set their sights beyond backyard conflicts. Many Indian nationalists consider a permanent seat for India on the UN Security Council to be a far more desirable price than giving Pakistan a military battering, especially since the nuclear stalemate between the two countries has clearly meant that the Kashmir issue cannot be resolved militarily. Similarly, rapidly growing Indian corporations are more likely to see India's neighbours, with their linguistic and cultural affinities, as potential markets rather than as enemies or minor pawns to be destabilized. The extraordinary push from South Asia's business community for a common market is testimony to this change. In addition, corporations are also likely to be concerned by the negative image conveyed to potential investors by perennial conflict in the region, even though such conflict may have little short-term economic impact.

Fourth, rapid economic growth is also likely to precipitate equally rapid changes—for the better as well as worse—in people's lives. While certain sectors of the Indian economy, most visibly the farmers, have borne the brunt of recent reforms, including the reduction of subsidies, others have seen their fortunes rise dramatically. Yet others, often among the lower middle classes, have become increasingly cognizant of the gulf in conspicuous consumption that separates them from the more fortunate sectors. Initial analyses of the voting patterns in the 2004 elections in India have revealed that in most instances voters punished governments and officials that they perceived as having let them down economically, nationalist rhetoric and the 'India shining' spin notwithstanding (in contrast, and ironically, many lower-income voters in the US elections later last year, and especially those whose incomes had seen precipitous drops since 2001, voted for the incumbent on nationalistic and religious grounds). Even in Gujarat, voters in districts that had seen heavy anti-Muslim violence punished the ruling BJP for the flight of investment from these areas. Given the almost obsessive economic focus of the Indian electorate, the new Manmohan Singh government can be forgiven for appearing to be in a hurry to settle matters with Pakistan, and move on with the business of growing the economic pie.

The growing constituency for peace in Pakistan has been prompted by an entirely different set of factors. Since this modus operandi for maintaining social peace was first perfected in the 1980s, segments of the Pakistani elite have used the lure of *jihadist* adventures abroad, in a manner similar to their counterparts in Saudi Arabia, as a safety valve for popular frustration over their economic and political failings. Public perceptions of an Islamic state under siege from non-believers have also been used to sustain internal cohesion. Several recent factors, as identified later for further exploration, have interrupted this dynamic, however.

First, the Musharraf government has actually shown a far greater recognition of the country's dire political and economic straits than its predecessors, and has launched and sustained a series of significant reform initiatives. This has boosted investor confidence as well as economic growth, although on a much smaller scale than in India, and prompted some of the same socio-economic results, including a growing middle class able to 'Internetwork' with a global hip-hop culture, as well as with similarly engaged counterparts in India. Indeed, since the advent of satellite television in South Asia in the early 1990s, a regional pop culture has been emerging. Musicians travel across borders performing and recording on either side of the India–Pakistan border. Many of the songs that have been topping regional charts in the last few years, have nothing to do with global hip-hop. They are homespun in one of two ways: either they are remixes of old Hindi (or other) hits or they are original tracks rooted in folk or classical music.

Second, many Pakistani policy makers appear to be convinced, especially in the aftermath of the Kargil conflict, that a strategy to support a long-term insurgency in Kashmir is just as unlikely to succeed as more conventional warfare. In addition, the insurgents have created a significant 'blow-back' factor, helping to radicalize and destabilize Pakistani politics. Pakistani concerns in this regard were clearly manifested recently in the form of strenuous efforts to keep malcontents from undermining the Afghan presidential election in 2004, and to enable Afghan expatriates in Pakistan to vote in the elections,[1] thus tipping the vote to Karzai.

Third, and perhaps most significantly, Pakistan has come under significant pressure from the US since the terrorist attacks of 2001 to control or eliminate violent groups operating on its soil, including

---

[1]International Organization for Migration, Press Briefing Notes, 17 September 2004.

remnants of formerly Afghan-based Taliban and al-Qaeda units. This pressure has not been without corresponding rewards for compliance; as in the 1980s, Pakistan has received significant economic and military assistance. In order to retain this assistance, however, as well as build momentum from ongoing reforms, Pakistan will need to find a lasting solution to the Kashmir issue, which continues to be a rallying cry for the *jihadists*.

While these factors may have created a greater receptivity for citizens' peace initiatives on the part of both Pakistan as well as India, it is not clear as to what extent ongoing initiatives might have generated this receptivity to begin with. A number of observations can again be outlined here, for further development and validation by interested scholars.

First, Indian and Pakistani foreign policy establishments have traditionally been impervious to inputs from civil society, including from think-tanks and academia, and largely continue to remain so, to the point where the latter have expended more efforts in influencing policy makers in the United States—the only external actor with significant leverage in both countries—to a much greater degree than their own policy makers. The latter view themselves to be a self-contained meritocracy, with little to gain from mingling with less qualified persons. There is no tradition in South Asia of the Washington-type revolving door, wherein officials and diplomats migrate back and forth between government service and academia, thus leading to a cross-fertilization of ideas (Chadha Behera 2003). To the extent that the members of the foreign service, and other elite policy makers, are likely to exchange ideas, and they are more likely to do so through old schoolboy networks centred on institutions such as Doon School and St. Stephen's College than through citizens' initiatives. That the ideas of the Neemrana Group, for instance, have recently found greater receptivity among foreign policy makers in both countries, may be due to the factors already outlined earlier than due to any intrinsic increase in receptivity to citizens' initiatives. The success of the Neemrana Group and select initiatives of this nature might also be due more to the types of individuals that constitute these efforts and their connections to the policy elite than to any generic increase in their possibilities for success.

Second, and given the earlier point, it is unlikely that citizens' initiatives have played a singularly significant role in prompting recent course changes by India and Pakistan. One area where initiatives such as cross-border visits and vigils are likely to have made an important contribution, however, and to a much greater degree than efforts by scholars and think-tanks, is in reassuring authorities in both countries that they might not have to pay a domestic political price for pursuing peace. While citizens' diplomacy has neither generated nor been systematically linked to mass movements in areas such as environment and local empowerment, it has nevertheless—as suggested before— captured the popular imagination. Representations of machismo in Bollywood, for instance, have morphed from gun-toting Rambo-type lyricists who wipe out entire platoons of enemy soldiers single- handedly, to starry-eyed idealists who bravely cross religious and national boundaries to seek out long-separated lovers or family members (and who, if they have to fire a weapon or two in the process, do so at shadowy bin Laden-type figures who are liable to mislead well-meaning Pakistanis and Indians, Hindus and Muslims, both; better still, they win their conflicts over cricket matches!). To put it briefly, citizen's initiatives might have played a significant role in 'humanizing' the other side, as the victims of common enemies and purveyors of instability themselves rather than as the real enemies.

Third, arguably, the scholars, civic activists, and media persons who have systematically promoted a peaceful solution to the Kashmir imbroglio have recently converged around a 'common sense' approach to this solution. In its broadest terms, this solution would leave the boundary question undefined, with the current Line of Control in Kashmir continuing to form a de facto boundary. India and Pakistan would guarantee the security and finances of their respective portions of Kashmir, which would enjoy a unified and autonomous government elected by Kashmiris from both sides of the boundary. A weaker version of this proposal still has India and Pakistan continuing to administer both sides of the boundary as they currently do, and ensuring free movement for the indigenous population across the Line of Control, which would serve as an international boundary (Mattoo 1999). The convergence of segments of elite opinion in both countries around this 'common sense' approach may have helped greatly in demonstrating to policy makers in both countries the viability of a negotiated win–win solution to the imbroglio. It is unlikely, however, that these proposals would have gained their greatly increased currency without the wider precipitating factors suggested earlier.

RECOMMENDATIONS FOR CITIZENS' INITIATIVES ON INDO–PAK RELATIONS

First, the nascent constituencies for peace in both countries remain extremely fragile, and the recent thaw in Indo–Pak relations can easily freeze over due to sudden political developments in either country, especially the opportunistic exploitation of nationalistic sentiments by the political opponents of the current leadership in both countries. Activists, scholars, and other advocates for a peaceful solution to the Indo–Pak issue, therefore, need to translate their enthusiasm into the beginnings of a mass movement. Their messages, campaigns, and deliberations need to be seen and heard at the local and provincial levels, especially through the vernacular media, and via forums at provincial universities instead of the usual round of elite think-tanks and schools. Conclaves at St. Stephen's College or the Indian Institutes for Management need to be mirrored by similar gatherings at the Haryana Agricultural University or Nagpur University. Given that the masses in South Asia tend to be best motivated—to their considerable credit—by material concerns (a fact that genuinely successful mass movements on issues such as dams and forest conservation have cleverly built on), they need to hear of, and debate and discuss, specific ways in which a 'peace dividend' will enhance their personal and professional horizons as well as their pocketbooks.

Second, while Indian think-tanks and networks of scholars have carried out a credible effort for engaging American policy makers, often with the support and encouragement of their counterparts in the US, American diplomats themselves have not made as systematic a use as they can of quasi-academic gatherings to promote creative ideas for the resolution of the Kashmir dispute. Averse as Indian and Pakistani foreign policy makers might be to a systematic engagement with their own constituents, they have always evinced a great interest in engaging their US counterparts, especially through semi-official gatherings such as fora and workshops that feature senior US officials (Shahzad 2004). The US should certainly use such opportunities in a more frequent fashion to provide detailed inputs into the ongoing Indo–Pak dialogue.

Third, government and non-governmental efforts to promote peace in between India and Pakistan have been conspicuous in their lack of focus on building the skills, aptitudes, and orientations of the key stakeholders, from foreign policy makers to political party leaders and parliamentarians, for constructive negotiation and consensus formation. Without the systematic prior acquisition of such skills, stakeholders are likely to continue to engage each other—even if they are persuaded to meet in order to negotiate or build consensus on certain issues—on the basis of skills and aptitudes that are suitable to the prosecution of conflict rather than its resolution. Ironically, in a number of tense and sensitive situations around the world, the United Nations and other international actors have been able to gain entry by initially offering to support all stakeholders in acquiring to certain useful skills, rather than in negotiating on specific issues. Once the latter have achieved a certain degree of knowledge of—and aptitude for—constructive methods for dialogue, as well as a greater appreciation for the win–win possibilities of negotiated solutions, they have then been able to generate dialogue initiatives of their own and invite UN and other international support as appropriate for such initiatives. This approach has led to a greater ownership of, and accountability for, the outcomes from such dialogue processes, and hence enhanced the prospects for lasting peace. Universities in both India and Pakistan, in particular, could play critical roles in providing such skills in a truncated fashion for otherwise busy policy makers and political leaders, and especially as a prelude to specific dialogue efforts.

IMPLICATIONS FOR CITIZENS' INITIATIVES IN NEPAL AND SRI LANKA

Both Nepal and Sri Lanka host a vibrant NGO community, including think-tanks and institutes, that seem to be perennially hosting seminars, with support for external donors, on the resolution and management of conflict. As is well known, these have had little or no impact on the civil conflict in Nepal. While Sri Lanka has had more success with its ceasefire, this may have less to do with civic energy than with a re-evaluation by the strategically sophisticated LTTE leadership of its objectives in the changed geopolitical environment following the terrorist attacks on the United States in September 2001, and with the availability of a donor state party in the form of Norway—with no other stake in the situation than global philanthropy—as a neutral mediator. The limited objectives of the LTTE as opposed to those of the Maoist insurgency in Nepal—independence, or autonomy approximating independence, versus large-scale social and political transformation—might also have contributed to their ability to adjust rapidly to a changing global environment. In addition, the Maoist insurgency's ideological pretensions, as opposed to the LTTE's ruthless pragmatism, have put them militarily at odds with the two international actors with the greatest influence in the country—the US and India. Barring the sudden acquisition of strategic brilliance by the Maoist leadership, and a makeover of their governing ideology from the promotion of Marxism to that of a free market democracy (which will immediately give them a public relations advantage against the tired and evident corruption of the current system), they are likely to continue to be at odds with the powers-that-be.

An additional factor in Sri Lanka, and one worth further exploration, is an evolution of the economy in directions similar to India's. Despite two decades of civil conflict in the north-east, Sri Lanka has sustained one of the highest growth rates in Asia, driven by a motley crew of investments, ranging from *maquiladora*-type factories to tourism and software development. Contrary to the indirect impacts of the Indo–Pak conflict on the Indian economy, however, the LTTE demonstrated in recent years a remarkable capability to attack vital institutions such as airports, and send the economy downwards on brief but intense spirals. The Sri Lankan middle class and the business community have, therefore, been among the most forceful champions of the peace process. Given the fact, however, that they do not yet constitute (and might do so to an even lesser degree in the post-tsunami period) a majority of the population, the country's economic fortunes notwithstanding, they cannot by themselves provide a firm basis for a lasting peace.

The missing ingredient in both countries is, in fact, quite similar, and can be provided by civic organizations in both instances. A key obstacle to a lasting ceasefire, and a sustainable peace process, in Nepal has been the extremely narrow terrain on which the government and the Maoists have engaged each other (International Crisis Group 2003). The brief engagements between the two sides have largely amounted to a flinging of their most extreme positions at each other, with little expert facilitation of the process, and minus any skills on the part of the participants in constructive negotiation or consensus formation that would allow them to conceive of the process any differently than as a game of one-upmanship. More glaringly, none of the other stakeholders in society—especially the political parties and civic organizations—has had its plethora of near-brilliant ideas for a national reformation taken into account during these brief forays into pre-negotiation. Aborted ceasefire talks have, therefore, been devoid not just of style but also of substance.

The government has also steadfastly refused international—especially UN—mediation prompted reportedly by India's fears that such efforts will set a precedent for third party involvement in the Kashmir issue. The continuing military aid from India and the US has also served to reduce the powerful army's interest in any real negotiations—the establishment of a peace secretariat by the government and Maoist control of three quarters of the country's territory notwithstanding—while the Maoists have been prompted by their ability to roam the countryside at will to persist in the conflict. Neither side, however, has the ability to completely vanquish the other.

In this bleak scenario, non-government organizations can play two types of positive role. First, a regional non-governmental institution with significant credibility with both India and the US could convene a multi-stakeholder dialogue featuring—among others—experts and academics who serve as proxies for the real actors, especially the military. Convened with the purpose of creating a consensual vision for the reform of governance in Nepal, and preceded by exercises that allow participants to acquire the requisite skills for consensus formation, a process of this nature could illustrate the possibilities for the reconciliation of differing views on the further evolution of the Nepalese polity, and also provide a common plan that could serve as a more productive template for the next round of negotiations. In fact, confidence and trust that is informally built through such a process would go a long way towards ensuring greater longevity for the next round of negotiations. In addition, more stakeholders are likely to have a stake in the resulting peace process and its results, and thus work harder to ensure its continuity.

Unfortunately, domestic conditions in Nepal are unlikely to permit such a process to unfold within the country. However, it could conveniently be held in other parts of the region, with Sri Lanka, ironically, offering the best possible locale.

Second, to the extent that a Track II process of this nature could provide an impetus for more successful Track II negotiations, one could hope that a non-governmental institution, with the backing of Norway or similar benefactors, could step up to offer its services. In fact, such initiatives have been briefly tried earlier in Nepal, but without many results. In order to have greater prospects for success, they will first need to be preceded by the wider dialogue detailed earlier.

The major lesson that civic engagement with the Indo–Pak relationship offers is that while modernity may have come to the logistics of officialdom in South Asia (the ubiquitous PC now graces the desk of every self-respecting *babu* in the subcontinent), bureaucratic conceptions of the state and its role with respect to other sectors in society remain mired in antiquity. When change occurs, it is either forced by global exigencies or by societal transformation. The transformation of political and bureaucratic habits that breed conflict into those that sustain peace is, therefore, unlikely to take place at the hands of officials alone, or those who mirror them among sundry insurgent groups. It is only when social sectors sit down together across group divides, with some expert facilitation, to develop common plans and ideas on contentious issues, a 'social pact' if you will, that officialdom is likely to notice and respond, and join them in order to 'boldly go where no bureaucrat has gone before'.

A similar point can be made with regard to Sri Lanka, which certainly does not lack a multitude of very good ideas on the long-term resolution of the issues that led to the Tamil insurgency. While the government in Sri Lanka has taken more steps than its Nepalese counterpart to seek the participation of other sectors in planning the peace, a vital national consensus on key governance questions remains glaringly absent. Though expertly supported by Norway, the peace process between the government and the LTTE belongs to the realm of traditional, albeit informal, high-level diplomacy, and may not be able to generate a wider consensus. Given that top officials on both sides remain inclined to support the peace process despite its fragility and the numerous blockages that define it, the moment is certainly ripe for an enterprising but credible non-governmental entity to support a national envisioning process, wherein different sectors can define a common agenda on vital socio-economic and political issues, including on the thorny question of autonomy or separation for the north-eastern regions. The poignant national moment created by the impact of the tsunami might provide a particularly opportune moment for such a dialogue. A dialogue of this nature does not corner the participants into premature negotiating positions, and allows for the requisite confidence, skills, and aptitudes to be built before the toughest issues are addressed.[2] More vitally, it allows them to acquire and communicate the tools through which they can address future potentially violent disputes without constant recourse to outside intervention, and do so in a participatory and consensual manner. Such capacities are essential so sustaining peace in the long run.

BUILDING AN ARCHITECTURE FOR PEACE IN SOUTH ASIA

The countries of South Asia lack an 'architecture for peace'.[3] By and large, school and university curricula do not include courses on the peaceful management of disputes and consensus formation, and these

---

[2]The Centre for Conflict Resolution of the University of Cape Town in South Africa has developed a methodology that allows diverse stakeholders in tense situations to engage in an interactive process of dialogue that is aimed, in the first instance, at the acquisition of the relevant skills and aptitude rather than the negotiation of specific outcomes. See Odendaal (2002).

[3]The term 'infrastructure for peace' has been coined by Tobi Dress of the United Nations Office in Geneva to indicate similar elements necessary for ensuring lasting peace within and among societies.

skills are not taught as part of the training imparted to administrators, the police, the militaries, or the foreign services in the region. While some curricula might include elements on traditional negotiations, they do not equip public leaders and officials to be able to engage with multiple sets of stakeholders in tense situations in order to build consensus on especially divisive issues. Members of forums where such consensus could be built, from special parliamentary committees and commissions to expert or advisory groups convened by governments to panchayats and other local councils, often lack such skills.[4]

State and local governments throughout the subcontinent lack access to trained mediators, mediation institutions, or networks of mediators when confronted with rising levels of violence or potentially explosive situations. While traditional dispute resolution mechanisms might sporadically be available to village and local councils, they are often overwhelmed by the pace of socio-economic change and the disputes consequently generated. Local governments, including law enforcement officials, have little training or competency in working effectively with civic organizations and community representatives to resolve potentially violent disputes, or to set up common monitoring and protection mechanisms in times of violent stress. The average American's first, second, and last resort in dealing with all disputes— an overused but effective judicial system—is often out of the reach of most South Asians. In sum, the countries of South Asia are highly deficient in those national capacities for conflict prevention, management, and resolution that are vital to ensuring both sustainable peace as well as lasting development.

The setting up of this architecture for peace is not a utopian enterprise. A network of South Asian academic institutions and think-tanks, with modest but sustained resources, could make a significant difference in this area over a five-year period, especially if they target select conflicts or conflict-affected areas, and particular stakeholders

---

[4]An exception, and a model, has been India's National Commission for Women, which has had a degree of success, through a series of public hearings and fora, in building participatory consensus on aspects of the agenda for the advancement of women.

involved in these situations.[5] The ripple effects from such a capacity building enterprise are often quite immediate, as stakeholders who have acquired these begin to apply them to generating dialogues, negotiations, and other consensus building exercises on the issues with which they are engaged. Recent experience suggests that in these situations, where they have taken the leadership on and responsibility—and hence accountability—for these efforts, they are likely to far more effective than external interveners, who can only provide short-run palliatives, or a 'breathing space' from ongoing conflict wherein such capacities can be built. The latter can also provide assistance once national stakeholders have accepted the need for or launched their own initiatives, and then requested such assistance. International development agencies have recently applied this approach with measurable successes in a range of countries with significant histories of tension,[6] and could assist with the development of the architecture for peace in South Asia.

BIBLIOGRAPHY

Balachanddran, P.K. (2005). Annan Hopes Relief Will Boost Peace in Lanka. *Hindustan Times,* 9 January.
Bidwai, Praful (2004). No Peace Without Civil Society. *Frontline,* 21(8), http://www.flonnet.com/fl2118/stories/20040910004511200.htm
Bose, Tapan Kumar (2004). Nepal: Context of Maoist Insurgency. *South Asian Journal,* 5, http://www.southasianmedia.net/Magazine/Journal/nepal_maoistinsurgency.htm
Chadha Behera, Navinita (2003). Need to Expand Track Two Diplomacy. *Asia Times Online,* 16 July, http://www.atimes.com/atimes/South_Asia/EG16DF03.html

---

[5]The South Asian Fellows Program of the Program in Arms Control, Disarmament and International Security (ACDIS) of the University of Illinois at Urbana-Champaign, directed at that time by Dr. Stephen P. Cohen with the support of the Ford Foundation, created in the early 1990s a network of alumni from different political and civic sectors in the region who had acquired some basic skills in conflict resolution. Subsequently, this network has been underpinned by various regional institutes, and could provide an initial basis for the type of capacity building envisaged here.
[6]Countries in Latin America, the Caribbean, and Southern Africa have received this assistance. Specific details remain confidential, but can be obtained by contacting the author.

Dev Rai, Ranjit (2000). Peace Hinges on Track Two Diplomacy. *Asia Times Online,* 6 April.

Economist (2004). Nepal, a Failing State. 2 December.

Economist. com (2004). All in a Game: The India–Pakistan Cricket Series. 18 Mach, http://www.economist.com/diversions/displayStory.cfm?story_id=2514575

International Crisis Group (2003). Nepal Obstacles to Peace. Asia Report No.; 57, 17 June, http://www.crisisgroup.org/home/index.cfm?id=1644&1=1

Mattoo, Amitabh (1999). Need to Line of Control the International Boundary. *India Abroad,* 9 July.

Mustafa, Seema. Track-Two Floats Andorra Model for J&K. http://www.countrywatch.com/cw_wire.asp?vCOUNTRY= 4&UID=1256713

Odendaal, Andries (2002). The Political Management of Ethnic Conflict in Africa: A Human Needs-based Approach. *Track Two,* 11(4).

Shahzad, Syed Saleem (2004). Keeping the Peace Initiative on Track. *Asia Times Online,* 16 February, http:// www.atimes01-atimes.com/atimes/South_Asia/FB16DF03-html

Waslekar, Sundeep (1995). Track Two Diplomacy in South Asia. ACDIS Occasional Paper, University of Illinois at Urbana-Champaign, June.

World Bank (2000). Experience with National Dialogue in Latin America: Main Lessons from a Roundtable Discussion. International IDEA, November, http://www.idea.int/documents/CDF_Nov 2000.pdf

Disasters in India: Patterns of Institutional Response

C.V. RAGHAVULU

Human beings have benefited from nature. They have also suffered its fury. Natural events like floods, cyclones, storm surges, earthquakes, tsunamis, or droughts occur within the various processes of nature; however, these events become disasters when they affect human lives and livelihoods or disrupt the wider functioning of a community or organization. Some types of human activity also contribute to their intensity. Moreover, some disasters are evidently man-made. With the growth of population, the increasing application of technology, and the disruption of the natural ecosystems, the scope for man-made disasters has been expanding. Disasters also differ in their speed of onset and their incubation period. The trend shows increasing losses from disasters, making people and societies more vulnerable. Living with risk, therefore, becomes an integral part of human existence. Considering the significance of the challenge posed by disasters, the United Nations declared the 1990s as the International Decade for Natural Disaster Reduction (IDNDR) with a view to promote strategies and solutions to reduce risk from natural hazards. Member countries, including India, took a number of initiatives in this regard. The Indian government implemented the policy of upgrading the technological capability for the early warning system for cyclones and river floods. Down the line, at state and local levels, the IDNDR strategy was implemented with mixed results.[1]

Despite the initiatives taken by multinational and national agencies, the international decade for disaster reduction witnessed a dramatic increase in the number of natural disasters and in the loss of human lives and property (ISDR 2002: 5) there has also been a 60 per cent increase in the number of victims dependent on humanitarian aid (Parasuraman and Unnikrishnan 2000: 3), touching 45 million by 2000. A recent study by a UN agency estimates that the number of people at risk has been growing by 70 to 80 million per year (ISDR 2002: 6). During the second half of the twentieth century the costs of disasters have increased fourteen-fold (IFRC 2001: 163). An Indian expert expresses the cynical view that 'continuing disaster impacts on humans reflect the inability of current management policies to reduce vulnerability' of communities (Sapir 2000: 28). In this context, studies of disaster situations and assessment of response from governmental institutions and non-governmental organizations (NGOs) gain priority. Keeping this perspective in view, this article presents a summary of information on the disaster scenario at the macro level, with a focus on major natural disasters that occurred during the last three decades. The nature of institutional response to these disasters is then assessed. At several points the chapter slides into a flashback of the issues and concerns, first raised in the Andhra Cyclone study of Cohen and Raghavulu (1979). In the final section on discussion and conclusions it is noted that several of these issues seem to persist, thereby providing a pattern to institutional response on disasters in India regardless of time, space, or the nature of the event. There have been a few changes for the better, but much has not changed in the politics of disaster.

DISASTER SCENARIO IN THE WORLD AND INDIA

Region-wise data for the period 1991–2000 (IFRC 2001: 182) show that about 39.3 per cent of the world's natural disasters have occurred

---

[1]The author is thankful to Professor B.P.C. Bose of the Department of Political Science & Public Administration of Nagarjana University, Guntur, AP, for his assistance in locating research materials.

in Asia; it is followed by the Americas (27.7 per cent), Europe (14.2 per cent), Africa (14.0 per cent) and Oceania (4.8 per cent).[2] The annual average number of people killed in the world during the period was 66,559 (IFRC 2001) and of them 83.3 per cent were from Asia, followed by the Americas (9.8 per cent), Europe (3.9 per cent), Africa (2.6 per cent), and Oceania (0.4 per cent) (ibid.: 174–79). Among disaster types, droughts/famines killed about 42.1 per cent, cyclones/ wind storms 30.9 per cent, floods 14.7 per cent, earthquakes 8.9 per cent, and other natural hazards 3.4 per cent (ibid.: 183). The annual average number of people affected by disasters in the world is about 211 million, the bulk (89.6 per cent) of whom were in Asia, followed by Africa as a distant second (6.2 per cent), Americas (2.3 per cent), and other regions (1.9 per cent). Floods account for more than two-thirds (68.5 per cent) of the people affected by natural disasters in the world; next are droughts/famines (18.0 per cent), cyclones/wind storms (12 per cent), earthquakes (0.8 per cent), and other natural disasters (0.7 per cent). On average, about 56 million people are affected each year by natural disasters in India. Asia also accounts for most of the people (85.5 per cent) rendered homeless by natural disasters. With an annual average death toll of 27,071 persons, North Korea tops this list of countries. It is followed by Bangladesh (14,775), India (5,913), and China (3,529) (ibid.: 186–96). The annual average estimated damage due to natural disasters for all regions of the world is Rs. 33.8 lakh crores or US$ 786.7 billion (ibid.: 185). Of this, Asia accounts for 50.9 per cent, followed by the Americas (26.4 per cent), Europe (20.9 per cent), Oceania (1.5 per cent), and Africa (0.3 per cent).[3]

The years 2004 and 2005 witnessed the worst of nature's fury, resulting in mega disasters. The Asian Tsunami (December 26, 2004), hurricanes Katrina (August 29, 2005) Rita (September 24, 2005) and

---

[2]There are wide variations in the data, periodicity; and composition of disasters of each of the databases presented by various sources.

[3]The figures are based on averages for the period 1991–2000, and compiled by the International Federation of Red Cross Societies and Red Crescent Societies. See IFRC (2001: 174–96). Given the increase in the number and intensity of natural disasters during 2001–5 (e.g., the Kutch earthquake in India, floods in China, and the Asian tsunami, hurricanes Katrina, Rita and Wilma in the Americas, and the South Asian earthquake), projections of damage would be twice as high for the world as well as Asia compared to averages of the preceding period.

the South-Asian earthquake (October 8, 2005) were the most devastating natural disasters with enormous human and property losses. The Asian Tsunami devoured nearly 300,000 people across 13 countries.

Three hurricanes (Katrina, Rita and Wilma)—which swept in quick succession within a short span of two months—had a cataclysmic effect on countries around the Gulf of Mexico and the southern United States. Hurricane Katrina was the most destructive and the most expensive natural disaster on record in the United States, with cleaning up and recovering costs estimated around US $250 billion. It was also the costliest tropical cyclone in recorded history.

The South Asian earthquake is the most lethal quake on record in this part of South Asia, with estimates of death toll (88,700) and displaced persons (2.5 million) being the highest. While the devastation was more extensive in the Pakistan controlled part of Kashmir, dozens of villages were flattened in the Indian province of Jammu & Kashmir.

Natural hazards are a recurring phenomenon in India and constitute a major source of human misery. However, we lack precise and adequate information about the proportion of each type of disaster, let alone data about the magnitude of losses in each category. Presented in the next section is a brief profile of various types of disasters with a focus on major ones that occurred during the last three decades.

Cyclones, Storm Surges and Tsunamis

The country's 7516 km coastline is continuously whipped by high-velocity winds, especially the east coast states of Orissa, Andhra Pradesh, and Tamil Nadu. From 1891 to 2004 about 560 cyclones/storm surges/tsunamis of varying intensity have ravaged the country. Nearly 80 per cent of them had their origin in the Bay of Bengal and caused maximum devastation in the states of Andhra Pradesh and Orissa. Some of the major cyclones before the twentieth century, with an estimated number of causalities in parentheses are: the Calcutta cyclone of 1737 (300,000), Bandar (Andhra Pradesh) cyclone of 1779 (20,000), Bengal cyclone of 1789 (20,000), Bandar cyclone of October 1864 (30,000), and Bengal cyclone of November 1864 (100,000) (Government of India 1971: 1). During the last three decades, twelve major cyclones/storm surges battered the Andhra coast, resulting in the loss of about 14,000 human lives, 6 million livestock animals, damage to 4.5 million dwellings, and crop damage to 9 million hectares (Subbiah 2004: 150). The estimated cost of the damage is about Rs. 2.46 lakh crores (US$ 56 billion). Although each disaster caused extensive human misery and physical damage, response to the Andhra cyclone of 1977, the Orissa super cyclone of 1999, and the Asian tsunami of 2004 deserve greater attention.

The Andhra Cyclone of 1977

The Andhra cyclone of 1977 generated a storm surge, ranging from 3 to 6 m feet high and about 80 km broad and 24 km deep. It swept the coast of Divi and Bandar *taluk*s of Krishna district around 2.30 p.m., on 19 November 1977. The storm surge was accompanied by a heavy downpour and winds estimated above 200 km. Acting in unison, they swept twenty coastal villages and engulfed fifty others within the core area. The quantity of water that moved from the sea to land mass within 90 minutes was about 27 million cusecs. In the core area of devastation the wall of water moved at a speed of about 30 km per hour. The cyclone and accompanying winds also caused unprecedented devastation in an area of about 600 sq km, affecting about 7.1 million people in 2,302 villages and towns in nine districts. The official count of human lives lost was 9,921. More than a million livestock animals were killed. Nearly a million houses were either destroyed or damaged. Infrastructure also suffered extensive damage. About a quarter million trees were uprooted. The fisherfolk in the coastal villages were the worst affected as most of them lost not only family members, but also their fishing vessels and equipment. The total damage due to the 1977 cyclone was estimated at Rs. 20 billion (US$ 2.2 billion).[4]

The Andhra cyclone is unique in several respects, the magnitude and colossal scale of devastation being only one of them. As Cohen and Raghavulu (1979) analyse, it became a political event embedded with a series of political controversies among various actors: between the Union and the state government over the quantum of aid, the role

---

[4]The exchange rate between US dollar and Indian rupee followed in this paper is the prevailing rate at the time.

of the military, and the performance of the India Meteorological Department (IMD) on the one hand, and the state of preparedness of the state government, the level of response, and the number of casualties on the other; between the ruling and opposition parties in the state over a number of issues; and among various factions within the ruling Congress Party within the state over political issues that had been simmering for quite some time for which the disaster context provided an alibi. Politicization reached its crescendo partly because elections to the state assembly were due within a few months—as was the case in the aftermath of the super cyclone of Orissa (1999). Despite the extraordinary politicization of the Andhra cyclone and many other handicaps, the institutional response to the disaster was credible.[5]

Super Cyclone of Orissa

The super cyclone which hit about 200 km of the Orissa coast around Erasama on 29 October 1999 had an unprecedented impact. With wind speeds reaching 300 km per hour and a storm surge several metres high, the 'severest' cyclone of the twentieth century, had catastrophic affects in three districts (Jagatsinghpur, Kendrapara, and Cuttack) and caused extensive damage in eleven others. It killed 9,893 persons and affected 15.7 million people. It destroyed or damaged 1.96 million dwellings; crops in 1.84 million ha worth about Rs. 17.5 billion (US$ 390 million) were destroyed. Estimates of total damage vary widely, from Rs. 100 billion (US$ 2.26 billion) to Rs. 400 billion (US$ 9.04 billion). The super cyclone remained anchored over land after hitting the coast for an unusually long period, causing heavy rainfall and consequent massive inland flooding. Hundreds of villages in the core area of the disaster remained marooned for over two weeks. Corpses and carcasses were floating all over. It took several weeks to restore power and communications in the affected areas.

---

[5]Severe disasters occurred in Andhra in 1979 (Chirala cyclone and flash floods), 1986 (Godavari floods), and 1996 (Kakinada cyclone). These caused extensive damage to the infrastructure and agricultural economy of the state. Floods in Vamsadhara in 1980 (Srikakulam) and Sriharikota cyclone of 1984 (Nellore) were disasters of moderate severity. The Asian tsunami of December 2004 had a limited impact on Andhra Pradesh.

Lack of anticipation and unpreparedness on the part of the state government left the political leaders and bureaucracy in disarray. One observer commented: 'It seemed as if the state administration was in hibernation' (Pattanaik 2000: 19). Chaos characterized the distribution of relief. Some survivors are reported to have died out of starvation (Bose 2003: 183). There was an outbreak of epidemics. In some of the affected areas the desperation of some victims led to food riots and looting of private commercial shops, government food godowns, and the relief supplies of the NGOs (Kanchan and Gwyhn 2000: 199; Pattanaik 2000: 19). Criminals and antisocial elements had a field day. A series of such unwelcome incidents had intimidated the NGO personnel from reaching out to the victims of the interior areas (Bose 2003: 183).

A couple of months after the super cyclone, campaigning for elections to the Orissa legislative assembly commenced. Deficiencies in the performance of the Congress government provided campaign material for the Biju Janata Dal (BJD) and Bharatiya Janata Party (BJP) opposition combine. The rout of the ruling Congress Party in the assembly elections held in February 2000 was largely attributed to lack of preparedness, corruption, bureaucratic ineptitude, and insensitivity of the political leadership in handling rescue and relief work in the cyclone aftermath (Mohapatra 2000: 1353–55).

Asian Tsunami: A Mega Disaster

Around 6.40 a.m. (IST) on 26 December 2004, a massive undersea earthquake (9.3 on the Ritcher scale) occurred in the Indian ocean, with its epicentre 257 km south-south-west of Banda Aceh of Sumatra island, Indonesia. The earthquake, the most powerful in the world in the last forty years, caused a tsunami (harbour waves) that affected thirteen countries of South and South East Asia, and five of them most severely. The US Geological Survey (USGS) records the death toll as 2,83,100 killed and 14,100 missing in this mega disaster.[6] Estimated death toll for India was 16,413.[7] Within India, Tamil Nadu,

---

[6]US Geological Survey, Earthquake Hazards Program. http://earthquake.usgs.gov/equinthenews
[7]Wikipedia, 2004. http://en.wikipedia.org/wiki/2004_IndianOcean_earthquake

the Andaman Islands and Pondicherry were the worst affected followed by Kerala and Andhra Pradesh. About 10,050 people were killed in Tamil Nadu.[8]

There was no warning until huge waves swept even those who were a couple of kilometres from the sea. Nagapattinam was the worst affected district, followed by Cuddalore, both in Tamil Nadu. In Nagapattinam three waves, 5 to 10 metres high, came in quick succession, between 7.45 a.m. and 9.45 a.m., wiped out the huts, sliced away buildings, and drowned entire families. The waves turned settlements into mass graves in the villages and on the beaches. Fishing boats anchored on the beaches were washed ashore to a distance of 1 km. In Nagapattinam district alone the casualties were around 6,000. A majority of the dead were women and children; more than a third of them were children. Nearly 200 people, mainly morning walkers and children playing cricket on the Marina beach in Chennai, were engulfed by the gaint waves. About 0.9 million people were affected by the tsunami in Tamil Nadu, the worst hit being fisherfolk.

The Tamil Nadu government swung into action quickly, first by the placement of two IAS officers, known for their dynamism, as collectors of Nagapattinam and Cuddalore, and then by establishing relief camps in the affected areas. It took steps for the cremation of corpses, located in mass graves or strewn over the beaches and elsewhere. Most of the victims also got a reasonable relief package within a week after the tsunami. The government's prompt and effective response to the victims of the Asian tsunami received widespread acclaim. However, the tsunami disaster led to stormy political controversies between Jayalalitha, the AIADMK chief minister of the state, and the Union government of the United Progressive Alliance (UPA). The state chief minister objected to the centre's move to provide direct funding—a subsidy-cum-loan package for the livelihood of the tsunami-affected fishermen through banks—bypassing the state government. She accused the centre of violating the norms of the federal structure in this regard. There were several other irritants over the sharing of political credit for relief and

---

[8]Particulars of the death toll for other states are Pondicherry–680, Kerala–166, and Andhra Pradesh–106.

reconstruction work, and even matters of protocol. Since elections to the state assembly were not far, each political outfit was keen to utilize the political fallout from the disaster to its advantage.

The effect of the tsunami was also severe in Pondicherry, but moderate in Andhra Pradesh and Kerala. The response was less than optimal in Pondicherry and Kerala. Their governments were slow to respond, relief camps were crowded, and distribution of relief was disorganized. Andhra Pradesh, which keeps an annual date with cyclones, responded to the needs of the tsunami victims quickly, and within twelve hours relief camps were organized in the affected areas. In the Andaman and Nicobar islands, which were nearest to the epicentre of the quake, the horror wrought by the tsunami was mounting. An estimated 5,000 people were killed, with another 2,000 reported missing. The government's response to the cataclysm was pathetic. There was a total collapse of the civilian administration, not to speak of logistical and transport problems, and breakdown of communications in Port Blair, the capital, and between the capital and the islands.[9] For the survivors of the tragedy it looked like the end of history. Two days after the calamity rescue and relief work were entrusted to the military. There was a scarcity of relief material, and the first consignment of relief from the mainland arrived only on the tenth day after the disaster.

Floods

India is one of the worst flood-affected countries in the world after Bangladesh and accounts for one-fifth of the global death count due to floods (Anon 1991: 1–7). During the second half of the twentieth century the area liable to floods has increased seven-fold, from less than 6 million hectares to more than 40 million ha—one-eighth of the country's geographical area (Roy 2000: 153). Floods affect, on an average, 56.6 million persons annually (Gupta et al. 2003: 199–200). Until the 1960s floods used to occur with a high frequency in only a few states—the north-eastern states, parts of Bihar, eastern Uttar

---

[9]The Andaman and Nicobar Islands number 572, and are dispersed over 700 sq km in the Indian Ocean; only thirty-five of these are known to be inhabited, with a combined population of 356,385 (2001 Census).

Pradesh, West Bengal, and Orissa. Now that areas of the Deccan plateau have also become flood-prone there are at least ten states that are chronically affected. The Ganga and the Brahmaputra rivers, flowing from the Himalayas, have annually inundated vast tracts of land for millennia. But floods changed their character by the middle of the twentieth century, from routine inundation to highly damaging disasters.

During the second half of the twentieth century major floods occurred in India in 1955, 1971, 1978, 1988, 1992, 1995, 1996, and 1998 (Kanwar 2003: 359). The annual average monetary damage for the period 1971–2000 is estimated at Rs. 21 billion (US$ 476 million). The annual average death toll from floods during the same period is 1,992 (IWRS 2001: 4–12). Floods may kill relatively fewer people, but the damage they render is pervasive and long term, the losses being exacerbated by rapid population growth, unplanned development, and unchecked environmental degradation. Evidence suggests that the intrusion of flash floods, as in the desert state of Rajasthan and in north Bihar, both in 1996, were largely due to man-made structures like dams, embankments, unplanned railway lines, and roads. Many feel that developmental planning had gone haywire (Mishra 2000: 157; Roy 2000: 149). About 15 per cent of the area in north Bihar is permanently waterlogged and 76 per cent of the area is flood-affected. In the 1996 floods 74 million ha of land in various regions of the country was submerged, causing an estimated economic loss of about Rs. 18 billion or US$ 473 million (Kanwar 2003: 259).

In spite of a flood policy and control schemes, flood damage has been increasing in India. One-third of the flood-prone area has reasonable protection due to structural and non-structural measures taken up. Yet it is clearly inadequate. There are also criticisms about relief and rehabilitation. First, the allocations made for these tasks are very low. Actual releases made by the Union government to the states are far lower than the demand and they do not exceed 3 per cent of the total of the demand made by the state governments. The second criticism relates to inefficient use of the allocations since a good chunk of the money is reportedly 'siphoned off by contractors, administrators and powerbrokers' (Roy 2000: 152). It is further observed that the tribulations of people affected by rivers in spate have always bowed to the technological and political exigencies of profits and power (ibid.: 147).

A new phenomenon—devastating floods—were witnessed in Hyderabad in 2000, and in Mumbai and Chennai in 2005. A cloudburst resulting in incessant rain (95 cm in 24 hours, the highest in recorded history), on 26 July 2005 caused unprecedented havoc in Mumbai, the financial capital of India, resulting in about 1,000 deaths and Rs. 150 billion worth of damage (Marpakwar 2005: 12; Menon 2005: 12). There was no forewarning about the deluge as the west coast did not have an efficient rain forecasting technological facility. Urban life came to a standstill. Commuters were stranded in trains, buses, and cars for up to 22 hours. Mumbai lost rail and air links with the outside world. All systems within the city—transport, telecommunications, water, power, drainage, health and medical facilities, gasoline, cooking gas, kerosene, food supplies, etc.— collapsed. What is worse, it lasted four days and there was no sign of any government presence. It took almost a week to distribute relief. However, people mobilized themselves to organize rescue and relief to the victims and providing help to those in distress (Sharma 2005: 11). Unregulated development, construction of buildings and roads, and location of slums on the basins, river banks, and mangroves, without accommodating the natural drainage patterns; and lack of modernization of a century-old sewerage system were responsible for the disaster (Ninan 2005: 16). Wide natural streams have been reduced to narrow *nullahs*. The state government has diluted, or made inoperative, the Coastal Regulation Zone (CRZ) rules, which restrict development on the city's coastline, at least seven times since 1991 in order to please builders (TNN 2005a: 10, 2005b: 8). The Mumbai floods (July–August 2005) expose the weaknesses of the system: politician–bureaucrat–real estate developers' nexus, leading to poor urban design, unfettered construction, and blindness to the city's ecology; poor infrastructure (water supply, drainage, transport, power supply, telecommunications, etc.); lack of professional management and incompetence in urban governance; and the infinite capacity of people to suffer instead of converting their anger into collective action.

Famines and Droughts

India is also a famine-stricken country with a history of several major famines that devoured millions of people. The Bengal famine of 1770 killed 1 million people and the next major famine (1837), which also occurred in Bengal, took a toll of 0.8 million people (Blair 1986: 111–34). During the nineteenth century famines and droughts killed large numbers of people in the Indian subcontinent. The total mortality officially admitted during 1854–1901 was 28.8 million (Digby 1901, 127–30; Kulkarni 1990: 22–23). The regions/provinces/districts of the subcontinent affected, the years during which major famines/droughts occurred, and the death toll particulars are: (*a*) north-west provinces, 1860–61, 0.5 million; (*b*) Orissa, north Bengal, Bihar, and Madras, 1865–66, 1.89 million; (*c*) Rajaputana, Punjab, north-west provinces, and central provinces, 1868–69, 2.1 million; (*d*) Bombay province and Hyderabad (Deccan), 1876–77, 0.97 million; (*e*) South India, 1876–78, 5.25 million; and (*f*) Ganjam, 1888–89, 0.15 million (Kulkarni 1990: 22–23).

Besides successive famine commissions and other government-sponsored committees, several studies (Aykroyd 1974; Bhatia 1967; Hanumantha Rao et al. 1988; Mishra 1991; Robson 1981; Sen 1981; Subbiah 2004) document how famines occurred in one part of the country or the other at regular intervals, affecting on an average about one-twelfth of the population of the country. They also deal with the causes of famine/drought and throw light on relief and rehabilitation policies, follow-up administrative actions, and their efficacy. India is affected by famine/drought more than any other country/continent in the world. Indeed, 1983 was the only year in recorded history when Africa had more drought victims than India (Naidu 1989: 1–14). Of the total cultivable area, an estimated 28 per cent is drought-prone in India.

Famine is defined as the failure of food production and distribution systems in the affected region, leading to sharply increased mortality due to starvation and associated diseases. The major causes of famines are identified as unfavourable weather like prolonged drought or excessive rain conditions, war or other catastrophic factors like cyclones, or a combination of them. There are three major theories of famine. The first indicates that a famine is caused by food grain availability decline; the second attributes it to lack of purchasing power; and the third combines the two. In his seminal study of the Bengal famine of 1943 Amartya Sen (1981: 154–66) demonstrated that non-availability or shortage of food grains was not the major cause of the famine; instead, it was a direct consequence of the deterioration in exchange entitlements or lack of purchasing power. Jean Dreze (1999) endorses Amartya Sen's view. Drought is a meteorological phenomenon. The IMD defines drought as a situation occurring in any area in a year when the annual rainfall is less than 75 per cent of the normal.

In the nineteenth century there were a dozen famines of which two were very severe with enormous loss of lives, cattle, and crops. The British government appointed three major famine commissions. Based on their recommendations, the British government evolved a famine policy involving the creation of a database on rainfall, crop statistics, etc., besides a famine code for relief and other assistance through employment facilities to the victims, and improvement of irrigation facilities and other infrastructure. The British had also established an administrative organization to handle various tasks relating to famine relief and associated operations. Yet the efforts made by them were considered half-hearted and totally inadequate, reflecting the failure of the British government's policy and its relief measures (Aykroyd 1974: 78; Bhatia 1967, 58–101; Blair 1986, 111–34; Mishra 1991: 325–40; Robson 1981: 2–4). Laxity on their part in developing irrigation facilities was considered a major reason for famines.

In the Bengal famine of 1943, which killed about 1.5 million, governmental neglect and administrative ineptitude, and inadequacy and delay in the provision of relief assistance are stated to have aggravated the misery of the victims (Bhatia 1967; Blair 1986: 111–34; Denhartog 1981: 158; Greengough 1982: 78). In the Bihar famine of 1966–67, it was pointed out, effective and prompt relief measures could have mitigated the distress and contained excess mortality (Mayer 1974: 98–100; Torry 1986:11–15).

Despite the expansion of irrigation facilities in post-independence India, drought remained endemic. About 50 million ha or 16 per cent of the geographical area is chronically drought-prone. Of the cultivable area, an estimated 28 per cent continues to be drought-prone. Areas subject to drought once in two to three years constitute more than 13 per cent of the country's area and about 19 per cent of its dry tropical area (Subbiah 2004: 52). In the post-independence period major droughts that affected more than one-third of the country occurred in 1951, 1966–67, 1972, 1979, 1987–88, 1994–95, 1999–2000, 2000–2001, and 2003–4. In 1999–2000 Gujarat experienced a severe drought, affecting 14,832 of the 18,356 villages in the state (Gupta and Sharma 2001a: 17). Rajasthan is one of the chronically drought-affected states because 61 per cent of the country's arid zone is located here (Gupta and Sharma 2001b: 28).

The Drought-Prone Areas Programme (DPAP) and the Desert Development Programme (DDP), both centrally-sponsored, have been in operation since the early 1970s as programmes of drought-proofing. The DPAP covers ninety-five districts and the DDP twenty-one districts. Unfortunately, these programmes have not made any dent into the basics of the problem. As an expert from the Indian Planning Commission admits, they have not been very successful mainly because of a thin spread of the investment in a widely dispersed area and non-integration of different activities to the core objectives (Rajan 1994: 30–31). The watersheds schemes, launched under various programmes, seem to be having a better rate of success.

The politics of drought relief in India has been analysed by a few writers. Writing on the Bihar famine of 1966–67, Paul Brass makes a generic observation that in a country where the politicians have to be concerned about popular support, 'crisis is defined by them ultimately in terms of the advancement of their own political interests' (1986: 245). In this process, adherence to canons of public accountability are forgotten. Lalu Prasad Yadav, the former chief minister of Bihar—and at present a minister in the Union cabinet—and several senior politicians and officers of the Bihar government were embroiled in a series of court cases with accusations of misappropriation of huge sums of public money meant for supplying fodder. The fodder scandal of Bihar lasted a decade. Meanwhile, Lalu Yadav was directed by the apex court to demit his office of chief ministership, which he did, in favour of his wife, though. The food-for-work programmes for which several millions of metric tons of wheat and rice have been released by the Union government to drought-affected states during the new millennium have also been mired in scandals with accusations of corruption; the beneficiaries are stated to be mainly ministers, MLAs, and local officials. The following observations of a senior journalist sound relevant: 'Drought relief, almost equally beyond question, [is] rural India's biggest growth industry .... Though relief can go to scarcity areas, those most in need seldom benefit from it .... In reality, the lion's share of drought funds is appropriated by the powerful' (Sainath 2000: 173–74). Year after year the same problems crop up all over again because the real issues were seldom touched. Drought relief is, therefore, ironically called the 'third crop' and flood relief the 'fourth crop', especially in Bihar and Uttar Pradesh. Other states are also falling in line with it.

There have been a number of studies and reports of committees and commissions on drought mitigation sponsored by the Union and state governments. The number is staggering. Their contents relating to diagnosis and prescriptions overlap a great deal. One can hardly dispute the major policy perspective shared by many of them, as also outside experts and multilateral agencies, that drought has to be tackled from a total canvas of sustainable development alongside measures for provision of infrastructure in the more vulnerable and poorer states (Hanumantha Rao et al.; 1988: 126–42; IBRD 2003: 59–123; Martin 2000: 63–64; Sen 1,988: 1523–24; Shah 1998: 66–79). If drought mitigation efforts are integrated with that of development, it is possible to make early interventions through contingency crop planning instead of relying on the earlier approach of entitlement of food through relief programmes. Indeed, such an approach was tried successfully in Uttar Pradesh (Subbiah 2004: 82).

Earthquakes

Earthquakes are the most disastrous of all natural calamities, and catches people unawares and unprepared. India's seismic belt is the largest for any country in the world. About 56 per cent of the geographical area of the country lies in the seismic zones of moderate to severe intensity (Vatsa 2002: 1,503). The Himalayan belt, Assam, Meghalaya, Gujarat, and Maharashtra are more prone to earthquakes of higher intensity than other seismic zones in the country. About twenty earthquakes occurred in India during the nineteenth century, the Assam earthquake of 1897 (magnitude 8.7) being the most devastating. Data for the previous century show that in India an average of three earthquakes of magnitude 6.0 or more on the Richter scale occurred each year (Arya 1994b: 130; Chopra 2000: 201). Earthquakes in India during the last century have taken on an average over 900 lives a year, 5 per cent of the world's average of 18,000 (Arya 1994a: 60).[10] Major earthquakes in the first half of the twentieth century include the Kangra earthquake of 1905 (magnitude 8.0), Bihar–Nepal earthquake of 1934, (magnitude 8.4) and Assam earthquake of 1950 (magnitude 8.6). The death toll in Kangra was over 20,000 (Chopra 2000: 203). The quake levelled every village from Dharmasala to Kangra. In Kangra town no official was alive to direct the rescue and relief operations. In the Bihar–Nepal quake of 1934 the official count of deaths was 1,100 (Arya 1994b: 132). But unofficial estimates place it around 25,000 (Chopra 2000: 203).

A series of earthquakes with moderate severity occurred during the third quarter of the twentieth century. They include Pardgo and Tanga, north-east India (1958), Koyna, Maharashtra (1967), and Kinnaur, Himachal Pradesh (1975). These earthquakes had a localized impact, with limited human and property losses. The Uttarkashi, Uttar Pradesh, earthquake (20 October 1991), which was of moderate severity, resulted in 768 deaths, but caused massive damage. About 90 per cent of the housing in the region was affected. The Uttarkashi experience highlights the lopsidedness in relief distribution, with relief trucks unloading goods at the accessible roadside villages and neglecting the victims in distant areas. Some relief goods were entirely inappropriate: summer clothes, high-heeled shoes, expired medicines— discarded junk of urban homes (Chopra 2000: 206). Often government supplies were routed through the village *pradhans / sarpanches* (elected chiefs), fattening them along the way. The Uttarkashi experience was an event of missed opportunities—by aid agencies and the government—in terms of learning how to handle quake relief and reconstruction work.

---

[10]The average is based on projections data from A.S. Arya (1994a) and other sources.

The Killari (Latur), Maharashtra, earthquake (30 September 1993), also of moderate severity, killed 7,928 people, injured about 16,000, and flattened houses in about twenty villages. Overall, the affects of the quake were felt in sixty-nine villages of Latur and Osmanabad districts. The initial response from the government and NGOs towards the quake victims was slow. It took two to four days to effectively organize rescue and relief operations. What then followed appeared to be well-organized and effective. Rescue and relief were hampered by heavy rains and the enormous quantities of debris. The narrow village streets were choked by rubble, which further hampered the rescue operations (EERI 1994: 1–2). The quake has brought about major changes in the community structure of some villages. An earthquake that hit Jabalpur, Madhya Pradesh, in May 1977 exposed the dismal inadequacy of relief and shelter despite potential for resource mobilization.

The Kutch (Gujarat) Earthquake

An earthquake of 7.7 magnitude struck the Kutch and adjoining regions of Gujarat, with Bhuj as the epicentre, on 26 January 2001. It is India's worst natural disaster in the last fifty years. The quake affected about 15.9 million people—nearly one-third of the state's population—in 7,633 towns and villages in nineteen districts. The number of human lives lost was 13,805 and about 167,000 persons were injured (Mishra 2004: 192). Over 348,000 buildings collapsed and about 844,000 were damaged. More than 10,000 small and medium enterprises stopped production. About 600,000 people were left homeless. Direct economic losses from the disaster were estimated at Rs. 192.3 billion or US$ 4.4 billion (Lahiri et al. 2001: 1320–23). Indirect losses due to the quake were estimated at Rs. 1,320 million or US$ 30 billion (Thiruppugazh 2003: 30). Kutch district, which suffered three disasters in the preceding three years (cyclones in 1998 and 1999, and drought in 2000), was the main target of the quake, accounting for about 92 per cent of the death toll and about 82 per cent of the injured. The loss of human lives in Kutch works out to 11.53 per 1,000 population.

Socio-cultural difficulties and the psychological trauma experienced by survivors due to the death of family members has been a critical issue in disaster after disaster. A demographic disequilibrium emerges in the affected communities, with a higher proportion of casualties among children and women. However, in the Gujarat disaster of 2001 a higher proportion of males, including male children (58.1 per cent) died (Lahiri et al. 2001: 1320–21). A break-up of the casualties by age shows that 62 per cent of the dead belong to the productive age group of 15–59 and the proportion of working adults is much higher than in other disasters. The post-disaster demographic profile results in a higher dependency ratio among the bereaved families.

As news of the devastation trickled in, the state administration went into action, but its response was slow, reflecting the bureaucracy's inertia and lack of preparedness. It took almost 48 hours for government agencies to take up relief work in an organized manner. In Bhuj, the district headquarters of Kutch, many key officials were themselves in trauma, having suffered either casualties in their families or damage to their property. The office of the district collector of Kutch was partially destroyed, records lost, and was without power. However, response from local volunteers was spontaneous. Within hours the calamity, rescue teams led by survivors became active in attempts to rescue victims buried under the rubble (Ray 2001: 132). They also tried to clear obstacles on the roads to enable the injured to be carried to physicians for first-aid. In places like Bhuj, where hospitals were destroyed by the quake, local doctors organized themselves, by makeshift arrangements, to provide first-aid to the injured. The army joined the effort in a big way, with transport planes, helicopters, rescue teams, medical teams, etc. But systematic rescue work began only 50 hours after the quake strike, when the Swiss search and rescue (SAR) team arrived. In the hours and days to follow, SAR teams from twelve other countries joined the effort. Foreign rescue teams brought sophisticated equipment (for example, heat-seeking laser sensors) and sniffer dogs to accurately locate the survivors under the debris. Incidentally, the Gujarat quake opened a new chapter in India's policy in permitting rescue and relief teams from abroad, including those sponsored by foreign governments to operate in disaster-affected areas in India. Foreign exchange norms were also relaxed to facilitate the flow of relief material and aid from abroad.

Kutch had a massive relief operation with material from thirty-eight countries besides several UN agencies and international and national non-governmental organizations. The participating organizations numbered 245, including ninety-nine international and fifty-five national NGOs. As elsewhere, visits by the high-profile political elite belonging to the ruling and opposition parties had the effect of diverting the attention of key functionaries from relief work. But such visits had a symbolic value as the victims were expecting VIPs to call on them in times of grief.

The lack of preparedness on the part of the state government and its knee-jerk reaction to the calamity have come in for criticism (Ray 2001: 130–31; Tonk 2003: 338–40). More specifically, no worthwhile disaster mitigation plans existed in the state to respond to such calamities. The Gujarat government did not act on preparedness though suggestions were made by experts after the Bhavanagar tremors of August–September 2000 (Ray 2001: 137). Having known the vulnerability of most buildings in the earthquake-prone area, seismic-proof construction norms were not enforced by the state government or local bodies. There was no attempt to build a proper decision support system for taking effective government actions after the quake. Relief work was, therefore, organized in an ad hoc manner in view of serious gaps in information about the locations of damage, in remote areas in particular. Several lapses occurred due to lack of planning, direction, and coordination. Relief personnel and material from outside flooded the affected area, but relief could not be delivered to the most affected groups in the interior or with speed. Medical aid was both inadequate and delayed. Delays in rescue and relief work were experienced due to slow mobilization of resources like technical equipment, tents/shelter material, and medicines and surgical equipment, as well as non-availability of adequate technical manpower. It was felt that some casualties could have been prevented if adequate and suitable rescue equipment for speedy clearance of debris was available within 24 hours after the quake.

Referring to the tardy distribution of relief and rehabilitation assistance in the Gujarat disaster of 2001, Lyla Mehta (2001: 2,934) observes that the government's initial failure to respond quickly was due to the massive scale of the tragedy and the failure of communication. She further notes that Kutch's marginal position in Gujarat also played a key role in the total collapse of the government machinery. The scale of the disaster does influence the level of response. The super cyclone of 1999 also had a crippling effect on the bureaucracy's response in Orissa. The suddenness of the disasters is perhaps another common reason. Studies of the Gujarat earthquake of 2001 (Mehta 2001: 2,934; Ray 2001: 138-39; Tonk 2003: 338–40) also note that while survivors in the roadside villages/towns got an excess of relief goods, victims in the interior locations did not receive any relief until after a week, and in a few cases they received only limited quantities.

ROLE OF NON-GOVERNMENTAL ORGANIZATIONS

There has been a growing interest and concern on the part of private groups and citizens towards disaster victims in India. Not only was this reflected in the presence of a large number of professional NGOs from abroad and India, ad hoc groups, political outfits, missionary/ religious organizations, etc. in the disaster area, but also in fundraising efforts through diverse ways. Besides some international NGOs that donated materials or cash, more than 150 NGOs participated in the relief work of the Andhra cyclone of 1977. In response to this the response of NGOs to the Chirala cyclone (1979) was far less; participation by international NGOs was also extremely limited. In both disasters government policy towards NGOs was unclear. Government agencies, which were preoccupied with multiple tasks, were unable to provide guidance and information to the NGOs (Cohen and Raghavulu 1979: 52–57; Raghavulu 1982: 30–39). Their perceptions and approach regarding relief were at loggerheads (Bose 2003: 188). In both the disasters the relationship between the government and the NGOs deteriorated further by the rehabilitation stage as there was a growing mistrust between them. Their enthusiasm was further dampened when, in 1979, the state government appealed (a euphemism for direction) for donations to the Chief Minister's Relief Fund, rather than allowing the NGOs to receive it directly. A common reaction among the NGOs was that the government could not be trusted to distribute relief without lining the pockets of many functionaries (Raghavulu 1982: 65). Despite all the odds, a few NGOs were successful in working in a hostile environment (Winchester 2000: 29).

In the super cyclone (Orissa, 1999) aftermath, the NGOs themselves faced rough weather from the survivors as a result of looting of relief goods; this has prevented many NGOs from spanning out into the interior villages. Notwithstanding the initial chaos, they moved quickly by building bridges with government agencies and by evolving efficacious strategies to organize rescue and relief to the victims. And they did commendable work under very difficult circumstances. An articulate observer of the NGO scene observes: 'I had never seen tragedy on this scale, But in my forty-plus Indian years, I have never seen selfless work on this scale either' (D'Souza 2002: 91). Most significantly, their work proved a morale booster to government relief agencies as well.

Professionally-oriented NGOs from India and abroad had a high visibility and made significant contribution in the relief, rescue, and reconstruction efforts of the Kutch earthquake in Gujarat. Up until the early 1990s direct participation by foreign government and international agencies and international NGOs in disaster relief and reconstruction was not welcomed by the Indian government. The latter's attitude had undergone a major change with the onset of the UN Decade for Disaster Reduction (1990–99), which also coincided with India's first phase of liberalization.

The Indian government had become more conciliatory towards the aforementioned organizations by the mid-1990s and positive by the turn of the new millennium. The results of the policy change were reflected in the presence of NGOs and aid agencies from abroad in high density in the super cyclone of 1993 and the Gujarat earthquake of 2001. Indeed, direct appeals were issued by the Indian government in the aftermath of the Gujarat quake, soliciting participation and aid from foreign governments, international NGOs, and multilateral agencies. Search and rescue (SAR) teams from thirteen foreign governments, including Pakistan, and relief and reconstruction teams from ten foreign governments, dozens of multilateral agencies, and ninety-nine international NGOs were involved in the post-disaster operations.

The Gujarat quake reconstruction phase marks a watershed in adapting approaches and strategies reflecting the influence of the processes of globalization. In fact, many international NGOs committed to the paradigm of disaster-resilient community[11] found in Gujarat a laboratory for experiments with models of capacity building of vulnerable communities, and cost-effective approaches for their speedy recovery (Nakagawa and Sharma 2004: 24–31; Sharma et al. 2003: 53–61).[12] In fact, the Gujarat government's reconstruction strategies also incorporated community participation and gender empowerment approaches to mitigation thanks to inputs from international disaster mitigation consultants sponsored by multilateral aid agencies (Thiruppugazh 2003: 30–38). By this time, the World Bank has established a Disaster Mitigation Facility (DMF) to mainstream disaster prevention and mitigation incentives into all its policies and aid packages. The World Bank persuaded the Gujarat government to evolve public policies with market incentives for risk management and risk reduction, especially through insurance (Lynch and Unnikrishnan 2000: 135). These developments signify the influence of the processes of globalization on disaster mitigation and preparedness strategies in India.

NGOs are still beset with their age-old problems. Very often they find it difficult to coordinate among themselves and with the government, the latter being the guilty partner (Bose 2003: 183–84; Mehta 2001: 2,935; Ray 2001: 132, 139; Sharma 2000: 124). There

---

[11]The disaster resilient community approach implies that since disaster prevention is not always possible, focus should be on minimization of losses and damage when a disaster occurs, speedy recovery, and paying attention to social, psychological, and economic variables. See Buckle et al. (2000: 8–14) and Paton et al. (2000: 173–179).

[12]Nakagawa and Shaw developed a model for bonding, bridging, and linking social capital from the Kobe experience—a tradition of community activities and collective decision making—with a successful and speedy recovery from disasters. This model was replicated in four communities in Gujarat and found the results encouraging. See Nakagawa et al. (2004: 5–34). Anshu Sharma et al. (2003: 53–61) report of a successful community-driven reconstruction project in Patanka (Gujarat) integrating development activities with capacity building, transfer of technology, risk reduction, promotion of livelihoods, and respect for socio-cultural attributes.

are inherent problems for achieving coordination among NGOs as there is a great deal of diversity among them in regard to size, degree of professionalism, approaches, resource base, experience, etc. They range from the highly professional NGOs like the International Red Cross, CARE, and OXFAM to ad hoc citizens groups and political outfits. In each disaster their efforts at coordination begin usually after the relief stage by which time most of the ad hoc groups, political outfits, and the smaller NGOs disappear from the scene. The difficulties encountered by NGOs with the bureaucracy on the one hand and with the leaders of some of the affected communities on the other in Uttarkashi (1991), Latur (1993), and Kutch (2001) are not dissimilar to those faced earlier in the Andhra cyclone (1977–78). Regarding Uttarkashi and Latur, Sharma (2000: 124) notes that the government and the NGOs tripped each other. In all these disasters, the bureaucracy, while making symbolic gestures of partnership with the NGOs, was unwilling to extend wholehearted cooperation to them. Displaying a condescending attitude, individual bureaucrats would ramble on about the legitimate authority of the government over the entire relief and rehabilitation process. Keeping a low profile, the NGO functionaries had to plead with the bureaucrats for guidance and cooperation.

The heightened expectations of the victims posed a problem, both in the Andhra cyclone and the Gujarat quake. In both cases villages were adopted by the NGOs for reconstruction work. But adoption meant different things to different people. The stakeholders in some of the villages proposed for adoption did not cooperate with the NGOs involved with the expectation of higher benefits either from the government or some other NGO. The bureaucracy was also not cooperative in resolving such problems. The predicament led to the withdrawal of many NGOs from the village adoption programme. The result was that the village adoption programme could not be implemented in all the affected villages. Politicization of the NGOs, at least some of them, could not be prevented. In the Andhra cyclone, the government advanced relief material to some political groups belonging to the ruling Congress Party for distribution to the victims in a few villages. While distributing relief material to the victims the political groups claimed that it was from their party. A similar practice was noted in the Gujarat quake aftermath. In Gujarat the Rashtriya Swayamsevak Sangh (RSS) was sanctioned, by the BJP government of the state, some funds towards relief work. The relief programme of the RSS was inaugurated by the state chief minister. The performance of this project did not progress as per expectations. Instead, it attracted criticism from the opposition parties that the RSS tried to inject communalism into the relief process (Ray 2001: 139).

In the aftermath of the Asian tsunami (2004–5) the Union government backtracked on its open door policy toward relief assistance from abroad. However, at a later stage, it welcomed foreign aid for reconstruction. In the post-disaster relief effort in Tamil Nadu and Pondicherry, the NGOs—mostly Indian and a few international ones functioning with offices in India—have participated on a large scale. The NGO scene is characterized by more or less the same tendencies noted in Andhra (1977–78) and Gujarat (2001): lack of coordination among NGOs themselves, and with government agencies, resulting in duplication of relief and wasted efforts. Unloading of unwanted goods, such as used clothing, reached intolerable limits in Tamil Nadu and Pondicherry. In this disaster greater attention was paid by professional groups and city-based volunteers towards relieving the trauma of the victims and providing other psychiatric care.

RESPONSE TO THE CHALLENGE OF DISASTERS

Disasters offer a unique opportunity to learn and innovate. The Union government and a few states have brought about technological or administrative improvements as part of disaster mitigation preparedness and management. Notable among them was the upgradation of the warning system by the Union government. Following the experience of the Andhra cyclone of 1977, and based on the recommendations of the CDMC (Government of India 1971: 18), a comprehensive satellite-based warning system was installed by the IMD. The warning system consisted of ten high-powered radar stations (six on the east coast and four on the west coast), besides ten high-capacity wind speed radars, including four doppler radar systems, and about 1,100 cyclone warning dissemination centres. The network of weather radar stations and early warning systems, linked to satellite, have been functioning effectively and facilitating a series of precautionary measures. Warnings are issued sooner and more accurately, saving lives. Inputs from other improved technologies also come in handy. In the matter of cyclones or floods, remote-sensing and satellite imageries have greatly helped in forecasting their behaviour. However, in the aftermath of the Mumbai floods (July–August 2005), it was pointed out that the west coast does not have any doppler weather radar systems to facilitate forecasting of cloudbursts or rainfall intensity.

There were a few critics who argued in the wake of the Asian tsunami of 2004 that the Union government dragged its feet in the installation of a tsunami warning system in the Indian Ocean despite recommendations in its favour by a high-power committee which submitted its report in 2001. The criticisms are somewhat unfair in view of the fact that, while cyclones are frequent, tsunamis are rare in the Indian Ocean. Between 1945 and November 2004 India had not seen one. Nevertheless, we tend to learn from the experience of major disasters. Following the December 2004 tsunami, twenty-six nations of the Indian Ocean region have come to a consensus over the installation of a tsunami warning system similar to the one in the Pacific Ocean. The Indian government will also install its own tsunami warning system by September 2007. The establishment of a national disaster management authority has been on the cards for several years. The havoc caused by the Asian tsunami hastened the decision of the Union government to establish, in January 2005, a National Disaster Management Authority (NDMA) and constitute it, in July 2005, to provide a framework for managing disasters. The disaster response system under the NDMA will have eight battalions, drawn from military and paramilitary organizations, to attend to rescue and relief activity of disasters. They will be given professional training in the relevant activities and provided with dedicated air support and equipment in the four metros of the country. They will maintain an online inventory system; and relief material will be stocked in major cities. Provision of a communication network with alternate satellite links is part of the disaster response system contemplated.

Another aspect of the Asian tsunami is relevant. This catastrophe has provided new diplomatic openings. India, although itself afflicted, has sent its rescue teams, relief material, medical teams, civil engineers, helicopters, and navy vessels to the affected countries of the region. Indeed, the rapidity with which the Indian teams moved into the affected areas and took up work was considered exceptional. The nations that received Indian assistance included Sri Lanka, Maldives, Indonesia, and Thailand. The Indian initiative would perhaps serve as an example of the need for multinational cooperation in handling mega disasters.

Based on the lessons learnt from the 1977 cyclone, the Andhra Pradesh government took a series of steps, including restoration of infrastructure, preparation of a contingency plan and manuals, and developed procedures for coordination and sensitization training programmes and field drills for officials. A long-term hazard mitigation policy was evolved on the basis of key hazard studies for coastal management, watershed and delta management, and geographic information system (GIS) data. Integration of disaster management with other developments in the application of information technology,[13] has been helpful for communication of information, decisions, and for interaction (Sahoo 2004: 104–6). After its experience with the super cyclone of 1999, Orissa has established a State Disaster Mitigation and Management Authority. Following the Latur earthquake, Maharashtra developed state-specific disaster management plans. Gujarat has created the Gujarat State Disaster Management Authority (GSDMA) in the immediate aftermath of the Kutch earthquake. Following the Jabalpur earthquake (1997), the Madhya Pradesh government got an earthquake preparedness plan for the Khandwa region.

Institutional Response in Andhra Pradesh and Orissa: A Comparison

Tropical cyclones constitute a permanent and recurring risk to both Andhra Pradesh and Orissa as both these states are contiguously in

---

[13]The system included computer networking of districts through a video-conferencing facility; provision of a computer network linking the state headquarters with twenty-three district headquarters, seventy-eight revenue divisions and 1,123 *mandals;* and arrangement of a very high frequency (VHF) network of the district headquarters with the *mandals* in each district.

the vulnerable zone on the east coast of India. It should be of interest to note that governmental response to cyclone/flood hazards in Andhra Pradesh has been much better than in Orissa. As noted earlier, in the case of Andhra Pradesh, sharper policies of disaster preparedness and institutional development and capability to deal with cyclone/flood hazards, especially in saving lives, has improved remarkably since 1978. This was evident in the performance of the disaster management system in Andhra Pradesh in handling the subsequent disasters, that is, the cyclones of November 1984 (Sriharikota), November 1989 (Kavali), May 1990 (Machilipatnam), and November 1996 (Kakinada). Of these, the 1990 and 1996 cyclones were very severe. Although the intensity of the 1996 cyclone matched that of 1977, the human loss was reduced to about one-tenth of the latter. In the 1996 cyclone 1,077 people were killed, but the physical damage was to the tune of Rs. 560 billion (US$ 14 billion). Preparedness measures in Andhra Pradesh include evacuation of large numbers of potential victims from vulnerable areas by government-arranged transport and an extensive alert in the target areas and mobilization of outside resources (army rescue teams, navy helicopters and machine boats, medical teams, etc.). Senior officers are dispatched to vulnerable districts much before a hazard occurs. Soon after the hazard strikes, adequate number of technical and non-technical officials are sent to handle the multifarious tasks. If it is a major disaster, several thousand government officials from unaffected districts are dispatched, along with vehicles, within 12 to 24 hours. Relief supplies and rescue equipment are also rushed to the affected areas on time.

It appears that the success of Andhra Pradesh in disaster risk reduction was not matched by either Orissa on the east coast or Gujarat on the west coast. The Gujarat coast was hit by two major cyclones, in 1978 and 1998. The state did not show evidence of any cumulative learning experience either in preparedness or in post-disaster operations. The Orissa government displays a record of serious neglect in preparedness. The Orissa coast has been subjected to frequent onslaughts by cyclones from the Bay of Bengal. The cyclone of 1971 (Balasore) was a severe one with a death toll of about 8,000. The Vamsadhara floods of 1980 also had a severe impact. A common observation of analysts is that in comparison with Andhra Pradesh, Orissa lagged far behind in learning from its earlier experience of handling natural disasters (1971, 1980, and 1982).

At this juncture, it is necessary to point out that while most observers were critical about lack of preparedness on the part of the Orissa government in facing the super cyclone of 1999, what has missed their attention was that the state government found itself helpless in the face of inadequate and unclear warnings from the IMD. It had parallels to what happened from the IMD side in 1977 (Cohen and Raghavulu 1979: 65–68). Despite the IMD's warnings on 18 and 19 November 1977, it was not known even to them when the storm surge would hit, at what depth, and at what point on the 985 km coastline of Andhra Pradesh. The ambiguities arising out of the limited technological capability of the IMD were compounded by the fact that the cyclone shifted its course twenty-seven times before crossing the Andhra coast.

While it was a problem of technological capability of the IMD in 1977, it was one of technical efficiency in 1999, the latter culminating in ineffective warnings. The ineffectiveness of the warnings, as Biswanath Dash (2002: 4,270) asserts, is because the IMD's approach was not user-driven. The warnings could not communicate specific information in order to assess the level of risk to the victims and that whether the storm surge—predicted to be 10 m high—would reach their village, located, for example, at a distance of 10 km from the coast. Given the ambiguities in the warnings, government officials as well as the victims remained indecisive about the need for evacuation. The IMD focuses on the technical aspects of the warning rather than upon helping the policy maker's or the victim's decision process. One of the UN agencies has suggested (UN 1997: 1–7) an integrated warning system emphasizing: (*a*) technical ability, that is, detection, forecasting, etc.; (*b*) identifying the extent to which the endangered population is vulnerable; and (*c*) effective communication and interpretation of the message in a manner that facilitates the decision-making process of the relevant government functionaries and the target population. The last item requires incorporation of social science inputs into the warning process (Dash 2002: 4,271).

DISCUSSION AND CONCLUSIONS

In the post-independence period, welfare ideology, democratic politics, and media focus on disasters have helped deepen the commitment of the Indian state towards disaster victims, a commitment originally rooted in *dharmik* notions of helping people in distress. An overview of the disaster scene of the last thirty years indicates that notwithstanding some initial hiccups and delays, the relief work of state governments in India is adequate, at least in the case of sudden disasters. While the burden imposed by disasters has been growing, the expenditure, especially on mitigation and preparedness, is not commensurate with the requirements. Improvements in the technology of warning systems with a rapid dissemination capability, coupled with satellite and remote-sensing imageries—the latter aimed at monitoring and hazard assessment and technical analyses—have been most helpful. So have the improved institutional capability of some state governments. Both these developments placed the disaster situation in a better state of preparedness and contributed to a dramatic reduction in human losses, especially with regard to cyclones and floods. Greater professionalism and participative approaches of the NGOs, despite their limited canvas of coverage, are a welcome trend. The conquest of famine, with the exception of stray cases, is also a remarkable achievement of independent India.

The relief scene presents a somewhat disorganized picture. Relief material were dumped at accessible places, resulting in iniquitous distribution, more so in disasters with an extensive geographical area of devastation. The tendency to inflate the relief rolls by splitting households for claiming excess relief was noted in almost all disasters in Andhra Pradesh, Gujarat, and Tamil Nadu. Very often, the village functionaries colluded with victims in this regard. Inordinate delays were reported in the delivery of relief assistance to victims in interior areas in the Orissa cyclone (1999), the quake-hit areas (Uttarkashi, Latur, and Kutch), and the Andaman islands (2004–5). Dumping of inappropriate and unwanted goods on disaster victims was common to all disasters. Medical services operated efficiently, except in the super cyclone of Orissa. It is also noticeable that in each disaster the survivors were the first to bother about rescue, medical aid, and relief to their family members and kin, followed by concern and help from neighbours and volunteers from unaffected villages of the area (Raghavulu 1982: 39; Ray 2001: 138–39; TNN 2005a: 10).

The NGO scenario has changed in a few respects. The Indian government's liberalization policy and the processes of globalization had some influence upon risk management and risk reduction strategies in India. Its open door policy has melted some of the earlier negativism towards international NGOs and foreign aid agencies. At the same time NGOs continue to be plagued by problems of coordination, lapses in relief work, and the heightened expectations of the victims in the adopted villages. NGOs are not happy about their relationship with the bureaucracy either. The symbolic gestures of partnership from the bureaucracy to NGOs stop short of offering a level playing field to the latter in the relief and reconstruction process, but instead turning them to play a second fiddle to the government.

Contrary to the prevailing stereotype that bureaucratic organizations and bureaucracies are rule conscious, inflexible, and suffer from red tape and other dilatory procedures, it is observed that they shed these characteristics to a large extent in disaster contexts. The emergence of inter-organizational alignments, temporary structures, as also improved acceptance of interdependence enable bureaucratic organizations cope with the new challenges posed by disasters (Raghavulu 1997: 401–6). This review concurs with the observation of Mathur and Bhattacharya (1975: 81) that bureaucracies tend to enhance their capability in disaster situations. The changes are mostly internal to the bureaucracy and are not sustained beyond the relief stage. Moreover, the political elite and NGOs do not perceive of any qualitative change in the attitude of the bureaucracy towards them as they perceive a relationship of conflict.

The Politics of Disaster Relief

A detailed review of institutional response to disasters indicates that the same issues and concerns that surfaced in the Andhra cyclone study by Cohen and Raghavulu (1979) seem to recur, though a few of them tend to be more salient than others. The phenomenon of conflict between different levels of the government and between various sets of functionaries has endured many a disaster regardless of time and space (Bose 1994: 119–34; Raghavulu and Bose 1992: 314–31). Conflicts between the Union government and the states in a federal context arise out of specific legal responsibilities and varying levels of access to information and resources. Controversies also arise due to conflict of political interests, more so when different political parties are at the helm at the Union and state levels, as was the case in major disasters in Andhra Pradesh in 1977, 1986, and 1996, and in the relief process of the Asian tsunami during 2004–5 in Tamil Nadu. In these instances, conflicts reached a high point of intensity between the Union government and the states concerned; the latter accusing the Union government about delay and inadequacy in the quantum of aid, anomalies in the modalities and procedures of assistance, and imposition of unreasonable conditions. For instance, during 1986–87, the Andhra government was directed to utilize the central grant within five days (*Hindu* 1987). The then governor of the state also floated an NGO and issued appeals for contributions; this practice was contrary to the norm of maintaining only one relief fund in the name of the chief minister. The state government accused the governor of running a parallel government (Bose 1994: 129). Most recently there were animated political controversies in the aftermath of the Asian tsunami between the AIADMK government of Tamil Nadu and the Union government. In contrast to the previous instances, a cooperative relationship prevailed between the Union and the states concerned with regard to the Latur quake of 1991 (Maharashtra), the super cyclone of 1999 (Orissa), and the Kutch quake of 2001 (Gujarat). In all the three disasters, the same party—Congress in 1991 and 1999, and the BJP in 2001—was in power both at the centre and in the states concerned.

Centre–state financial relations in the sphere of disaster mitigation have been contributing to an anomalous situation in the federal system as states are responsible for performance, but the centre, which holds the purse strings, lords over them. A careful and detailed examination of the Union government's record, regardless of the party in power, demonstrates that partisan political considerations received undue weightage in its dispensation of aid (Raghavulu and Bose 1992). While it is not entirely possible to pre-empt political considerations from disaster contexts, it is not difficult to depoliticize contentious issues and limit the scope for overtly political approaches. Clear norms should, therefore, be evolved for the quantum of central assistance by quantifying a number of parameters of a disaster besides the modalities of aid so that the affected states are not placed at the mercy of the Union government. Of equal importance is the demarcation of the spheres of authority and responsibility between the Union and the states.

Conflicts between the political elite and bureaucracy are over goals and perceptions of each other's role in disaster situations. While the bureaucracy advances uniform criteria for relief and rehabilitation assistance, politicians suggest departures from the rational model to subserve partisan considerations. In the Andhra disasters of 1977 and 1979 and in the Asian tsunami (2004–5) in Tamil Nadu, the ruling party's local elite were able to divert more relief to groups and individuals that form their support structures. The political elite of the ruling party and their constituents have also cornered a disproportionate share of reconstruction assistance such as pucca housing. Further, the bureaucracy was pressurized to provide aid at an optimal level to areas that were only marginally affected. It was observed that political interference in relief distribution has increased, in some cases to the extent of rendering the whole exercise a mockery (Reddy 2000: 196). In the conflict that ensued, the bureaucracy had to yield (Raghavulu 1997: 405). Where organized political groups were persistent, the bureaucracy made amends to the criteria.[14] Obviously, there is need for a clear demarcation of the realms of authority between politicians and bureaucrats, while ensuring coordination among the various participating agencies, including NGOs.

The Andhra cyclone was intensely politicized. The term 'corpse politics', first popularized in the Andhra cyclone study, gained wider currency in characterizing the political discourse of each of the subsequent major disasters in India. The tendency for the ruling party elite to promise aid—and more aid—and for the opposition to attack the government of negligence, inefficiency, and even corruption, has

---

[14]Recent experience with food-for-work schemes under drought mitigation indicates that in a vast majority of cases politicians and bureaucrats cooperated with each other in deals relating to misappropriation of funds or material.

now become common to the political rhetoric of disasters. Politicians are alert to the opportunities a disaster situation offers for purposes of political mobilization. No major disaster since the Andhra cyclone of 1977 has escaped controversies over the number of causalities, estimates of the costs of damage, or the quantum of central assistance. Over the years major disasters have generated a number of controversies, augmenting the political heat of electoral campaigns or galvanizing political realignments or changes in leadership. Many such politically motivated controversies have only contributed to deterioration of the quality of political discourse in India. The political landscape of disasters provides adequate political space for other types of actions of political embarrassment such as resignations by cabinet ministers or feelers to that effect by opponents to the chief minister concerned with a view to intimidate or blackmail or increase their bargaining power for immediate or long-term political gain. The Andhra cyclone triggered resignations by as many as ten ministers citing inept performance by the bureaucracy and the chief minister. One of them withdrew it later. In the super cyclone of Orissa (1999), in the Kutch quake (2001), and in the Mumbai floods (2005) the chief ministers of the respective states were the focal points of attack from leaders of the opposition as well as factions within the respective ruling parties. Indeed, the incumbent chief minster of Gujarat who was from Kutch even offered his resignation, though it was not accepted.

From Relief to Preparedness, Mitigation and Development

The Indian disaster response system has also remained impervious to new approaches, in spite of the fact that a growing body of literature, backed by documentation by academicians and experts, besides recommendations from multilateral agencies, is stimulating governments and disaster organizations to reinvent disaster response strategies. Many experts suggest a gradual shift from relief to preparedness and integration of mitigation and preparedness with development. Natural and man-made hazards are inevitable, but they need not transform into disasters. However, disasters seem to recur in the same areas with a high frequency, causing more human and property losses. For the poor every one of them represents an increase in vulnerability. Response by way of relief and rehabilitation in the aftermath of each disaster does very little to protect them against subsequent disasters; they only help reinforce the 'dependency' syndrome. It is, therefore, suggested that a disaster mitigation policy should be built into strategies of socio-economic development, environmental management, and, broadly speaking, sustainable development (Bjerregaard 1994: 201; ISDR 2002: 6; Mileti 1999: 155–207; Indo-French Seminar 2002: 5; Wisner 2003: 135–45).

In the Indian context, disaster mitigation and prevention are not conceptually linked with development planning. Nor is there a long-term strategy for mitigation and development of hazard-prone areas for disaster reduction (Sharma 2003: 141–42). The series of recommendations made by experts in the aftermath of each major disaster reflect the tenets of sustainable development. The United States Geological Survey reckons that the economic losses from natural disasters in the 1990s could have been reduced by US$ 280 billion by investing just one-seventh of that sum in disaster risk reduction measures. In India the need for a shift of focus from relief to disaster reduction and linking the latter with development planning has not received adequate attention though it is filtering, albeit slowly, into the policy rhetoric. Of late, there has been some realization on the part of the Union government that 'disaster mitigation concerns/ aspects may be made an essential term of reference for every plan project/development scheme in the areas vulnerable to disasters' (Government of India 2004b: 51). The policy frame leaves it to the option of the state governments to incorporate disaster risk reduction into development instead of making it a mandatory strategy. The conceptual shift has not materialized so far not because of lack of awareness and knowledge among policy makers; it has not happened because of such factors as shortage of public and private funds, and a political leadership wedded to projects of visibility and vote bank calculus. Despite the Union government formally regulating construction and development within 500 m of the coast by declaring it as Coastal Regulation Zones (CRZs) through a notification in 1991, ecosystems in these areas continue to be under threat on both the east and west coasts. Aqua farms, industries, tourist resorts, residential buildings, and several other private ventures have been permitted by the state governments concerned, offering relaxations to the central notification or by simply ignoring it. Relevant verdicts of the apex court have also been outmanœuvered in the process.

There is a widely held view that international NGOs and multilateral agencies are committed to long-term disaster reduction. Prevailing practices do not, however, support this view. International or national NGOs do not have budgets for long-term disaster reduction. Multilateral agencies and international financial institutions, despite their wide acceptance of the idea, seem to be biased towards short-term, high-impact, and visible projects (Dixit 2003: 105). Assistance that they provide for long-term disaster reduction projects is not extensive. It is, therefore, necessary to have a consensus among NGOs and international financial institutions for an optimal investment for long-term mitigation. Sustained efforts by lobbies committed to disaster mitigation can break the vicious circle of vulnerability.

It is disturbing to note the progressive depletion of the forest cover, not to speak of the lack of any concerted approach to increase natural vegetation on the coast and aforestation in the interior. Equally pathetic is uncontrolled environmental degradation and unchecked development on the sea coast and river banks. A casual approach in the construction of dams, layout of roads, railway lines, and drainage structures in the flood plains, and location of slums on river banks/ basins and drainage structures had the effect of accelerating floods. Non-implementation of earthquake-resistant building regulations and codes in seismic zones is all pervasive. Earthquakes do not kill: buildings do. A.S Arya[15], a seismic expert, observes that almost 85 per cent of the country's buildings are vulnerable to damage from earthquakes. Inadequacy of public and private funds, poor engineering practices, weak regulation capacity, rampant corruption, and collusion between political and bureaucratic elite on the one hand and powerful private investors on the other are resulting in non-observance of safety measures in building construction in the seismic zones and vulnerable coastal areas. The Gujarat government's action in protecting the interests of the builders by issuing two ordinances regularizing

---

[15]Quoted from *The National Vulnerability Atlas* (prepared for the Government of India by a committee headed by A.S. Arya) by Rajesh Ramachandran in 'Danger from Earthquakes: A Hundred Ground Zeroes' in *Outlook,* Mumbai (January 17, 2005), XLV (2), pp. 42.

illegal constructions in the aftermath of the Kutch earthquake exposes the weaknesses of the political system.

The problem is not amenable to any 'quick-fix' solutions as it is intrinsic to the democratic process and the functioning of public institutions in India. In most cases comprehensive legislative enactments exist, but the tragedy is that they remain unenforced or relaxations are obtained by interested parties. One can only hope that with the passage of time democratic processes themselves will undergo a qualitative transformation to impact upon the functioning of public institutions in ways favourable to disaster reduction. Influence from extrinsic sources, as it happened in the arena of economic policy, may also have a salutary effect in enhancing the commitment of public authorities towards disaster reduction. Improvement in standards of living,[16] increasing public awareness and participation to reduce vulnerability to disasters, judicial activism in regard to enforcement of environmental legislation, and media focus on patterned violations of law would help in improving institutional response to disasters in India.

BIBLIOGRAPHY

Asian Disaster Reduction Center (ADRC). (2000). *Data Book on Asian Natural Disasters in the 20th Century.* Kobe: ADRC.

Anon (1991). *Floods, Flood Plains and Environment Myths: State of India's Environment, A Citizen's Report.* New Delhi: Centre for Science and Environment.

Arya, A.S. (1994a). Action Plan for Earthquake Disaster Mitigation. In Vinod K. Sharma, ed., *Disaster Management*, pp. 60–73. New Delhi: Indian Institute of Public Administration.

———— (1994b). Case Study in India: Diagnosis, Repair and Strengthening of Damaged Buildings. In Vinod K. Sharma, ed., *Disaster Management*, pp. 129–48. New Delhi: Indian Institute of Public Administration.

Aykroyd, W.R. (1974). *The Conquest of Famine.* London:Chatto and Windris.

Baria, Farah (2005). Metropolis on the Brink. *Indian Express* (Mumbai), 5 August, p. 9.

Bhatia, B.M. (1967). *Famines in India: A Study in Some Aspects of the Economic History of India.* Bombay: Asia.

---

[16]One Japanese scholar argues that a society that can raise funds from its own economic surplus will have considerably greater disaster-coping capacity and resilience. He cites the case of Japan, which used to suffer from disasters every year until the early 1960s. Since then economic growth made it possible to allocate sizeable amounts for disaster preparedness. See Watanabe (2003: 96).

Bjerregaard, Ove (1994). Keynote Address: Natural Disasters vis-à-vis National Development. In Vinod K. Sharma, ed., *Disaster Management*, pp. 7–12. New Delhi: Indian Institute of Public Administration.

Blair, Charles (1986). *Indian Famines: Their Historical Aspects, Financial and Other Aspects.* New Delhi: Agricole Reprints.

Bose, B.P.C. (1983). Disaster Preparedness in Andhra Pradesh. *Disaster Management*, 3(3), (July–September), pp. 153–57.

———— (1994). The Politics of Disasters. *Indian Journal of Political Science*, 60(2), (April–June), pp. 119–34.

———— (2003). NGOs in the Disaster Context of India: Some Issues. *Loyola Journal of the Social Sciences*, 42(2), (July–December), pp. 171–91.

Brass, Paul R. (1986). The Political Uses of Crisis: The Bihar Famine of 1966–67. *Journal of Asian Studies*, 45(2), pp. 245–67.

Buckle, Philip, Graham Mars, and Syd Smale (2000). Approaches to Assessing Vulnerability and Resilience. *Australian Journal of Emergency Management*, 15(2), pp. 8–14.

Chaturvedi, A. (1988). *District Administration: The Dynamics of Discord.* New Delhi: Sage Publications.

Chopra, Ravi (2000). Earthquakes: Reconfiguring Lives and Landscapes. In S. Parasuraman and P.V. Unnikrishnan, eds., *India Disasters Report*, pp. 201–8. New Delhi: Oxford University Press.

Cohen, Stephen, P. and C.V. Raghavulu (1979). *The Andhra Cyclone of 1977: Individual and Institutional Responses to Mass Death.* New Delhi: Vikas.

Dash, Biswanath (2002). Lessons from Orissa Super Cyclone: Need for Integrated Warning System. *Economic and Political Weekly*, 37(42), pp. 4270–71.

Denhartog, Adel P. (1981). Adjustment of Food Behaviour during Famine. In John R.K. Robson, ed., *Famine: Its Causes, Effects and Management*, pp. 156–62. New Delhi: Gordon and Breach Science Publications.

Digby, William (1901). *Prosperous British India.* London: T. Fisher Unwin.

Dixit, Amod M. (2003). *Regional Development Dialogue*, 24(1), pp. 102–06.

Dreze, Jean (1999). *The Economics of Famine.* New York: Edward Elgar Publishing.

D' Souza, Dilip (2003). The Attitude of Relief. *Seminar*, 509 (January), pp. 90–94.

Earthquake Engineering Research Institute (EERI) (1994). *Special Earthquake Report* (EERI Research & Information Newsletter), 28 (January), pp. 1–4.

Gopal Raj, N. (2005). Flood Forecasting Possibilities and Problems. *Hindu* (Hyderabad), (8 August), p. 10.

Government of India (1971). *Cyclone Distress Mitigation Committee Report* (CDMC Report, Appendix iii). New Delhi: Ministry of Irrigation and Power.

———— (2004a). *Drought 2002, Chattisgarh, Madhya Pradesh and Orissa, Part 2, Vol.iii.* New Delhi: Ministry of Agriculture.

———— (2004b). *Disaster Management in India: A Status Report, August 2004.* New Delhi: Ministry of Home Affairs.

Greengough, P.R. (1982). *Prosperity and Misery in Modern Bengal: The Famine of 1943–44.* New York: Oxford University Press.

Gupta L.C. and V.K. Sharma. (2001a). *Drought in Gujarat 1999–2000.* New Delhi: Indian Institute of Public Administration.

———— (2001b). *Drought in Rajasthan, 1999–2000 and 2000–2001.* New Delhi: Indian Institute of Public Administration.

———— (undated). *Orissa Super Cyclone '99.* New Delhi: Indian Institute of Public Administration.

Gupta, Sujata, Akram Javed, and Divya Datt (2003). Economics of Flood Protection in India. *Natural Hazards,* 28(1) (January), pp. 199–210.

Guardian, (2005). 29 January, http://www.guardian.com.uk London Quoted in New HTML Article on Indonesia/Nicobar/Andaman Earthquake (updated March 7, 2005).

Hanumantha Rao, Ch. (1987). Unstable Agriculture: Lessons from Current Drought. *Monthly Commentary on Indian Economic Conditions,* 30(1) (August), pp. 41–47.

Hanumantha Rao, Ch., S.K. Ray, and K. Subba Rao (1988). *Unstable Agriculture and Droughts.* New Delhi: Vikas.

Hindu (1987). 16 February.

IBRD (2003). *World Development Report 2003: Sustainable Development in a Dynamic World.* Washington, DC: World Bank.

Indo–French Seminar on Earthquake Prevention, Preparedness and Mitigation, Background Material (mimeo.). 2002 (18 November). New Delhi: The Embassy of France in India.

International Federation of the Red Cross and Red Crescent Societies (IFRC). (1998). *World Disasters Report 1998.* New York: Oxford University Press.

———— (IFRC) (2001). *World Disasters Report 2001.* New York: Kumarian Press.

ISDR Secretariat (2002). *Living With Risk: A Global Review of Disaster Reduction Initiatives* (Preliminary version). Geneva: ISDR Secretariat (United Nations).

Indian Water Resources Society (IWRS) (2001). Theme Paper on Management of Floods and Droughts. IWRS, Roorke, pp. 4–12.

Kanchan, A. and J. Gwynn (2000). The 1999 Super Cyclone in Orissa. In S. Parasuraman and P.V Unnikrishnan, eds., *India Disasters Report,* pp. 199–200. New Delhi: Oxford University Press.

Kanwar, Rakesh (2003). Disaster Management. In Shivraj Singh, P.P.S. Gill, S.S. Chauhan, and S.K. Mahajan, eds., *Public Administration in the New Millennium: Challenges and Prospects,* pp. 335–53. New Delhi: Anamika Publications.

Kulkarni, N. (1990). *Famines, Droughts and Scarcities in India.* Allahabad: Chugh Publications.

Lahiri, Ashok K., T.K. Sen, R. Kavitha Rao, and P.R. Jena (2001). Economic Consequences of Gujarat Earthquake. *Economic and Political Weekly,* 36 (21 April), pp. 1319–32.

Lochan, K. and S. Avasthi (2000). Lessons from Eastern Uttar Pradesh. In S. Parasuraman and P.V. Unnikrishnan, eds., *India Disasters Report,* pp. 161–63. New Delhi: Oxford University Press.

Lynch, Simon and P.V. Unnikrishnan (2000). A Profile of Agencies Involved in Disaster Response. In S. Parasuraman and P.V. Unnikrishnan, eds., *India Disasters Report,* pp. 130–37. New Delhi: Oxford University Press.

Marpakwar, P. (2005). Mumbai's Damage Bill: Rs. 15,000 Crores. *Times of India* (New Delhi) (3 August), p. 12.

Martin, Max (2000). Environmental Disasters. In S. Parasuraman and P.V. Unnikrishnan, eds., *India Disasters Report,* pp. 59–65. New Delhi: Oxford University Press.

Mathur, K. and Mohit Bhattacharya (1975). *Administrative Response to Emergency*. Delhi: Concept.

Mathur, Kuldeep and Neeraja G. Jayal (1993). Parliamentary Response to Drought 1987. *Indian Journal of Political Science*, 54(3 & 4) (July–December), pp. 352–68.

Mayer, Jean (1974). Coping with Famine. *Foreign Affairs*, 53 (October), pp. 98–130.

McEntire, David A., C. Fuller, C.W. Jonston, and R. Wefer (2002). A Comparison of Disaster Paradigms: The Search for a Holistic Policy Guide. *Public Administration Review*, 62(3) (May–June), pp. 267–81.

Mehta, Lyla (2001). Reflections on the Kutch Earthquake. *Economic and Political Weekly*, 36(31) (4 August), pp. 2931–36.

Menon, Meena (2005). Mumbaikar Agony Aggravates. *Hindu* (New Delhi), (1 August), p. 12.

Mileti, Dennis S. (1999). *Disasters by Design: A Reassessment of Natural Hazards in the United States*. Washington, DC: Joseph Henry Press.

Mishra, D.K. (2000). Bihar: Breaches of Promises. In S. Parasuraman and P.V. Unnikrishnan, eds., *India Disasters Report*, pp. 155–57. New Delhi, Oxford University Press.

Mishra, H.K. (1991). *Famines and Poverty in India*. New Delhi: Asish.

Mishra, Pramod K. (2004). *The Kutch Earthquake 2001: Recollections, Lessons and Insights*. New Delhi: National Institute of Disaster Management.

Mohapatra, Bishnu (2000). Politics in Post-Cyclone Orissa. *Economic and Political Weekly*, 35(16) (15 April), pp. 1353–55.

Mohapatra, P.K. and R.D. Singh (2003). Flood Management in India. *Natural Hazards*, 28(1) (January), pp. 131–43.

Naidu, B.R. (1989). Disaster Management. In B.R. Naidu, ed., *Disaster Management*, pp. 1–14. Kavali: SVUPG Centre.

Nakagawa, Y. and R. Shaw (2004). Social Capital: A Missing Link to Disaster Recovery. *International Journal of Mass Emergencies and Disasters*, 22(1) (March), pp. 5–34.

Ninan, Oommen, A. (2005). India Inc. Hype Stands Exposed. *Hindu* (Hyderabad), (8 August), p. 16.

Parasuraman, S. (1995). The Impact of the 1993 Latur–Osmanabad (Maharashtra) Earthquake on Lives, Livelihoods and Property. *Disasters*, 19(2), pp. 156–69.

Paton Douglas, Leigh Smith, and John Violantic (2000). Disaster Response: Risk, Vulnerability and Resilience. *Disaster Prevention and Management*, 9(3) (July), pp. 173–79.

Pattanaik, P.K. (2000). A Blue Print for Effective Management of Natural Disaster. *Yojana*, 44(7), (July), pp. 19–25.

Raghavulu, C.V. (1978). Disaster Management: A Study of Bureaucracy—Voluntary Groups. In *Seminar Report on Lessons Learnt from the Andhra Cyclone*, pp. 65–70. Vijayawada: ARTIC/INTERTECT.

———— (1980). Disaster Management and Organisational Adaptation. In T.N.Chatruvedi and Shanta Kohli Chandra, eds., *Social Administration, Development and Change*, pp. 63–81. New Delhi: Indian Institute of Public Administration.

———— (1982). *Disaster Preparedness: A Study in Community Perspectives*. Hyderabad: ARTIC/UNICEF.

———— (1985). Disasters, Development and Foreign Aid: Some Issues and Concerns. *Journal of Social and Economic Studies*, 2(4) (October–December), pp. 343–59.

———— (1989). Disaster Management. In B.R. Naidu, ed., *Disaster Management*, pp. 19–26. Kavali: SVUPG Centre.

———— (1997). Disaster Management. In V.A. Pai Panandiker, ed., *A Survey of Research in Public Administration 1980–1990*, pp. 392–426. New Delhi: Konark.

Raghavulu, C.V. and B.P.C. Bose (1992). Centre–State Relations in Disaster Mitigation and Preparedness. *The Indian Journal of Political Science*, 53(3) (July–September), pp. 314–31.

Rajan, K. (1994). Natural Disasters Management in National Development: An Indian Perspective. In Vinod K. Sharma, ed., *Disaster Management*, pp. 26–37. New Delhi: Indian Institute of Public Administration.

Ray, C.N. (2001). Earthquake Relief and Rehabilitation in Gujarat: Issues in Disaster Management. *Indian Journal of Public Administration*, 47 (April–June), pp. 129–51.

Reddy, A.V.S. (2000). Cyclone Mitigation Measures: Interview with Captain A.V.S. Reddy. In S. Parasuraman and P.V. Unnikrishnan, eds., *India Disasters Report*, pp. 195–97. New Delhi: Oxford University Press.

Robson, John R.K. (1981). Introduction. In John R.K. Robson, ed., *Famine: Its Causes, Effects, and Management*, pp. 1–4. New York: Gordon and Breach Science Publications.

Roy, Dunu. (2000). A Small Matter of History. In S. Parasuraman and P.V. Unnikrishnan, eds., *India Disasters Report*, pp. 147–54. New Delhi: Oxford University Press.

Sainath, P. (2000). Everybody Loves a Good Drought. In S. Parasuraman and P.V. Unnikrishnan, eds., *India Disasters Report*, pp. 173–76. New Delhi: Oxford University Press.

Sahoo, M. (2000). Andhra Pradesh Government Policy on Disaster Management. In S. Parasuraman and P.V. Unnikrishnan, eds., *India Disasters Report*, pp. 104–6. New Delhi: Oxford University Press.

Sapir, D.G. (2000). Disasters in South Asia. In S. Parasuraman and Unnikrishnan, eds., *India Disasters Report*, pp. 25–28. New Delhi: Oxford University Press.

Sen, A.K. (1981). *Poverty and Famines in India: An Essay on Entitlement and Deprivation*. Oxford: Clarendon Press.

Sen S.R. (1988). Coping with Droughts. *Economic and Political Weekly*, 23 (23 July), pp. 1523–24.

Shah, A. (1998). National Development Programmes in India: Emerging Issues for Environment Development Perspectives. *Economic and Political Weekly*, 33(26) (January), 66–79.

Sharma, Anshu, M. Gupta, R. Bajaj, and R. Shaw (2003). From Disaster to Sustainable Community Recovery: Challenges and Lessons Learned. *Regional Development Dialogue*, 24(1) (Spring), 53–61.

Sharma, Kalpana (2005). Should Mumbai Govern Itself. *Hindu* (New Delhi), (3 August), p. 11.

Sharma, Vinod K. ed., (2003). Disaster Management: Approach and Emerging Strategies in India. *Vision: The Journal of Business Presepective*, 7 (January), pp. 135–44.

———— (2000). NGO–Government Collaboration. In S. Parasuraman and P.V. Unnikrishnan, eds., *India Disasters Report*, pp. 124–25. New Delhi: Oxford University Press.

Shaw, Rajib (2003). The Role of Non-Governmental Organizations in Earthquake Disaster Management: An Asian Perspective. *Regional Development Dialogue*, 24(1) (January), pp. 117–29.

Shaw, Rajib, M. Gupta, and A. Sharma (2003). Community Recovery and its Sustainability: Lessons from Gujarat Earthquake in India. *Australian Journal of Emergency Management*, 18(2) (January), pp. 28–34.

Sinha, A. and V.K. Sharma (1999). *Culture of Prevention Natural Disaster Management*. New Delhi: Indian Institute of Public Administration.

Subbiah, A.R. (2004). *State of the Indian Farmer; A Millennium Study—Natural Disaster Management*. New Delhi: Ministry of Agriculture, Government of India.

Thiruppugazh, V. (2003). Training and Capacity Building with the Policy Perspective of a Rehabilitation Programme: Experiences from Gujarat, India. *Regional Development Dialogue*, 24(1) (Spring), pp. 30–38.

Times News Network (TNN) (2005a). Analysing the Deluge. *Times of India* (New Delhi), (4 August), p. 8.

———— (2005b). Faulty Policies Led to Mumbai Mayhem. *Times of India* (New Delhi), (1 August), p. 10.

Tonk, V.S. (2003). An Approach to Disaster Management. In Shivraj Singh, P.P.S. Gill, S.S. Chauhan, and S.K. Mahajan, eds., *Public Administration in the New Millennium: Challenges and Prospects*, pp. 335–53. New Delhi: Anamika Publications.

Torry, W.I. (1986). Drought and the Government: Village Emergency Food Distribution System in India. *Human Organization*, 45 (Spring), pp. 11–23.

United Nations (1997). National and Local Capabilities for Early Warning, Geneva: IDNDR Secretariat

UNDP (1998). *Human Development Report, 1998*. New York: Oxford University Press.

US Geological Survey, Earthquake Hazards Program. http://earthquake.usgs.gov/equinthenews.

Vatsa, Krishna S. (2002). Reducing Earthquake Losses: Towards a National Perspective. *Economic and Political Weekly*, 27 (20 April): pp. 1503–05.

Watanabe, Masayuki (2003). A Core Concept for a Disaster Preparedness Plan for Developing Countries. *Regional Development Dialogue*, 24 (Spring), pp. 90–101.

Winchester, Peter (2000). Cyclone Mitigation, Resource Allocation and Post-Disaster Reconstruction in South India: Lessons from Two Decades of Research. *Disasters*, 24 (January), pp. 18–37.

World Bank (1994). *Report on Marathwada Earthquake, India (mimeo)*. New Delhi: Maharashtra Earthquake, Reconstruction Credit Appraisal Mission. Washington D.C.: World Bank.

———— (2003). Social Capital for Development. http://www.worldbank.org/poverty/scapital.

Wisner, Ben (2003). Sustainable Suffering? Reflections on Development and Disaster Vulnerability in the Post-Johannesburg World. Regional Development Dialogue, 24 (Spring), pp. 135–48.

List of Publications by Stephen Philip Cohen

Books

2004.   *The Idea of Pakistan* (Washington, DC: Brookings Institution Press).

2003.   *The Compound Crisis of 1990 Perception, Politics, and Insecurity.* With Pervaiz Iqbal Cheema and P.R. Chari (London: Routledge).

2001.   *India: Emerging Power* (Washington, DC: Brookings Institution Press; New York: Oxford University Press 2001). Revised paperback edition (Washington: Brookings 2002). Japanese, Taiwanese and Chinese editions (2001). Choice award for academic book of the year, 2002.

1995.   *Brasstacks and Beyond: Crisis Perception and Management in South Asia.* With Kanti Bajpai, P. R. Chari, Pervez Cheema and Sumit Ganguly (New Delhi: Manohar). Pakistan edition (Lahore: Vanguard Publishers, 1996). US Edition (Columbia: South Asia Books 1996).

1993.   *South Asia After the Cold War: International Perspectives.* Co-edited with Kanti Bajpai. (Boulder: Westview Press).

1991.   *Nuclear Proliferation in South Asia: The Prospects for Arms Control.* Editor (Boulder: Westview Press). Indian edition (New Delhi: Lancers Publishers).

1987.   *The Security of South Asia: American and Asian Perspectives.* Editor (Urbana and Chicago: University of Illinois Press). Indian edition (New Delhi: Vistaar Publications, 1988).

1984.   *The Pakistan Army* (Berkeley: University of California Press). Second revised edition (New York: Oxford University Press, 1998). Urdu translation (Karachi: Oxford University Press, 2002).

Reprint editions (New Delhi: Himalayan Books 1984; Karachi: Oxford University Press, 1992). Pirated editions published by the Pakistan Army (1985) and in Chinese by People's Liberation Army (1993).

1979. *The Andhra Cyclone of 1977: Institutional and Individual Responses to Mass Death.* With Chitturi V. Raghavulu (New Delhi: Vikas).

1978. *India: Emergent Power?* With Richard L. Park (New York: Crane, Russak and Company).

1971. *The Indian Army: Its Contribution to the Development of a Nation* (Berkeley and London: University of California Press and Oxford University Press). Second revised edition (New York: Oxford University Press, 1990). Third paperback revision (New York: Oxford University Press, 2001).

Book Chapters

2004. 'Nuclear Weapons and Nuclear War in South Asia: An Unknowable Future.' In Ramesh Thakur and Oddny Wiggin, eds., *South Asia in the World: Problem Solving Perspectives on Security, Sustainable Development, and Good Governance*, pp. 39–57 (Tokyo: United Nations University Press).

2004. 'Indo–Pak Track II Diplomacy: Building Peace or Wasting Time?.' in P.R. Kumaraswamy, ed., *Security Beyond Survival: Essays for K. Subrahmanyam*, pp. 192–217 (New Delhi: Sage Publications).

2003. 'India, Pakistan and Kashmir.' In Sumit Ganguly, ed., *India as an Emerging Power*, pp. 32–60 (London: Frank Cass).

2002. 'South Asia.' In Richard J. Ellings and Aaron L. Friedberg, eds., *Strategic Asia, 2002–03: Asian Aftershocks*, pp. 263–308 (Seattle: National Bureau of Asian Research).

1998. 'The United States, India, and Pakistan: Retrospect and Prospect.' In Paul Kreisberg, Dennis Kux, and Selig Harrison, eds., *India and Pakistan: The First Fifty Years*, (Washington, DC: Woodrow Wilson Center and New York: Cambridge University Press).

1998. 'India.' In Robert Chase, Emily Hill, and Paul Kennedy, eds., *The Pivotal States: A New Framework for US Policy in the Developing World*, pp. 40–63 (New York: W.W. Norton & Co.).

1998. 'Pakistan's Search for Security and Prosperity.' In Roger Kanet, ed., *Resolving Regional Conflicts*, pp. 105–34 (Urbana: University of Illinois Press).

1997. 'South Asia: The Origins of War and the Conditions for Peace in South Asia.' In Roger Kanet, ed., *Regional Conflicts and Conflict Resolution: Essays in Honor of Jeremiah Sullivan*, p. xx (Urbana: University of Illinois, 1997).

1996.   'America and India: A New Approach.' In Williamson Murray and Alan R. Millett, eds., *Brassey's Mershon American Defense Annual, 1996–97: Current Issues and the Asian Challenge*, pp. 158–85 (New York: Brassey's).

1995.   'Regional and International Dimensions of South Asian Nuclear Proliferation.' In David Law, ed., *Regional Security in South Asia*, pp. 21–25 (Kingston: Centre for International Relations, Queen's University).

1995.   'Kashmir: The Roads Ahead.' In Chetan Kumar and Marvin Weinbaum, eds., *South Asia Approaches the Millennium: Reexamining National Security*, pp. 127–44 (Boulder: Westview Press).

1995.   'Images of Peace and War in South Asia.' In Kanti P. Bajpai and Harish C. Shukul, eds., *Interpreting World Politics*, pp. 309–36 (New Delhi: Sage Publications).

1994.   'Cooperative Security and South Asian Insecurity.' In Janne Nolan, ed., *Global Engagement: Cooperation and Security in the 21st Century*, pp. 447–80. With Kanti Bajpai (Washington: Brookings Institution Press).

1994.   'Conflict in South Asia: An American Perspective.' In Leo A. Rose and Jasjit Singh, eds., untitled volume on superpower and South Asian relations, p. xx (Berkeley: University of California, and New Delhi: Institute of Defence Studies and Analysis).

1993.   'The Military in India and Pakistan: Contrasting Cases.' In Myron L. Cohen and Roberta Martin, eds., *Asian Case Studies in the Social Sciences*, pp. 282–97 (New York: Columbia University Press).

1992.   'Trends in US–Indian Relations: The Security Dimension.' In Leo A. Rose and Eric Gonsalves, eds., *Toward a New World Order: Adjusting India-US Relations*, pp. 105–14 (Berkeley: Institute of East Asian Studies, Research Papers and Policy Studies).

1992.   'The Reagan Administration and India.' In Sumit Ganguly and Harold Gould, eds., *The Hope and the Reality: US–Indian Relations from Roosevelt to Reagan*, pp. 137–54 (Boulder: Westview Press).

1992.   'The Future Indian Security Role in the Asia-Pacific-Indian Ocean Region.' In Jasjit Singh, ed., *Indo–US Relations in a Changing World: Proceedings of the Indo–US Strategic Symposium*, pp. 65–84 (New Delhi: Lancers Publishers).

1992.   'Controlling Weapons of Mass Destruction in South Asia: An American Perspective.' In Shelley A. Stahl and Geoffrey Kemp, eds., *Arms Control and Weapons Proliferation in the Middle East and South Asia*, pp. 197–220 (New York: St. Martin's Press in association with the Carnegie Endowment for International Peace).

1991.   'India as a Great Power: Perceptions and Prospects.' In Philip Oldenburg, ed., *India Briefing, 1991*, pp. 7–73 (Boulder: Westview Press).

1990.   'US–Soviet Cooperation in South Asia.' In Roger Kanet and Edward Kolodziej, eds., *The Cold War as Cooperation*, pp. 281–309 (London: Macmillan and Baltimore: Johns Hopkins, 1991).

1990.   'Solving Proliferation Problems in a Regional Context: South Asia.' In Joseph Nye, Jr., et al., eds., *New Threats: Responding to the Proliferation of Nuclear, Chemical, and Delivery Capabilities in the Third World*, pp. 163–96 (Aspen and Washington: Aspen Strategy Group and University Press of America).

1990.   'Political Leadership in Asia.' In Robert H. Taylor, ed., *Handbooks of the Modern World: Asia and the Pacific*, p. xx (New York: Facts on File Publications).

1989.   'The Soviet Union and South Asia'. In Roger Kanet and Edward Kolodziej, eds., *The Soviet Union and the Third World*, pp. 201–26 (Baltimore: Johns Hopkins University Press).

1988.   'The Military and Indian Democracy.' In Atul Kohli, ed. *India's Democracy: An Analysis of Changing State–Society Relations*, pp. 99–143 (Princeton: Princeton University Press).

1987.   'The Security of South Asia: Regional Conflicts and External Induction.' In Robert S. Litwak and Samuel F. Wells, eds., *The Third World and International Security: Competing East–West Policies and Perspectives*, pp. 153–78 (Boston: Ballinger).

1987.   'South Asia in 1986.' In Barry Blechman and Edward Luttwak, eds., *Global Security: A Review of Strategic and Economic Issues*, pp. 213–36 (Washington: Center for Strategic and International Studies and Boulder: Westview Press).

1987.   'Partners or Friends: US–Pakistan Security Relations Revisited.' In Leo Rose and Noor A. Husain, eds., *US–Pakistan Relations*, p. xx (Berkeley: Institute of East Asian Studies).

1987.   'Growing Soviet Interests in South Asia.' In Ray S. Cline, James Arnold Miller, and Roger E. Kanet, eds., *Asia in Soviet Global Strategy*, pp. 131–42 (Boulder: Westview).

1986.   'The Role of the Military in Contemporary Pakistan.' In Edward A. Olsen and Stephen Jurika, Jr., eds., *The Armed Forces in Contemporary Asian Societies*, pp. 285–308 (Boulder: Westview Press).

1986.   'State Building in Pakistan.' In Ali Banuazizi and Myron Weiner, eds., *The State, Religion, and Ethnic Politics: Afghanistan, Iran, and Pakistan*, pp. 299–332 (Syracuse: Syracuse University Press).

1985. 'US–Pakistan Security Relations: Bases, Arms Sales, Nuclear Policy.' In Leo Rose and Noor A. Husain, eds., *US–Pakistan Relations*, pp. 15–33 (Berkeley: Institute of East Asian Studies).

1985. 'Militarization in South Asia.' In Jagat S. Mehta, ed., *Third World Militarization: A Challenge to Third World Diplomacy*, pp. 93–106 (Austin: LBJ School of Public Affairs, University of Texas).

1985. 'India, South Asia, and the Superpowers: War and Society.' In Paul Wallace, ed., *Region and Nation in India: Essays in Memory of Richard L. Park*, p. xx (New Delhi: Oxford University Press and American Institute of Indian Studies).

1984. 'Defense Planning in Pakistan, Comments.' In Stephanie Neuman, ed., *Defense Planning in Less Industrialized States*, pp. 231–38 (Lexington: DC Heath).

1983. 'Regional International Relations and Foreign Policy Analysis: South Asia.' In John Stremlau, ed. *International Relations Research: Emerging Trends Outside the United States, 1981–1982*, pp. 1–27 (New York: Rockefeller Foundation).

1983. 'Pakistan: Coping with Regional Dominance, Multiple Crises, and Great Power Confrontation.' In Raju G. C. Thomas, ed., *The Great Power Triangle and Asian Security*, pp. 47–63 (Lexington: DC Heath).

1982. 'Pakistan.' In Edward A. Kolodziej and Robert E. Harkavy, eds., *Security Policies of Developing Countries*, pp. 93–118 (Lexington: DC Heath).

1981. 'Image and Perception in India–Pakistan Relations.' In Shivaji Ganguly and M.S. Rajan, eds., *Great Power Relations, World Order, and the Third World*, p. xx (New Delhi: Vikas).

1980. 'Towards a Great State in Asia?' In Onkar S. Marwah and Jonathan Pollack, eds., *Military Power and Policy in Asian States: China, India, Japan*, pp. 9–41 (Boulder: Westview Press).

1980. 'The Strategic Imagery of Elites.' In James M. Roherty, ed., *Defense Policy Formation: Towards Comparative Analysis*, pp. 153–73 (Durham: Carolina Academic Press).

1977. 'India's Security: Process and Policy.' In Giri Raj Gupta, ed., *Main Currents in Indian Sociology, Volume 3: Cohesion and Conflict in Modern India*, pp. 237–61 (New Delhi: Vikas and Durham: Carolina Academic Press).

1976. 'The Military.' In Henry C. Hart, ed., *Indira Gandhi's India*, pp. 207–39 (Boulder: Westview Press).

1976. 'Civilian Control of the Military in India.' In Claude E. Welch, Jr., ed., *Civilian Control of the Military: Theory Cases from Developing Countries*, pp. 43–64 (Albany, State University of New York Press).

1974.   'The Security Policy Process in India.' In Frank B. Horton III, ed., *Comparative Defense Policy*, pp. 156–68 (Baltimore: Johns Hopkins University Press).

1974.   'Military Ideology: South Asia.' In Frank B. Horton III, ed., *Comparative Defense Policy*, pp. 73–87 (Baltimore: Johns Hopkins University Press).

Articles

2003.   'The Jihadist Threat to Pakistan.' *Washington Quarterly*, 26(3), pp. 7–25.

2002.   'The Nation and the State of Pakistan.' *Washington Quarterly*, 25(3), pp. 109–21.

2002.   'India, Pakistan and Kashmir.' *Journal of Strategic Studies*, 25(4), pp. 32–59.

2002.   'India, Pakistan and Kashmir.' *Journal of Strategic Studies*, 25(4), pp. 32–60. Reprinted in Sumit Ganguly, ed., *India as an Emerging Power* (London: Frank Cass, 2003).

2001.   'Moving Forward in South Asia.' *Brookings Policy Brief*, 81 (May).

2000.   'India: Old Issues and New Opportunities.' *Brookings Review* 18(4) [Fall]: 30–33.

2000.   'India Rising.' *Wilson Quarterly*, 24(3), pp. 32–49.

2000.   'A New Beginning in South Asia.' *Brookings Policy Brief*, 55 (January).

1998.   'The United States and India: Recovering Lost Ground.' *SAIS Review*, 18(1), pp. 93–107.

1997.   'The Critical Dimensions of a Possible U.S. Strategic Partnership with India.' *United Services Institution of India Journal* (New Delhi), 127(530), pp. 491–501 (The First Pyaralal Memorial Lecture).

1997.   'South Asia: The Origins of War and the Conditions for Peace.' *South Asian Survey*, 4(1), pp. 25–46.

1995.   'The South Asian Nuclear Arms Competition: An American Perspective.' *South African Journal of International Affairs*, 2(2), pp. 38–50.

1994.   'A Generational Change.' *Seminar* (New Delhi), October, pp. 17–20.

1993.   'Kashmir: The Roads to Peace.' *Journal of Peace Studies* (New Delhi), 1(1), pp. 59–68.

1993.   'Is There a Road to Peace in South Asia? An American Perspective.' *United Services Institution of India Journal* (New Delhi), April, pp. 146–53.

1993.   'The Reagan Administration and India: Right for the Right Reasons?' *India International Center Quarterly* (New Delhi), 20.

1992.   'A Season of Separatism.' *Bulletin of the Atomic Scientists*, 48(6), pp. 28–32.

1990.   'The Possibility of Arms Control in South Asia.' *Strategic Studies Journal* (New Delhi), 3(1/2).

1989.   'Our Bomb and Theirs.' *Swords and Plowshares*, 3(3), pp. 3–7.

1988.   'Pakistan and its Army: the Road Ahead.' *Far Eastern Economic Review*, 27 October, 'Fifth Column.'

1987.   'Balancing Interests in South Asia.' *National Interest* (October), pp. 74–84.

1985.   'South Asia after Afghanistan.' *Problems of Communism*, (January–February), pp. 18–31.

1983.   'Pakistan: Army, Society and Security.' *Asian Affairs: An American Journal*, 10(2), pp. 1–26.

1983.   'Pakistan in 1982: Holding On.' *Asian Survey,* 23(2), pp. 123–32 (With Marvin Weinbaum).

1983.   'India: New Elements of Understanding or Continuation of the Confrontation.' *Journal of South Asian and Middle Eastern Studies*, 6(4), pp. 55–65.

1983.   'India Within the Region.' *Seminar* (New Delhi), July, pp. 31–38.

1983.   'Geostrategic Factors in India–Pakistan Relations.' *Asian Affairs: An American Journal*, 10(3), pp. 24–31.

1982.   'Pakistan in 1981: Staying On.' *Asian Survey*, 22 (2), pp. 136–46 (With Marvin Weinbaum).

1982.   'Identity, Survival, Security: Pakistan's Defense Policy.' In *Punjab Journal of Politics*, 6(1), pp. 50–77.

1981.   'Pakistan and America: The Security Dimension.' *Defense Journal* (Karachi), 7(8), pp. 7–11.

1978.   'Defense and Détente: The Problem.' *Seminar* (New Delhi), May, pp. 10–12.

1978.   'American Security Interests in South Asia.' *Strategic Studies* (Islamabad), 2(1), pp. 13–21.

1977.   'ROTC Revisited.' *Inter-University Seminar on Armed Forces Newsletter* (March), p. 4.

1977.   'Indian Ocean or Madagascar Sea?' *Journal of the United Services Institution of India*, (April–June), pp. 101–8.

1976.   'US Weapons and South Asia: A Policy Analysis.' *Pacific Affairs*, (Spring), pp. 49–69.

1975.   'Security Issues in South Asia.' *Asian Survey*, March, pp. 203–15.

1975.   'South Asia and US Military Policy.' In Lloyd and Susanne Rudolph, eds., *The Coordination of Complexity in South Asia*

(Washington, DC: US Government Printing Office). Papers prepared for the National Commission on the Organization of the Government for the Conduct of Foreign Policy. Appendix 5, Vol. 7, pp. 149–158. Reprinted Manohar Publishers, New Delhi, 1978.

1974. 'Japanese Security Policy.' *Japan Foundation Newsletter*, March, p. xx.

1973. 'Japanese Security Policy.' *Japan Foundation Newsletter*, November, p. xx.

1971. 'India's China War and After.' *Journal of Asian Studies*, 30(4), pp. 847–57.

1969. 'The Untouchable Soldier: Caste, Politics, and the Indian Army.' *Journal of Asian Studies*, 28(3), pp. 453–68.

1969. 'Army and Society in India.' *Journal of the Institute of Defense Studies Analysis* (New Delhi), July, pp. 12–29.

1968. 'Issue, Role, and Personality: The Kitchener–Curzon Dispute.' *Comparative Studies in Society and History*, April, pp. 337–55.

1965. 'The Bomb: Strategic Considerations.' *Seminar* (New Delhi), January, p. xx.

1964. 'Rulers and Priests: A Study in Cultural Control.' *Comparative Studies in Society and History*, January, pp. 199–216.

1964. 'Officer and Tradition in the Indian Army.' *Journal of the United Services Institute of India* (New Delhi), January–March, p. xx.

1964. 'Arms and Politics in Pakistan: A Review Article.' *India Quarterly*, October, pp. 403–20.

1963. 'Subhas Chandra Bose and the Indian National Army.' *Pacific Affairs*, Winter, pp. 411–29.

Monographs, Reports, and Speeches

2001. 'Problem Solving.' Interview Transcript. *Harvard Asia Quarterly*, 5(4), p. xx

1993. Amarnath Kakkar Memorial Lecture. Inaugural Speech, Allahabad University, Allahabad, India, September.

1992. Nuclear Weapons and Nuclear War in South Asia: An Unknowable Future. United Nations University Conference on South Asia, Tokyo, May.

1990. Towards a Nuclear Verification Regime in South Asia. Study for the Los Alamos National Laboratory, April.

1989. The Nuclear Futures of South Asia. Program in Arms Control, Disarmament, and International Security, University of Illinois. *Occasional Paper*, 89–92, February.

1987.   Security, Peace and Stability in South Asia: An American Perspective. Centenary Lecture to Allahabad University. Allahabad, India.

1983.   Pakistan's Security Policy. Briefing paper prepared for the United States Department of State, Bureau of Intelligence and Research, December.

1982.   Security Decision-Making in Pakistan. Report for United States Department of State, Office of External Research, September. Reprinted, Office of Arms Control, University of Illinois, Urbana.

1979.   Perception, Influence, and Weapons Proliferation in South Asia. Report for the United States Department of State, Bureau of Intelligence and Research, August. (Contract #1722-920184)

1978.   The Andhra Cyclone: Individual and Institutional Responses to Mass Death. Report to the Indian Council of Social Science Research, New Delhi, 19 February. Co-authored with C.V. Raghavulu, Andhra University, Waltair, India.

1977.   The Military in Pakistan: Origins, Structure, Prognosis. United States Department of State, Office of External Research, Bureau of Intelligence and Research, 22 April, Paper prepared for a Colloquium on Pakistan.

1976.   Report on the Conference on Current Developments and Future Trends in India. United States Department of State, 23 January.

1973.   Arms and Politics in Bangladesh, India, and Pakistan. SUNY at Buffalo, Council on International Affairs, Special Studies Monograph.

1970.   The Indian Security Policy-Making Process. Report prepared for the United States Arms Control and Disarmament Agency, July.

About the Contributors

Kanti Bajpai is currently headmaster, The Doon School, Dehra Dun, India. He was awarded his Ph.D. in political science from the University of Illinois, Urbana-Champaign, in 1990. Under Steve Cohen's guidance, he wrote his doctoral thesis on the South Asian Association for Regional Cooperation. He has taught political science and international relations at the Maharajah Sayajirao University of Baroda and Jawaharlal Nehru University, New Delhi, and has held visiting positions at Wesleyan University, the University of Illinois, Urbana-Champaign, the University of Notre Dame, the Brookings Institution, and the Australian Defence Force Academy, Canberra. His collaboration with Cohen includes a co-authored article on cooperative security, a co-edited volume on South Asian security, and a book he and others co-wrote on the Brasstacks crisis between India and Pakistan.

Sunil Dasgupta, Steve Cohen's last doctoral student at the University of Illinois, is Visiting Assistant Professor and a core faculty member in the Security Studies Program in Georgetown University's Edmund A. Walsh School of Foreign Service. He researches and teaches security studies and international relations with an emphasis on military organization, civil–military relations, and unconventional warfare. He is writing a book on the rise of paramilitaries and military decentralization. Previously, he was a research associate in the Foreign Policy Program at the Brookings Institution and national security correspondent for *India Today* magazine in New Delhi, and an economics reporter and editorial writer for *Financial Express* newspaper, also in New Delhi.

Sumit Ganguly is a professor of political science and holds the Rabindranath Tagore Chair in Indian Cultures and Civilizations at Indiana University in Bloomington. He received his Ph.D. in 1984 and was a Ford Foundation Dual Competence Fellow at Columbia University during the 1985–86 academic year. He has previously taught at James Madison College at Michigan State University, Hunter College of the City University of New York, and the University of Texas at Austin. Professor Ganguly serves on the editorial boards of *Asian Affairs*, *Asian Survey*, *Current History* and the *Journal of Strategic Studies*. He is the founding editor of the *India Review*, the only refereed American social science journal devoted to the study of contemporary India and the co-editor of *Asian Security*, a refereed journal dealing with contemporary Asian security issues. His most recent book (with Devin Hagerty), is *Fearful Symmetry: India and Pakistan in the Shadow of Nuclear Weapons* (New Delhi: Oxford University Press and Seattle: University of Washington Press, 2005). He and Steve Cohen co-authored the chapter on India in Robert Chase, Emily Hill, and Paul Kennedy's *The Pivotal States: A New Framework for US Policy in the Developing World* (New York: W.W. Norton and Company, 1999).

Amit Gupta is an associate professor in the Department of International Security Studies at the United States Air Force Air War College, Maxwell AFB, Alabama. He got his Ph.D. in 1995.

Kavita Khory is an associate professor of politics at Mount Holyoke College, where she has taught since 1990. She worked with Professor Cohen from 1985–1990. Her teaching and research focus on international relations and comparative politics, with a regional specialization in South Asia. More specifically, she works on regional security issues and political violence, especially in the context of nationalist movements and insurgency groups in Pakistan, India, and Sri Lanka. Presently, she is working on two rather different projects: one is on diaspora politics and activism, and the other is on Baluch nationalism and its implications for Pakistan domestic politics and foreign policy.

Chetan Kumar currently works for a UN agency. The views expressed in this volume are strictly his own and not those of any UN department or agency. He has previously worked for the Office of the Special Representative of the UN Secretary-General for Children and Armed Conflict, and for the International Peace Academy in New York. He is the author of *Building Peace in Haiti* (Lynne Rienner, 1998), and co-editor of *Peace-Building as Politics: Cultivating Peace in Fragile Societies* (Lynne Rienner, 2000) and *South Asia Approaches the Millennium: Re-examining National Security* (Westview, 1995). He holds a Ph.D. in Political Science from the University of Illinois at Urbana-Champaign (1995).

Dinshaw Mistry is assistant professor of political science and director of Asian Studies at the University of Cincinnati. He completed his Ph.D. in political science from the University of Illinois in 1999. He is author of *Containing Missile Proliferation* (University of Washington Press, 2003). His other publications include 'Nuclear Asia's Challenges' (*Current History*, April 2005); 'The Strategic Significance of India's Nuclear, Missile, Space, and Missile Defense Programs' (book chapter in *South Asia's Nuclear Security Dilemma*, 2004); 'The Unrealized Promise of International Institutions: The Test Ban Treaty and India's Nuclear Breakout' (*Security Studies*, Summer 2003); 'Beyond the MTCR' (*International Security*, Spring 2003); 'Technological Containment: The MTCR and Missile Proliferation' (*Security Studies*, Spring 2002); 'The Geostrategic Implications of India's Space Program' (*Asian Survey*, November–December 2001); and 'Diplomacy, Sanctions, and the US Nonproliferation Dialogue with India and Pakistan' (*Asian Survey*, September–October 1999).

C.V. Raghavulu obtained his B.A.(Hons.) from the Andhra University, M.D.P.A. from the Indian Institute of Public Administration (New Delhi), M.P.A. from the University of New Mexico (1971), and Ph.D. in political science, from the University of Illinois (1976). He was on the faculties of the Andhra and Nagarjuna Universities; served as dean of social sciences and director of the Disaster Mitigation Centre at the Nagarjuna University. He was the recipient of several prestigious fellowships, including the Indo-American Senior Fellowship (University of Texas, Austin, 1986–87). He was vice-chancellor of Nagarjuna University (1998–2001) and Vice-Chancellor (IC) of Andhra University (March–October 2001). Dr Raghavulu was editor of the *Indian Journal of Political Science* (1993–94); general secretary and treasurer (1994–97) and president of the Indian Political Science Association (1997–2000); and is currently president of the Indian Public Administration Association. He is the author of six books and eighty-five research papers. Dr. Raghavulu is the co-author, with Dr. Stephen P. Cohen, of the Andhra Cyclone of 1977.

Swarna Rajagopalan is an independent political and security analyst based in Chennai, India. She was educated at Elphinstone College, Bombay, Syracuse University, and the University of Illinois, where she studied with Professor Cohen for her doctorate in political science (1992–98). She has taught political science and South Asian politics at Sophia College, Bombay, the University of Illinois, James Madison College at Michigan State University, and Yale University. She is the author of *State and Nation in South Asia* (Lynne Rienner, 2001), co-editor of *Re-distribution of Authority:*

A Cross-Regional Perspective (Praeger, 2000), and *Women, Security, South Asia: A Clearing in the Thicket* (Sage, 2005), and author of several articles and chapters besides.

Shonali Sardesai works with the Conflict Prevention and Reconstruction Unit of the World Bank in Washington, DC, USA.

Index

Printed in the United Kingdom
by Lightning Source UK Ltd.
113513UKS00003B/4-18